Foundations of Theology

Gerald O'Collins, S.J.

LOYOLA UNIVERSITY PRESS
Chicago   60657

Nihil obstat: Rev. Msgr. Matthew P. Stapleton
                Diocesan Censor
Imprimatur: + Richard Cardinal Cushing
                Archbishop of Boston
October 1, 1970

Cover photograph
"U.S. Pavilion
New York World's Fair"

from
Photographs/Algimantas Kezys, S.J.
© 1966 Loyola University Press

CONTENTS

TO
Jim, Kevin,
Posey and Stephanie
With much love
From their brother-in-law.

Preface

A theological examination of the Christian Church, the doctrines about Jesus Christ and the nature of the sacraments presupposes that certain foundations have already been laid for such study. What are these foundations? Where and how does theology begin?

In this book I attempt to create a basis for discussion in theology by exploring some fundamental notions which must affect the full development of any theology. From the outset it is worthwhile trying to get things straight about the nature of theology itself, theological procedure, revelation, salvation history, and the link between Christian faith and history. To investigate the meaning of these first categories in theology and try our hand at expressing them accurately should help to shut off later false understanding and yield greater intelligibility.

It could be misleading to do no more than expose some basic notions to a searching scrutiny. That approach would too readily suggest that we are justified in elaborating a priori such categories as revelation and faith without paying proper attention to the concrete event of divine self-disclosure in Jesus Christ. More than a mere nod must be paid to the fact that Christian revelation is rooted in history. From the beginning theologians ought to attend to the ineradicable particularity of Christianity's origins. Hence I devote two chapters to the life, death, and resurrection of Jesus Christ.

Without question, one helpful way of approaching theology is to offer an analysis of Christian faith. In accord with such plan we would investigate the fides qua, the faith by which man appropriates God's saving self-manifestation and responds with personal commitment. This present book by no means buries this (subjective) aspect of faith in a blanket of neglect. But I have chosen to concentrate on the objective pole, examining those categories which provide the basic structure for the fides quae (that which is believed). It is vital to map carefully the areas within which ultimate questions affecting one's personal existence are to be raised. How we understand the basic elements of Christian revelation will determine whether we will be willing to accept it.

The contents of this book are as follows. Part one deals with some fundamental notions of theology, part two with two contemporary theological statements on revelation, part three with Christ's resurrection and our knowledge of the historical Jesus. I am well aware that many important questions connected with such terms as dogma, Christian proclamation, tradition, ecclesiastical teaching authority, hermeneutics and theistic language are hardly touched on in part one. The choice of Wolfhart Pannenberg and Gerald Downing for discussion in part two may not commend itself to all readers. In part three a full discussion of serious questions like the relation of Jesus to Paul is not offered. This book is necessarily selective. It is not meant to constitute an exhaustive account of theological foundations, even supposing that such an account were possible. Various contributors to the June 1969 volume (n.46) of Concilium, an issue devoted to the theme of "Fundamental Theology," illustrate how other options remain open--both as regards the general area of study and the particular selection of themes. A complete "Fundamental Theology" would require a complementary elaboration of ecclesiological themes such as (1) the Word of God in the preaching, teaching, dogma, and confession of the Church, and (2) the mission of believers to the world which God's self-revelation summons them to serve.

This book unashamedly involves the reader in recent German theological discussion. To do this, I realize, is to risk alienating two groups. Those anxious to apply the Christian message to the urgent task of changing a sick society can readily grow impatient with technical theology. But ultimately any strong and lasting program of action can only rest on true insights into the way things are. I hope that by precisely stating some basic elements of Christian revelation, this book will help to yield the basis for such a program. Second, there are those who may resent any German or even any European leadership in theology. Such a reaction is particularly understandable on the part of intelligent students confronted with an uncritical and "faddish" promotion of the latest continental trends. However, in the area of revelation, faith and Christian origins theological literacy demands familiarity with the positions of Barth, Bultmann, and the post-Bultmannians. We ignore their debates at our peril, and that not merely because of the intrinsic value of what they have to say. Their views have widely influenced present theological convictions in various Christian communities, including the Catholic Church itself.

As it happens, I am writing this preface at the Berghaus Hügel in Tübingen. A few hundred yards along the bank of the Neckar stands the home of Ernst Bloch, the great Marxist philosopher of hope. In the summer of 1967 I wrote an article on the relation between Bloch's thought and the contemporary theology of hope. That article ended as follows:

> In his Tübingener Einleitung in die Philosophie he takes up Thomas Mann's statement that writers are people who find writing more difficult than other people do and adds that philosophers find thinking more difficult than others. We can carry on this thought and suggest that theologians are those who find it more difficult to believe than other people do. In a strange kind of way Bloch can help the theologians to believe and go on believing, and through belief to find courage for their hope.
> (Scottish Journal of Theology 21 [1968], p. 144)

Far beyond what I guessed in that lovely Tübingen summer when painful theological problems still seemed no larger than a tiny cloud above the Black Forest, those words have proved true. This book and other studies form an attempt to explain to myself and others why Christian revelation and life still make sense.

ix

To all who have in one way or another contributed to the making of this book I am grateful. Between March and August 1969 I tried out many of these ideas on the students of Corpus Christi College, Glen Waverley, and the Jesuit Theological College, Parkville. (Both colleges are situated in the State of Victoria, Australia.) I wish to acknowledge the stimulus, corrective influence and insights these students provided. My lectures for the Jesuit Theological College coincided with its relocation at Melbourne University and the start of close cooperation with the joint theological hall of Ormond College (Presbyterian) and Queen's College (Methodist). I would like to record my personal thanks to the faculty and students of that hall for the kind welcome which made the beginning of our common venture so successful. Finally, I wish to express my deep appreciation to Mrs. Marie Cutler who typed nearly all of the original manuscript.

Tübingen, West Germany
February 17, 1970

PART ONE

Fundamental Notions

We theologize either as Catholic or as Protestant theologians, to name only the most outstanding difference.
It is doubtful whether the attempt to avoid either of these
alternatives, and to find a position outside of, or beyond
the confessional differences, can be called theology.

Gerhard Ebeling

Theology is what theologians do--no more, no less. It
has no more security of tenure as a phenomenon than
"science" has. And science as Polanyi and others have
pointed out, is a tissue of personal appropriations,
personal priorities in attention, affirmation, neglect.

Peter Steele

Chapter I

Theological Procedure

In the preface to <u>The</u> <u>Theologian</u> at <u>Work</u>, Roy Eckhardt points
out that "a sensible way to discover what an enterprise means is
to look at what its practitioners do."[1] Eckhardt then presents a
selection of writings from those whom he rates among the best contemporary practitioners of theology. This kind of procedure is in-
dubitably sound. To study those commonly reckoned among the
greatest Israelite-Christian theologians and to let all minor theologians await later attention would make a helpful initial orientation to theological thinking. The curriculum in a theology school
could profitably prescribe a "great books" course which would
confront the beginner with the work of Ezechiel, Paul, Irenaeus,
Origen, Augustine, Anselm, Aquinas, Luther, Calvin, Barth,
Rahner, and others. In the particular field of the theology of faith
Newman's <u>Grammar</u> <u>of</u> <u>Assent</u> suggests an oft-neglected approach
by recommending that we ask how in fact people come to Christian

1

faith.[2] Too frequently what purports to be an examination of faith turns out to be an answer to the question: "How in my opinion should people come to Christian faith?" A "great books" course that formed the introduction to the study of theology could go a long way towards ensuring that the future theologian addresses himself to the right questions. Rather than lay down guidelines on how theologians ought to go about their business, he will ask how theologians (both past and present) do in fact practice their profession.

Accounts of theological procedure

Provided that we remain alert to the type of reasoning being followed, even a brief sampling of theological writing should alert us to the rich variety of procedures at work. Theological method is no simple, easily grasped phenomenon. One commonly held formula, from St. Anselm, states that theology is the exercise of "faith seeking understanding." Theology is faith engaged in a reflection upon itself. There are a number of things to note about this formulation of the theological task. Firstly, it should not be taken to suggest that faith by itself lacks all understanding, as if the theological task involved finding something of which faith had previously been deprived. Rather faith engages in systematic reflection upon realities which it already spontaneously, if confusedly, appreciates. This search can never yield definitive insights and statements which might put an end to further interrogation. Faith remains endlessly engaged in seeking to articulate itself. What Kierkegaard said about Christianity applies to theological reflection: "There is no such thing as being a Christian; there is only becoming a Christian." Secondly, this approach means that the theologian finds a starting point within the circle of faith itself. Not even initially does he take up a position outside faith in an attempt to understand it better or justify it more successfully. In these terms theology may be described as "essentially the conscious effort of the Christian to hearken to the actual verbal revelation which God has promulgated in history, to acquire a knowledge of it by the methods of scholarship and to reflect upon its implications."[3] It should be remarked, however, that not all theologians agree that their work begins from within the circle of faith. Wolfhart Pannenberg, for example, adopts a methodologically neutral standpoint, subjecting God's alleged self-revelation in Christ to "the test of man's matured understanding as such."[4] He holds that at least in principle man can know and speak of revelation from an uncommitted point of view which is logically prior to faith. In that case the procedure expressed by the axiom credo ut intelligam ("I believe in order that I might understand") would be reversible.

Thirdly, the formulation "faith seeking understanding" may indicate one or other of two closely related goals. If "understanding" is taken strictly, our concern is with intellectual insight into and conceptualizing of one's lived Christian faith. Or else interest may be directed primarily towards the language which expresses an understanding of faith. Thus Gerhard Ebeling at times treats theology as the language school of faith.5 In this case it might be preferable to speak of "faith seeking expression" (fides quaerens linguam). Fourthly, if we are to appreciate two divergent ways of doing theology which can both adopt the motto "fides quaerens intellectum," we need to ask: "Faith seeking understanding about what?" It is open to the theologian to seek understanding about faith itself, about the conditions under which faith becomes a reality, and about faith's effect on the life of the believer. In other words, the theologian may focus his attention on man and only indirectly raise the question of the God towards whom faith is directed and who is acknowledged as the ultimate cause of faith. On the other hand, faith may directly seek understanding about God and the divine self-communication in Christ. The first style of approach can be called anthropocentric theology and the second theocentric theology--to use two much overworked and easily misunderstood terms. But in the last analysis we cannot speak of God adequately unless we speak of man and vice versa. In spite of Karl Barth's denials, ultimately anthropocentrism and theocentrism are, or should be, the same.6 As his son, Markus Barth, put the matter, "a theology that is not human and humane is not theology at all. Theology has to deal with God Incarnate. . . . Theology deals with God who contacts humanity."7 Conversely, an "anthropology that remains unconcerned with God is ultimately no account of the real man who in his origin, existence and destiny is essentially related to God. In the next chapter we will return to this theme when discussing the correlation between revelation and faith. It is worth noticing here the extreme theocentrism which Karl Barth, particularly in his earlier writings, championed. He described the task of theology as that of bringing "the Christian sermon to reproduce in human words what is said to man about God by God himself--in opposition to all that man can say for himself about God."8 Despite the later shift to an unqualified dominance of Christology in Barth's thought, man's side of the divine-human relationship remained comparatively

3

neglected. Ebeling rightly took issue with Barth for failing to offer anything more than a merely peripheral discussion of faith.[9] It was only late in his Church Dogmatics that Barth declared: "We shall give to the Christian individual and his faith the attention which he demands, but it must be at this point--not at the beginning of our way, but very briefly at the end."[10]

In place of "faith seeking understanding" some theologians prefer to view their task as that of "love seeking understanding" or "hope seeking understanding." Thus Augustine thinks of existence in love as a search for the knowledge of love: "Tantum cognoscitur, quantum diligitur." For Jürgen Moltmann faith and love are bound together under the primacy of hope. Moltmann proposes "spes quaerens intellectum" or "spero ut intelligam" ("hope seeking understanding" and "I hope so that I may understand") as mottos which express most appropriately the theological task.[11] The thrust of his theology, however, is not so much a search for theological understanding as a missionary call into the future.

What has to be noted is that these three basic accounts of theological procedure are open to either an individualizing or a social orientation. The theologian may confine his attention largely to the individual Christian's faith, love, and hope, or else he may be thoroughly conscious of the community which is established and coheres through faith, love, and hope. Let me give one example to substantiate this point. There is a world of difference between Ebeling's concern with the individual conscience[12] and Markus Barth's insistence that justification through faith creates solidarity between those formerly estranged.[13] Yet both writers are in a real sense engaged in the work of elucidating the meaning of faith.

What holds true of the theological procedures mentioned above is the case also with a further group of explanations which in various ways bring theology close to religious activity as such. Their explanations may highlight either the individual Christian or the community. For Heinrich Ott "all theological speech must in its cause and execution be internally and really (if not externally and obviously) prayer."[14] In his Secular Christianity the late Ronald Gregor Smith may have spoken of "the business of theology" as "reflection about faith" and--what is not quite the same thing--"a description of what goes on in Christianity,"[15] nevertheless, in a private conversation he described theology as a "reflective account of what goes on when the Christian is at prayer." In this view theological statements are derived from prayer and lead

4

back to prayer.[16] Dietrich Ritschl's account of theological procedure aims to do justice to the role of the community and community worship. The language of theology is "doxological," by which
Ritschl means language expressing worship of the risen Christ
present in the Church. Doxological language is rooted in community prayer which recalls our Christian past and manifests our
hopes for the future. Ritschl sets his face against any separation
of scholarship and piety as a failure to grasp how theology is a
call to worship and is practiced in the context of prayer.[17] Those
who interpret theology as closely related to Christian prayer and
worship will profess to acknowledge God rather than to know him,
to address God rather than to express him.

Theology can also be identified with preaching or at least
understood as reflection upon preaching.[18] If theologians are
not preachers of the Christian gospel, they watch their language
in the presence of preaching. This poses the question: What is
to count as Christian proclamation? (A similar question may be
asked about the other accounts of theology outlined above: What
is to count as Christian faith, love, and hope and as the Christian
community or individual at prayer?) We would probably require
that preaching should on the one hand be drawn from the revelation
recorded in scripture and on the other hand it should touch the
particular life situation of those to whom it is addressed. Ebeling,
after explaining that theology is "responsible reflection on proclamation," adds at once that "proclamation, properly speaking,
is eo ipso church proclamation," "that which makes the church
the church" and "that in which the church is seen to be the church."[19]
From the context it is clear that Ebeling expects proclamation to be
biblical, as well as ecclesiastical. He then enlarges this account:
"If the task of the theologian is to reflect on the event of proclamation as one who shares responsibility for it, this means that one's
reflections will be directed both towards proclamation which has
already taken place and towards proclamation which is to take
place in the future."[20] Here we run up against various issues:
What is the proclamation in which "the church is seen to be the
church?" What proclamation that "has already taken place" meets
with the theologian's approval? What kind of proclamation does he
wish to take place in the future? And--most important--what is
"biblical" proclamation?

There has always been a debate about "the meaning" of scripture, not only about the meaning of particular texts, but about the
interpretation of whole books of scripture and the bible as a whole.
Theologians are anything but uniform in their assessment and use

of different biblical traditions both for the construction of theology and the enlightenment of Christian preaching. Proclamation which is based on Luke-Acts and the Pastoral Epistles will differ from proclamation which takes the fourth gospel as its major guide. A theology which claims to be a reflection on Christian proclamation is probably going to be shaped decisively and ultimately by judgments about scripture. It will test and interpret Christian preaching and life against the bible. There is nothing new, of course, in holding that theology is properly understood as systematic reflection on the revelation recorded in scripture. At the beginning of his Summa Theologica Aquinas announces that theology is "the science" of the scriptures.

Two points ought not to escape us here. Firstly, a theology which understands itself to be engaged in scriptural reflection is likely to be closely related to those theologies which profess to be an elucidation of Christian liturgy and prayer. "Every prayer," Heinrich Schlier writes, "is based on direct or indirect scriptural interpretation and on direct or indirect understanding of scripture. Liturgy is scripture transposed into prayer and action."[21] Secondly, reflection on scripture moves between the poles of the past and the present. The biblical texts were written then and their meaning must be investigated with all the techniques of historical criticism. But they also have a message for us now. In the task of theology there is the hermeneutical gap to be bridged. Continuity in meaning may often demand discontinuity in language. If the biblical text is to "reveal and transform reality,"[22] it must itself be transformed into our spoken word today. This work of interpretation may gain such importance that the word "hermeneutics" can be used as synonymous with "theology."[23] In the interpretation of texts modern hermeneutics often shows a positive attitude to tradition. Hence the theologian's ultimate procedure may involve operating with three factors: the text, the tradition, and our understanding now. By invoking tradition he acknowledges a role of the Christian community in interpreting scripture.

This brings us to yet further approaches to theology, namely those in which traditional considerations are paramount. Many theologians--no matter what formal explanation they offer regarding the ultimate nature of their work--are really engaged on the task of preserving and elucidating what they understand to be traditional Christianity. Sometimes they incidentally let slip remarks that let us glimpse the ultimate grounds for their theological positions. Thus David Jenkins questions whether Schleiermacher's Christology is "an approach to Jesus Christ" that "maintains and does

justice to his uniqueness and centrality as it has usually been understood in the Christian tradition."[24] Theologians of the Reformation
churches can on occasions appear to be intent upon justifying the
so-called "spirit of the Reformation"[25] or at least traditional
doctrines encapsulated in particular classical slogans. Roman
Catholic theologians may announce that their task is to reflect
on the divine self-revelation in Christ. But what many of them
have in fact been busy about was the investigation, explanation
and vindication of conciliar and papal formulations. Their theology could deteriorate into a commentary on and justification of
ecclesiastical texts. Too often it was forgotten that these statements were essentially incomplete, dependent on circumstances
and mostly negative rather than positive contributions. All the
approaches to theology mentioned in this paragraph can be
described as traditio quaerens intellectum ("tradition seeking
understanding"). Inasmuch as Ebeling maintains that the reflection on proclamation (which he considers to be theology's proper
task) should also be concerned with the "proclamation which has
already taken place," he can write: "The task which theology is
given to do is identical with the gift it receives from tradition."
Hence "the task of handing on this tradition . . . is clearly
constituted for theology."[26] It may seem astounding that a theologian who is so consciously loyal to the Reformation as Ebeling
should be finally bracketed among those who approach theology
in the spirit of traditio quaerens intellectum. What we see here
is the effect of H. G. Gadamer's contribution to hermeneutics
in incorporating tradition into interpretation and seeing it as a
necessary context for the recovery of meaning rather than an
obstacle.[27]

Now that we have surveyed briefly the most important accounts
of theological procedure, it should be clear that so far from being
mutually exclusive the procedures are often deeply interrelated.
Furthermore, no procedure may claim definitive preeminence.
The factors are too diverse. To expect any single theologian in
the practice of his enterprise to preserve a perfect harmony
between all the relevant elements would be illusory. Ideally the
theologian ought to reflect (1) as an individual member of the
Church, (2) using the data of past, present, and future, and (3)
conscious that he must find some middle ground between turning
theology into mere religious activity on the one hand and simple
self-critical analysis on the other. He has to keep renominating
for himself what the balance shall be between the claims of the
community and the demands of his intellectual and spiritual

vivacity. He may not become a theological armadillo, encased in the narrow shell of his own ponderings. But, correspondingly, a zeal to sink oneself in the community and common traditions deprives precisely the community of a necessary creative and disturbing challenge. Preoccupation with the right relationship between past, present, and future requires that theological procedure refrain from conniving at nostalgic reaction, from the flight to an eternal present or from an attempt at absolute revolution-- according to whether a paramount role is ascribed to past, present, or future respectively. To drift into preoccupation with theology's function as a religious activity can lead to pietism, while self-reflection is not immune against lapsing into an agnosticism where an "intellectus dubitans de fide" (intellect doubting about the faith) replaces a "fides quaerens intellectum."

Subject matter of theology

Closely linked to the issue of theological procedure is the question of theology's subject matter, a theme already touched on above when we examined the formulation "faith seeking understanding." It should hardly be necessary to point out that theologians do not always make the divine reality their primary object of attention. Paul Tillich examined the answers given by religious symbols to religious questions. Rudolf Bultmann's concern lay with the ontic state of the individual man of faith.[28] Despite Ebeling's formal affirmation that theology's subject matter is "the Word of God,"[29] he has devoted so much attention to a sensitive analysis of faith that his theology appears transmuted into "pistology." Much contemporary Roman Catholic theology seems to take the corporate self-understanding of the Church as the subject matter of theology. John Knox values "the corporate reality of the Church" so highly that he interprets the task of the Christian theologian as that of "trying to say as accurately and adequately as possible what Christians--that is, sharers in the life of the Church--find true in their common experience."[30] Pre-Vatican II Catholic theology was frequently so preoccupied with conciliar and papal formulations that instead of being talk about God it lapsed into being talk about talk about God. Dr. John Robinson is not too far from this position when he explains that the work of theology is to deal with a history of religious discourse. The theologian is to coordinate this talk about God and draw conclusion from it, but not to deal directly with God and state whether this traditional discourse is true or false.[31]

8

In this century no one has been more tirelessly insistent than Karl Barth that theology ought to be true to its name. Its subject matter is firstly God and his redeeming agent Jesus Christ and only then the self-understanding of the believing man. Confronted with what he took to be Bultmann's reduction of theology to anthropology, Barth asked: "Are the New Testament's affirmations about God's saving act and about man's being in Christ primarily statements about man's subjective experience? Is not this reversing the New Testament?"[32] Basically Vorgrimler and Rahner are in agreement with Barth when they explain that the subject matter of theology is "God who by his salvific dealings with men in Jesus Christ reveals himself . . . in his own glory--otherwise necessarily hidden from man--. . . communicates himself in grace."[33] Oscar Cullmann's position approaches that of Barth when--as we will see--he formulates the "plot" of God's saving acts in history as the subject matter of theology.

To simplify greatly, we can contrast anthropocentric and theocentric types of theology, or if you like the Bultmannian and the Barthian styles of theology. The first devotes its attention to man as responding to God in Christ, the second to God as communicating himself to man in Christ. Mediating positions are obviously feasible. Thus Luther indicates that the subject matter of theology is both "man the sinner and the God who justifies" (homo peccator et deus justificans). Provided that a given theology continues to deal with a real God and a real man, it merits its name. But once a certain point has been passed in whittling down the reality of either God or man, what is being done is better expressed by a different name. Paul van Buren's reflections[34] in which "God" is taken as a personified ideal about whose real existence we can afford to remain agnostic do not deserve to be entitled "theology." They are better understood as essays in the reinterpretation of religious language. Conversely, such Roman Catholic writings which repeat traditional doctrine in an apparently "orthodox" fashion but present (or imply) an unrecognizable account of man fail to merit the name of "theological." Call them confessional books or collections of historical documents. But we ought not connive at the situation in which works are deemed theological in which either God or man ceases to be recognizably real. One way in which the human reality is (partly) falsified in contemporary theology is by the fiction of "the modern man," a splendid creation of the theological imagination.

Criteria for theological argument

Even where the subject matter of theology was agreed upon,
there has always been a debate about the criteria for theological
argument. What are these criteria? And what is their relative
order of importance? This subject is so vast and the possible
issues so complex that we are obliged to seek some simplifying
approach. Our question is: How do we know that this or that theological assertion (or series of assertions) is both true and valuable? Every theologian seeks to provide some satisfaction to such
a questioner. This is the case even with such theologians who appear to renounce reason in what looks like the spirit of "credo quia
absurdum" (I believe because it is absurd). In his famous exposition of the Epistle to the Romans, Barth declared that "all the
articles of our Christian belief are, when considered rationally,
impossible and mendacious and preposterous. Faith, however,
is completely abreast of the situation. It grips reason by the
throat and strangles the beast."[35] Barth's willingness to affirm
Christian truth without apology prompted Bonhoeffer to stigmatize
this position as a "positivist doctrine of revelation which says,
in effect, 'Like it or lump it.'"[36] Nevertheless, Barth gave a
clear exposition of his views, presented them with their scriptural
credentials and allowed Calvin, Kierkegaard, Luther, and other
voices from the Christian past to be heard. Clarity, biblical warrant, and appeal to Christian tradition were operating here to
recommend and justify Barth's assertions.

Theology and Scripture   Christian theologians have always acknowledged their obligation to justify their positions by producing
scriptural backing for them. If it was once considered a straightforward matter to offer biblical authority for an assertion, it has
become increasingly obvious how many problems this procedure
must face. Let me set out the major problems in brief. If we take
up some particular biblical text, what is to count as a proper
explanation of it? Is the bible to be interpreted in accordance with
normal hermeneutical principles or is it subject to special, even
completely special, hermeneutics? A related issue in the work
of interpretation involves the focus of our attention. Will it be
(a) the text itself, or (b) the mind which produced it, or (c) what
the text is supposed to be "about" (for example, the subject matter)? The differences can prove by no means inconsiderable.
Thus Ernst Fuchs detects a serious gap between the subject matter (the "purity" of St. Paul's faith) and the apostle's actual reflections offered in I Corinthians 15:3 ff. Here the "purity" of

Paul's faith does not "coincide with the purity" of his statements about faith.37 Further, we must also confront the difficulties which arise from the fact that the scriptures are culturally conditioned and (frequently) "occasional" writings. They are usually addressed to meet specific needs of particular groups. They may also be deeply determined by personal presuppositions and cultural circumstances. We will need to decide whether and in what way some position stated in the scriptures was intended to embody a doctrine of lasting importance which has a direct message for us today. Let me illustrate this issue by two examples from St. Paul.

Romans 13:1 ff. is a passage which has often been cited as a piece of straightforward scriptural backing for the duty of obedience towards those who enjoy power in civil society. It is invoked in this way by Vatican II.38 But how general was the apostle's injunction "be subject to higher authorities" meant to be? Was it intended as an injunction for all Christians and for all ages? To what extent was this injunction shaped by Paul's political situation and conceptual background? A church leader in the first century faced the practical necessity of proving that Christianity meant good citizenship, so that the Roman civil authorities would not harass the Christians as adherents of a subversive, revolutionary movement. Further, the structure of the apostle's thinking seems to have run along the lines of hierarchic principles of subordination. It was part of his world of ideas to acknowledge human authorities as counters to a heavenly hierarchy and to urge the duty of subordination. In support of his argument he alleged that obedience would meet with praise from the civil authority; it was only those who proved insubordinate who needed to fear punishment. Clearly Paul was taking an unrealistic view of how civil authority was often exercised then and can still be exercised today. Wrongdoers could be left untouched; the good might have much to fear from corrupt, despotic rulers. Finally, civil obedience under the imperialistic Roman rule was clearly a very different thing from civil obedience under democratic rule in advanced industrial society. Romans 13:1 ff. can enjoy only an indirect application in an argument about contemporary Christian duties in society.39

The second example is the Pauline doctrine of justification by faith. We might decide that this doctrine is not only the heart of Paul's gospel but also just as important today as it was in the first, fifth, and sixteenth centuries. Or we might join Krister Stendahl in declining to regard justification by faith as the central Pauline doctrine 40 and then go on to accept as well Markus Barth's argument that the attempted justification by self-achievement against which Paul fought in Galatians is no longer a temptation today.[41]

More problems crop up if we ask whether and how the bible is to be understood as a whole. What purports to be a simple piece of biblical warrant for some theological assertion may presuppose that a series of important positions have already been adopted. Do we view the bible as first and foremost a missionary book, a religious document, the word of God in its written form, the book of the Church, or as something else? Further, do we regard the relationship between the two Testaments as principally a matter of continuity or of discontinuity? Our position one way or the other can decisively modify subsequent theological arguments as well as our appeal to scripture in support of those arguments. However the role of the Old Testament is assessed, it remains a pre-Christian book and it is on the New Testament that the theologian focuses in evaluating conflicting theological assertions. This appeal to scripture will be deeply affected according to whether he is already convinced or unconvinced that there exists an ultimate unity between the expressions of Christian faith found in the various New Testament traditions. In other words, does the theologian accept the whole canon of the New Testament as that against which he is ready to test his assertions? Ernst Käsemann for one exempts himself from the authority of the fourth gospel by concluding that it was due to "man's error and God's providence" that this book found its way into the canon.[42]

Even when the theologian is convinced that the whole canon should command his respect and allegiance, he is hardly going to grant equal value to all the books of the New Testament, let alone to all the books of the Bible. Almost certainly he will agree that all scriptures are equal but some scriptures are more equal than others. Thus Heinrich Schlier may warn against the danger of making "the theology of one book or group of books the norm of what is 'Theology of the New Testament.'" "The theology of the New Testament," he insists, "is built on the basis of all the New Testament writings," but adds significantly, "though of course not all of them contribute in the same proportion."[43] If not all contribute in the same proportion, then some books become a more important norm than others. Hans Küng objects to Käsemann's procedure of establishing a "canon within the canon" through arguments that only a portion of the New Testament expresses the pure gospel. (As well as rejecting John's gospel Käsemann detects in such books as Luke-Acts and the Pastoral Epistles a deterioration

12

into "early catholicism." By this term he designates the emergence of a structured Church which dispenses salvation according to principles of ordination, apostolic succession, traditional doctrine, and reestablished law. We will return to this subject in a later chapter on salvation history.[44] Küng protests strongly against Käsemann's selectivity: "What actually is at issue here? Nothing but the fundamental renunciation of a comprehensive understanding and a serious acceptance of the whole New Testament in favor of a concentrated selection, that is, the rejection in principle of a 'Catholic' understanding of Scripture in favor of 'heresy.'"[45] At the same time, however, Küng himself gives strong preference to certain books, even if he does not exclude the others from the canon.

Küng proposes to us the principle of "originality" as a criterion for evaluating the relative importance of New Testament writings. There is originality of "chronology": I Corinthians is earlier than Ephesians. There is originality of "authenticity": we know that I Corinthians was actually written by Paul himself, whereas the Pauline authorship of the Pastoral Epistles is extremely doubtful. There is originality of "relevance": I Corinthians is nearer in content to the gospel of Jesus than is the epistle of James.[46] I must confess serious doubts about the value of the principle of "originality," at least as expounded by Küng. What is chronologically earlier need not necessarily express the essence of Christianity more aptly than what comes later. Is Mark's gospel necessarily more valuable because it is more original (chronologically) than John? Compared with later writers, an earlier writer may prove to be an inferior judge of the significance of the events in question. As for authenticity, the fact that the authorship of ever so many biblical books is unknown or doubtful indicates that originality of authenticity can scarcely be taken as a very important factor. At first glance originality of relevance looks like a valuable criterion. Küng picks an easy example for himself in asserting that I Corinthians is nearer in content to the gospel of Jesus than is the epistle of James. But what is the position if I Corinthians is contrasted with Ephesians or the Pastorals? It becomes more difficult to say which is nearer in content to the gospel of Jesus, and--if we grant that there is a long gap between the writing of I Corinthians and the Pastorals--it is a less meaningful thing to say. Even if we suppose that the author or authors of the Pastorals knew I Corinthians, it may have taken them further from the gospel of Jesus to have merely repeated the message of that letter. In a changed situation fidelity to the gospel could have demanded fresh statements and new moves. It is precisely the shifting nature of the situation which makes Küng's "originality of relevance" a vulnerable and unsatisfying criterion. In any case an appeal to the so-called "gospel of Jesus" compels one to adopt certain positions regarding the relevance of the historical Jesus for faith, as well as regarding the shift from the preaching of Jesus to the teaching of Paul. We will return to these themes in a later chapter.

Finally, when we test a theological assertion against scripture, two procedures may be at work. Scripture may be understood to be the way (or perhaps even the unique way) to shape one's personal understanding. Where the believing self-understanding of the Christian becomes the subject matter which theology is to describe and analyze, scripture will bear directly on the religious life of the user of scripture but only indirectly on theology. Alternatively, scripture can be interpreted as bearing directly on theological assertions. We can instance Bultmann as one scholar in whose theology scripture operates in the first way. Rahner would be another example. At the same time it is worth adding that scripture may operate in both ways: the theologian could conceivably both appeal directly to scripture as well as take the believing self-understanding of Christians as his subject matter.

Theology and Tradition   The work of the Christian theologian goes beyond any merely "private" study in which the sole test for his conclusions would be the sacred writings of his religion. Theology is a community affair in which the theologian listens to and engages in dialogue with present and past Christians. For a proper appreciation and appraisal of his work it is important to hold before one's attention the manifold ways in which Christians have already articulated their faith in teaching, preaching, liturgy, sacred art, and various styles of life. Every theologian acknowledges, at least implicitly, some role of tradition. Yet no theologian argues that he ought to respect all tradition. None uphold the principle of tota traditio, as almost all uphold the principle of tota scriptura. In appropriating tradition the theologian must make a whole series of choices. Some tradition he will dismiss as a debased development. Where his argument takes account of traditional teaching, he will give a certain preferential value to certain writers, to certain centuries, to certain councils, and to certain Christian communities. Vatican II shapes current Roman Catholic theology more deeply than Vatican I and much more deeply than the Council of Florence.

To assess theological positions on the basis of tradition is to expect the theologian to take account of the Christian community and of the Christian past. It is certainly not to require that he reproduce with verbal correctness what is deemed the acceptable line of tradition. The classical formulation of Vincent of Lerins ("What is believed everywhere, always and by all--this is truly and properly catholic."47) could suggest that tradition excludes progress and change. But is that the proper effect of the norms of universality, antiquity, and general consent which Vincent of Lerins invokes? At stake is what is "believed" (creditum) and not what is "said" (dictum). Possibilities for generous growth and development in theological understanding must be allowed for.

The Ethical Norm   Let me touch briefly on four further grounds for assessing theological assertions. The ethical consequences of a given position can provide concrete evidence for its truth and value. The New Testament and in particular the later books of the New Testament link erroneous doctrine with debased morals. This line of argument was implicitly raising the question: How will Christian ethical response be shaped when this or that theology is made the point of departure? This kind of test is particularly applicable when--as is the case with such theologians as Barth, Bultmann, and Rahner--we can follow up the moral consequences of their doctrine which emerge in their sermons.

The Norm of Internal Consistency   The previous three criteria attempt evaluation on the basis of factors extrinsic to theological views. They ask: In what way do these views do justice to the evidence of scripture and tradition? What effects in moral behavior could these views produce? But we ought also to look at the clarity and internal consistency with which given theologians are articulated. Here we reach the issue of a successful application of philosophical categories in theology. As a matter of historical fact the Christian religion has proved the greatest employment agency for philosophers the world has ever seen. It is worth reflecting that if the Incarnation had taken place in the late nineteenth century, theologians might perhaps have used predominantly Weberian, Marxist, Durkheimian, or Freudian categories in their work of elucidating the Christian gospel. Sociological, anthropological, and psychological concepts could help to provide a clear and coherent account of theological belief. Success in the application either of these or of strictly philosophical concepts can be evaluated by the degree of intelligible self-consistency attained. The only proviso is that the theological argument is being elucidated and not controlled by categories drawn from nontheological disciplines. At the deepest level, of course,

15

the use of philosophical (or other nontheological) notions does not represent the intrusion of alien matter into theology. To the extent that philosophy deals with man's ultimate reality it does not come to theology from without. This holds true whether one adopts a theocentric or an anthropocentric approach to theological reflection.

Relation to Contemporary Men   In the face of the actual human reality theology remains very weak unless it speaks to the contemporary situation. Hence there is a further (practical) criterion for judging the value of given theological positions: Are they keeping pace with man's self-understanding at this point in his history? This is not to suppose that there exists such a thing as the modern man with his particular self-understanding. The theologian ought to be conscious of the diversity in contemporary cultures and not be content to find a hearing merely with the modern man of his own country or--even worse--of his own theological faculty and school of thought. In seeking to conceptualize the experience of the divine revelation in Christ which elicits human faith, the theologian must be attuned to contemporary men's knowledge of themselves and talk in terms that make a meaningful communication to a wide audience. Otherwise what he says may sound incredible or simply unintelligible even to the sympathetic, educated hearer.

The Personal Aspect   A last basis for judgment is the individual, the solitary "one" among the mass of modern men. Does this or that theology illuminate "my" self-understanding and clarify (or provide) my perspective on life and history? Does it show how God is pro me (for me)? My response to a given theology should hardly provide the major, let alone the sole, criterion for assessment. Nevertheless, the fact that--despite my sympathetic attention--certain theological claims fail to speak to me and my situation is more than a mere matter of personal disenchantment. It is concrete evidence of a failure or at least a limitation in the theology with which I am confronted.

Is theology a science?

To elaborate theological procedures, criteria, and subject matter is to touch on the issue whether or not theology is rightly called a "science." In Roman Catholic circles and beyond, theology is frequently so described. Aquinas begins his Summa Theologica with the affirmation that "theology is a science" (sacra doctrina est scientia).[48] M. D. Chenu assures us that "theology is the science which deals with God."[49] Louis Bouyer defines theology as "the science of divine

16

things, "[50] and Karl Barth regards theology as "a science" which has for its subject "the word of God."[51] Yves Congar is a little more reserved when he explains that "theology is a reflection on the faith intent upon reaching the status of a science."[52] In their account of the nature of theology Rahner and Vorgrimler state that "this methodical effort to acquire knowledge of a complete, internally unified subject must be called a science."[53] Theology, in Ebeling's judgment, is a science, albeit a "responsible science" rather than a "calculating science."[54] If we look at specific areas of theology, we find that Gabriel Moran offers "a scientific theology of revelation."[55] Dr. John Robinson asserts that the formulation of statements in the field of eschatology concerns "the final sovereignty of God as it must be understood if the data of Christian existence are to be scientifically explained."[56] Previously he assures us that in general "the conclusions of theology" enjoy a "scientific" validity.[57]

I cannot regard this terminology with complacency. In English "science" used without qualification means the so-called natural sciences. It is misleading to translate the Latin "scientia," the French "science" and the German "Wissenschaft" by "science." All of these terms have a wider area of meaning than the English word "science." They denote an organized body of knowledge in which critical methods of investigation and argument are applied. To an extent Aquinas,[58] Chenu, Bouyer, Rahner, and others suffer misrepresentation at the hands of their translators. Moreover, we find various qualifications being introduced which indicate great differences between theology and science (that is, the natural sciences). Thus Chenu reflects: "Theology is not just any kind of knowledge about a supreme being who is called God but only knowledge through and in faith in revealed truth. The believer adheres to God revealing himself. . . . The result is a knowledge-structure unknown to the scientist." "This science," he adds, "is unique in another sense too, for it is by definition provisional. It is a mere preview to a direct vision."[59] Barth poses the claim of theology to enjoy a quite "unscientific" autonomy in which there would be no obligation to harmonize the findings of theology with those of secular thought. "Theology," he writes, "is a science and a teaching which feels itself responsible to the living command of this specific subject and to nothing else in heaven and on earth, in the choice of its methods, its questions and answers, its concepts and language, its goals and limitations."[60] Rahner and Vorgrimler qualify their account of theology as a "science" (that is, a Wissenschaft not a Naturwissenschaft) by adding that "the way in which its object first presents itself for study, its primary principles, and to some extent its methods of investigation are different from those of the profane sciences."[61]

Theology may be compared with the natural sciences in that it deals critically with facts of concrete reality which it seeks to systematize and generalize. It does not deal with abstractions as mathematics and logic do. In being an "historical" religion Christianity is linked with history. Some writers want to assimilate history to science.[62] If we agree that history is truly "scientific," theology would have a relationship with science through Christianity's connection with history. (In later chapters we discuss the "historical" nature of Christianity.) Moreover, theology is like scientific theory in that we can specify validity conditions. The Christian religion and its theology would cease to be valid if, for example, it were demonstrated that Jesus of Nazareth never existed or that he was in fact a malicious criminal.

However, on many counts theology remains irreducibly different from science. First, theology starts from the so-called data of revelation which it seeks to articulate, explain and relate. The subject matter of theological reflection is God communicating himself to men in Jesus Christ, an ultimately personal "given" which cannot be compared with the "given" in such sciences as inorganic chemistry or nuclear physics. Second, a particular science offers an accumulated body of knowledge which can be enriched by further discoveries. There is a sense in which theology accumulates information by drawing on the fresh findings of scripture and historical studies. But in its essential "given" theology does not tolerate an increase. It is not a progressive science. Foundational revelation closed with the apostolic age and the faith which responds to this revelation "no longer experiences any real increase from outside. . . . The new justifies itself always and only through its origin from the old; the new truth is the old truth and not a truth added to the old one from outside."[63] Third, science proceeds by observation and experiment to explanations and predictions which it co-ordinates in laws expressed in mathematical notation. The claims of science are subject to immediate confirmation or refutation in controlled experience. The particular scientific methods of argument and modes of verification are not applicable in theology.

The theologian as believer

We began this chapter by recommending the need to examine what the great practitioners of theology actually do. As one of my students once observed, given theologies are always a species of autobiography, with some of the enigmas that attend more overt forms of autobiography. There is no theology apart from the lives of individual theologians. Sooner or later we have to pose such questions as: How does the theologian's own faith affect his professional work? What is the link between his theology and his denominational adherence? Can he carry on his professional work while withholding any personal belief in God and Christ? If Christians take it upon themselves to elucidate and explain non-Christian religions, can a non-Christian do the same effectively with Christian theology? If theology is an activity of "fides quaerens intellectum," can it be someone else's faith that we seek to understand?

In Ebeling's judgment the theologian must be a believing Christian. In reflecting on "the event of proclamation" he "shares responsibility for it."

> [He] identifies himself with the subject matter of theology. For he can only speak of this in the form of assertions, affirmatively. He allows himself to be engrossed by it, he takes responsibility for it. . . . No matter how learned he may be, he is of no use unless he is certain of what he is saying. . . . One cannot speak about God in a disinterested, objective and neutral way. If one does, then in effect one is no longer speaking about God. . . . Theology ceases to be theology if it is no longer concerned to bring God to expression, and so to make the claim to speak the truth in the sense of the simply necessary.64

But why must this be so? We might point out that as a matter of fact theologians have always been believers and were expressing their personal faith in their theological statements. Or we might decree that unless someone is a believer, he is not to count as a theologian, whether or not he calls himself a theologian and does work that looks like theology. Or again we could argue that unless a man is a believer, he is likely to lack the interest and motivation to engage himself in serious theological work. But these answers at best remain on the surface and fail to reach the heart of the matter. To expound serious knowledge of and pass worthwhile judgments on something requires a measure of real communion with the "object." It cannot remain something alien to oneself towards which one continues indifferent. The theologian too must know God if he is to expound him. Belief is part of the theologian's equipment, whether his focus of attention is on God disclosing himself to man or on man responding to the self-revealing God. The theologian is a Promethean figure struggling to know and say more about God than he has a right to. He is not a spokesman for God; it is just that he watches his language in the presence of God.

There are, however, two riders to be added. Belief and unbelief are not two mutually exclusive, entirely complete entities which one either experiences totally or not at all. It is arguable that no one is the complete believer or the complete nonbeliever. For the theologian, as for other Christians, there are many possible gradations. Secondly, theology may obviously be studied after a fashion by one who professes unbelief. The theologian can engage in serious academic discussion with him, just as the preacher can put some account of what the Christian message is to the ordinary nonbeliever.

We should also recall that the theologian remains always a child of a particular form of Christian tradition. His personal life and commitments will exercise a more intrinsic influence upon the positions he espouses than is the case with chemists and lawyers. The particular way in which he lives Christianity will affect decisions about the subject matter of theology, the warrants to which he appeals and so forth. Ebeling judges this factor so important that he takes as "the most outstanding difference" between theologians the fact that "we theologize either as Catholic or as Protestant theologians."[65] Only a Christian still preoccupied with the Reformation, however, could make such a judgment. There are clearly far more vital differences than the one Ebeling mentions. Let us note two of them. We can divide theologians according to whether they retain the traditional Christian conviction that Jesus is unique and definitive or are ready to see him as exchangeable at least in principle in his function as the initiator of our faith. Fritz Buri falls into the second class when he dismisses Bultmann's insistence on the unique and decisive saving act of God in Christ as a "mythological remnant," an "illusion of exclusiveness," and a "Christ-myth" which is unjustified.[66] Secondly, a few theologians challenge the common conviction that Christian faith involves our subjective survival after death. Thus Schubert Ogden declares: "What I must refuse to accept, precisely as a Christian theologian, is that belief in our continued subjective existence after death is in some way a necessary article of Christian faith."[67] Such differences go much deeper than the traditional Protestant-Catholic controversies which Ebeling has in mind.

Revelation is God's self-interpretation.

Karl Barth

Theologians are always trying God on for size, and this
they do whether they do it reverently or otherwise. In
either case, they are also trying themselves on for size:
if they are Christians, they cannot but claim that the two
"tryings" are simultaneous, and that at best the one is
the other.

Peter Steele

Chapter II

Revelation:

Introduction to the Discussion

Christians are convinced that God has made himself known to us in the history of the Old and the New Testament, manifesting himself through Jesus of Nazareth as our merciful, loving Father. Christianity is a revealed religion. Revelation is the constant presupposition to all discussion of particular events or details of the Christian religion. Our doctrine of revelation encloses and affects the whole of theology. Along with such expressions as "the word of God" and "salvation history," "revelation" is among the most general terms available, designating comprehensively the "object" of faith and the "content" of theology. The study of revelation is in a sense coextensive with theology. After considering theological procedures and criteria it is logical to begin with the subject of revelation.

Right from the outset, however, we should renounce an unwarranted claim that the notion of revelation gives the most

23

profound expression to the Christian gospel. This category does not enjoy some privileged immunity from limitations and ambiguity. Perhaps more than any other theological idea it carries with it the danger of an intellectualism which would suggest that man's essential predicament is his lack of knowledge of God rather than his sinfulness and total need before God. "We are saved through God's merciful love; therefore, we are Christians"--is a fuller and more appropriate confession than: "We know God through his revelation; therefore, we are Christians." If we wish to use such slogans, it is preferable to describe Christianity as a religion of redemption than as a religion of revelation.[1] There is no room here for a Cartesian-style affirmation, "Scio, ergo Christianus sum."

Propositional or personal revelation?

In opening up the topic it may help to begin by putting the case against pre-Vatican II Roman Catholic theology for treating revelation as if it were identical either with the communication of a set of divinely authenticated truths or with the body of information thus communicated to man. The Lutheran theologian, Gerhard Gloege, described the Catholic position as follows: "Revelation is the communication of hitherto unknown truths or facts which on the basis of divine authority are accepted in the act of rational assent."[2] His fellow Lutheran Paul Althaus characterized Roman Catholic theology as having "entirely depersonalized and materialized the concept of revelation. . . . The depersonalization of the idea of revelation is evident from the fact that they never say, 'God has revealed himself.' Revelation is intellectualized."[3] A more benign critic could point out how there never was an entire depersonalization of revelation in Catholic theology. Vatican I did speak expressly of God "revealing himself."[4] But the trend to depersonalization was unmistakably there, so that revelation was presented as the disclosure of new truths about God, the communication of a body of doctrine, a privileged enriching of our knowledge about God. The upshot was that revelation came to be closely associated with notions of creed, correct doctrine or a collection of doctrines. The assent of faith was understood as assent to doctrine. It was believing "the things" to be true which God has revealed.[5] From here it was only half a step to allowing "correctness" of verbal expression and the sterile recitation of creeds to predominate over the lived experience of self-commitment to God. Faith became orthodoxy.

The case against these earlier trends in Catholic thinking on revelation would include unfavorable comments on the teaching of Vatican I which both exemplified and promoted the trends. However benignly or harshly we judge the doctrine of Dei Filius, the Council's dogmatic constitution on Catholic faith,[6] the suppositions about man, his knowledge and his language bear some responsibility for the limitations in the formulations proposed about faith and revelation. The platonic-scholastic style of anthropology envisages the process of man's believing affirmation of revelation in a hierarchy--with intellect and will in partnership at the top and the passions in a kind of helotry at the bottom. The document is pre-Freudian in its understanding of man. There is no recognition of human emotions and instincts, not to mention the experimental nature of man's response to life in which he is always "trying things on for size." The intricate, fundamental and often highly obscure relationship between overt and covert awareness and assent is not touched upon. An idealizing account of man is presupposed which gives scant recognition to the way in which the capacities of people and their grasp of truth vary. Revelation is credited with making it possible for naturally knowable truths about divine things to be known "by all with facility, with firm assurance and with no admixture of error (ab omnibus expedite, firma certitudine et nullo admixto errore)." Despite the fact that the Council has just invoked "the present condition of the human race (in praesenti quoque generis humani conditione)," it fails to acknowledge that inescapable ambiguity which attends man's acquisition of truth.[7] Furthermore, the Council Fathers appear to employ contestable notions about the capacity of language to encapsulate truths (whether natural or revealed). It seems to be taken for granted that language enjoys an independence of cultural presuppositions and can form a kind of noncreative medium for the preservation and transmission of revelation. "This supernatural revelation, according to the faith of the universal Church, declared by the Sacred Synod of Trent, is contained in 'the written books and unwritten traditions which have come down to us, having been received by the apostles from the mouth of Christ himself, or from the apostles, by the dictation of the Holy Spirit, having been transmitted, as it were, from hand to hand.'"[8] Revelation is here portrayed as something which endures and remains rather than as something which happens. What remains is truth or rather a collection of truths. The questions are not raised: How does someone in the nineteenth century know that a parcel of revealed truths dispatched in the first century is reaching him intact? What is it for such truths to

"remain intact" in the required sense? As the text of the Council
document invokes on occasions the work of the Holy Spirit within
the Church, a benign interpreter might mount answers in those
terms. Our experience now somehow guarantees that what we know
now is what was known back in the first century. This reply, by
effectively highlighting the present and personal nature of divine
activity, would shift away from the main thrust of the Council's
interpretation of revelation as truths to be handed down.

In his survey John Baillie sharply contrasted Roman Catholic
teaching on revelation with the views of Wilhelm Herrmann, Dr.
William Temple and others, on the grounds that whereas the latter expressed revelation as the personal self-disclosure of God,
the former offered us a theory of propositional revelation, that
is to say, a theory that God has disclosed a set of truths otherwise inaccessible to human reason.[9] He cited with approval the
observation of J. M. Creed: "For Scholasticism, whether in its
original form or as modified by teachers of our own time, the
concept of Revelation as the supernatural and infallible communication of propositional truths is indispensable."[10] (Scholasticism
is here identified by Creed with Thomism and Roman Catholic
theology.) It was certainly understandable that Creed in 1938
and Baillie in 1956 could identify Catholic theology with Scholasticism. It is now no longer possible to assert that a propositional
view of revelation is indispensable for Catholic theology. In the
documents of Vatican II[11] and the writings of Heinrich Fries,[12]
René Latourelle,[13] Gabriel Moran,[14] Avery Dulles,[15] and others
revelation is set out as God's personal self-revelation.

Such is the kind of account which has been commonly given of
pre-Vatican II Catholic thought on revelation--a story with a happy
ending as the change takes place from the derided propositional
view to the proper personal explanation. The so-called propositional view comes in for severe strictures at the hands of Gabriel
Moran. He represents this view as maintaining that what God has
revealed is a set of propositions to be believed.[16] Characterized
in such a way, the view is clearly silly. But what theologian of
any real standing ever held precisely that? Gloege who--as we
noted above--rejects the older Catholic view describes it correctly as holding revelation to be "the communication of hitherto
unknown truths or facts." Revelation was taken to be the disclosure of facts about God, man and God's plan for man. Dissatisfaction with this view is no excuse for caricaturing it. Moran
maintains that the so-called propositional view implies that there
is a finite, numerable set of statements to be believed.[17] There

is no such implication. About any object whatever--and a fortiori about "the things" which God has revealed--an indefinitely large number of true statements can be made. Moran's criticism suggests that the so-called propositional view carries the implication that there is no real contact between man and the revealed reality. (As we have seen, Althaus complains that this view "entirely depersonalizes" the idea of revelation, on the grounds that it fails to include the affirmation that "God has revealed himself.") However, among the things revealed is the fact that the triune God wishes to communicate himself to man in grace with a view to man's reaching the supernatural goal of the beatific vision. Even if the so-called propositional view does not identify revelation as self-revelation, it is far from entirely depersonalizing revelation and implying that there is no contact between man and the revealed reality.

I certainly have no desire to deny that there is much truth in the common story about the shift in Catholic theologies of revelation. But let us look carefully at a key feature of this story, the distinction between the personal and the so-called propositional view of revelation. Suppose we agree that revelation is properly understood as the saving self-disclosure of God who calls us in Jesus Christ to enter by faith into a new relationship with him. Is there no room left for talk of "revealed truths" and the "content" of revelation? With regard to this question we should recall that the relationship of the revealing God and the believing man is first and foremost a living experience which shapes man's personal history. But this experienced reality is not so wholly incommunicable that it remains locked up in inarticulate subjectivity. The faith which arises in encounter with the self-revealing God feels the need[18] to formulate true statements of faith both within the community of those who share this experience and also for outsiders. This is all part of the social dimension of revelation, faith and human life.[19] Faith talks about itself and what it experiences of God: "Since we have the same spirit of faith as he had who wrote, 'I believed, and so I spoke,' we too believe, and so we speak" (II Corinthians 4:13).[20] Provided that these formulations give some insight into the lived event of revelation, they may be described as expressing revelation. In this sense revelation could be called propositionable. It can find expression in true propositions about God's self-communication to man.

This is the kind of analysis which I offered in my book, Theology and Revelation.[21] Some points need to be added. Man's ex-

27

perience of revelation does not merely give rise to true statements about revelation, as if the role of language in this case were simply to put into words what had already been experienced in some wordless state. We do not enjoy such a separate inner life. Revelation comes about because man is addressed--in sermons, in the scriptures, in doctrinal pronouncements, in the sacraments, in sacred art, and in any other account which Christians give of their gospel. Men encounter the divine self-revelation indissolubly linked with the Jewish-Christian community's traditional discourse about their God and his relations with man. The truths which make up that tradition supply the word which is a constitutive element of the revelation encountered in faith. In John's gospel the experience of Christ's self-manifestation does not take place in inarticulate silence but is mediated through what he says. Thus his statements (and questions) play an essential role in his self-disclosure to the Samaritan woman (4:7 ff.). This divine revelation does not occur through Jesus being manifested in some silent epiphany or wordless transfiguration.

In principle we could postulate some figure(s) who stood at the very beginning of what we know as the Jewish-Christian religion. After some experience(s) of God they give expression to their faith and thus began a history of religious discourse. This community of faith with their traditional language was instrumental in bringing about revelatory situations and initiating the faith of new adherents. Even the apostles, despite the directness of their experience of God in Christ, brought to this revelatory experience a traditional understanding that at least partly guided their interpretation of what it was they were experiencing. The God whom they met in these new disclosures was a God they had known and of whom they had heard before. This prior knowledge was now called into question. Their subsequent confession of faith came to expression through the interplay of the old tradition and the new experiences. A tradition of language continues to surround and enter into faith's experience of the self-revealing God.

A further point that I wish to add concerns the element of experience. It would be inaccurate to suppose that in my earlier book I was proposing that man's experience of revelation is monolithic. There is no need to appeal to William James or his successors to establish the manifold variety that is involved. One experience can be that of finding through revelation a new perspective on life and history and thus coming to Christian faith for the first time. The hearing of a sermon might bring fresh insight into one's sinfulness before God. Through the Eucharist one could vividly experience the nearness of God and the truth of the community's union in Christ. Short of the face-to-face experience which is the final vision, the ways in which God's revelatory activity can be encountered seem indefinitely many and various.

In this context it could be enlightening to introduce some comparisons and contrasts between the experience of divine revelation and the confessional language of faith which both gives rise to this experience and issues from it. The language of faith like the living experience itself is provisional and characterized by a hope which looks forward to fulfillment. Both in the formulation of his faith and in his faith itself "the Christian" is, as Luther put it, "not in a perfect state but in a process (Christianus non est in facto, sed in fieri)." The theology which has to deal with such formulations can be no more than a theologia viatorum. The personal engagement of faith which responds to revelation must be renewed and grow, even as faith's doctrinal utterances need constant reformulation. Of course, such very simple confessions of faith as that "God is three" and "Christ is present in the Eucharist" survived by being less culturally conditioned and thus transcending the normal provisionality. But they say very little. The two confessions cited leave open the kind of presence and trinity which faith knows and announces.

The faith which revelation calls forth is directly concerned with God in Christ. Properly speaking, it is knowledge of God rather than a knowledge that God is such and such. To quote Aquinas: "The act of the believer terminates at the object itself, not at what is to be enunciated (actus credentis non terminatur ad enuntiabile, sed ad rem)."22 As such, reflection on the confession of faith deals with our notions of God in Christ and is not in immediate contact with the divine reality. Furthermore, the statements of faith which can be multiplied indefinitely are always partial and fragmentary. In faith itself one encounters God as a personal being and hence as whole. While the commitment and knowledge generated by the encounter can deepen and grow, there is a certain wholeness even about the initial coming to faith. It is an interpersonal experience, a subject-to-subject encounter. If we ask what is revealed, we might come up with such answers as: "Through a salvation history culminating in Christ's death and resurrection God affords a glimpse of the mystery of his absolute love." Or perhaps: "Man's greatness consists in allowing God to become the partner of his nature; God alone can free man for genuine humanity so that life is to be defined in terms of God." Or again: "God offers life in Christ to all men, even though

29

they have done nothing to deserve his offer." Yet there is nothing final or finally satisfying about these formulations. They are replies to the question, "What is revealed?", rather than to the question which is ultimately the only appropriate one, "Who is revealed?".

The difference between revelation itself and the language of revelation can be expressed from the side of revelation's direct correlate, faith. The "object" of faith is Christ's person more than Christ's doctrine, Christ himself rather than propositions about Christ. In the case of a Socrates, once the disciple is in possession of the doctrine, he can forget about the teacher. But what Christ does as a teacher--as John's gospel shows clearly-- is to reveal precisely himself and his Father. When he asks "the twelve," "Will you also go away?", Peter does not reply: "We shall stay because we have understood your testimony, realize its truth and can verify it." Rather his answer is deeply personal: "To whom shall we go? You have the words of eternal life" (John 6:67 f.). Aquinas was almost echoing Peter's declaration when he observed: "What seems to be decisive in any act of faith is the person to whose words approval is given."23 We may not, of course, allow ourselves to think of this personal relationship as if it were some mysterious encounter, which either lay beyond description or of which we could not say that one description is better than another. If that were so, there could in no sense be a "content" to Christian revelation or else the "content" would be so ambiguous that no accounts of it would be instructive. But at the same time the objective communication that is an essential aspect of revelation remains at the service of personal encounter. As Aquinas' remark suggests, one ought not remain satisfied with an assent to truths about God but should come by means of these formulations into a close relationship with God himself.

Renewed theology of revelation

After these initial disclaimers and observations, I want to look at earlier theological work which has helped to shape current reflection on revelation. When assessing the factors that have contributed to the renewal in Catholic theologies of revelation, Latourelle draws attention to the stimulus of Protestant theology, the biblical and patristic renewal, the Catholic debate on the nature of theology itself (1936-1939), the contribution of the so-called kerygmatic theology from Innsbruck and work on the development of dogma.24 It occasions surprise to find nothing said about the philosophical influences which were operative in the renewal. Even granted that it would be difficult to plot the precise effect of any particular philosophical contribution, certain points are clear. Catholic theologians have been compelled to join their Protestant counterparts in facing up to the fact that since Kant the problem of religious knowledge has become acute. Theologies of revelation have been elaborated in an attempt to come to terms with this problem. Through Philipp Marheineke and A. E. Bieder-mann, Hegel has encouraged first Protestant and then Catholic theologians to interpret revelation as the divine self-manifestation.[25] The category of "encounter" and talk of revelation in terms of an "I-Thou" confrontation have gained popularity in Catholic theology. Besides seeing here the influence of Martin Buber we should not allow Ferdinand Ebner's contribution on the "I-Thou" relationship of speech to be forgotten.[26] What Latourelle has to say about the renewal of the theology of revelation in Protestantism is very sketchy and surprisingly fails even to mention the decisive con-tribution of Karl Barth.[27] It seems that it would have some value to offer here a critical account of the consensus about revelation that obtained in so-called "dialectic" theology founded by Barth.[28] Contemporary Protestant and Catholic work remains in explicit or implicit counterpoint with this consensus.

Revelation in dialectic theology

Karl Barth more than any other single theologian brought about after World War I a renewed concern to elucidate the nature of divine revelation.[29] The importance of his commentary on Romans lay essentially in his rediscovery of "the revelation of God as the decisive category of theological thought."[30] To prevent this chapter becoming confused and confusing I want to set out schematically the basic motifs found in the writings of the dialectic theologians on revelation.

1 Both in his exposition of <u>Romans</u> and in other early works Barth vehemently protested against the current liberal Protestant theology which assimilated the gospel to European bourgeois culture and treated Christian faith as a phenomenon in the history of reli-gion. Barth assaulted with passion this reduction of faith to the "highest possibility of reason," revelation to the "highest possi-bility of history" and Jesus' consciousness of God to the highest possibility of human religiosity.[31] Christianity had been presented as a pious tradition, a piece of eclecticism and a cult of "the inner attributes of personality."[32] Against this distortion Barth argued

31

that the task of theologians is to speak not about the man of Christian religion, his faith, his piety and his experience, but about
God, and the only God we know is the God who reveals himself.
Barth called for a return to the proper sources of faith and theology, the revealed word of God witnessed to in the bible. God must
be allowed to be God, the "wholly other," who is separated from
man by the "infinite qualitative distinction between time and eternity"[33] and remains inaccessible unless he speaks and discloses
himself. Barth's call was "to take revelation seriously,"[34]
namely as that "penetrating and ultimate crisis"[35] which con-
fronts man when God makes himself known from above.

For the other dialectic theologians too, "the only possible
theme of an honest theology" was--in Gogarten's words--"to
restore to the word of God its due position" and to maintain that
attitude in carrying through the theological task.[36] Brunner's
stance was similar. The standard for judging a theology was "the
energy and clarity with which the thought of God's divinity or of
the divine revelation is adhered to. For "revelation is not only
the content, but at the same time the basis of all theology."[37]
Hence "the great theme of Christian thought is the defining and
establishing of the Christian concept of revelation."[38] Even before the second edition of Barth's <u>Romans</u> made such a lasting
impression on him,[39] Bultmann was insistent that the true foundation of Christian theology lay in revelation. "Protestantism," he
wrote in 1920, "must recognize the specific aspect of religious
life and bring it to consciousness." This meant, he explained,
that Protestantism "must be able to speak of God's revelation."[40]
Later he took the motif of revelation as the central theme for his
greatest work, the commentary on John. Because he understood
the developed presentation of "the revelation event" to form the
content of the gospel,[41] he summed up chapters 2-12 under the
heading "the revelation of the <u>doxa</u> before the world" and chapters
13-20 under the heading "the revelation of the <u>doxa</u> before the
community."

2 From the beginning of dialectic theology it was agreed that
divine revelation is essentially God's self-revelation and not a
supernatural communication of truths,[42] mystical experience,
or anything else. Despite later disagreement as these men elaborated various theologies, the understanding of God's revelation
as self-revelation became "almost universal in contemporary
Protestant theology."[43]

3 Man's response to revelation was recognized to be faith.
"Faith and revelation are correlatives," declared Brunner.[44]

Barth agreed: "To the miracle of revelation corresponds the miracle of faith."[45] So too did Paul Tillich, a critic, albeit a friendly critic, of dialectic theology: "Faith is always revelation faith (Offenbarung-sglaube)."[46] This consensus included Bultmann, who, as we shall see, understood revelation to be the proclamation that precipitates our decision of faith. God's revealing word and man's responding faith were taken to be absolutely coordinate: there is no revelation outside faith and no faith without revelation.

4 The divine revelation which makes faith possible was widely characterized as a word to be heard rather than as an object to be seen or a truth to be possessed. In his commentary on John, Bultmann declared: "It is only in the word that Jesus was the revealer, and it is only in the word that he will be the revealer."[47] Faith came and continues to come by hearing. "Revelation," Brunner wrote, "is not man opening his eyes so that he now sees the sun which, nevertheless, was always shining; rather it is God's giving himself to be known, a self-giving which is to be understood in word."[48] "God has spoken"--over and over again Barth recalled this revealing word of God which the believer hears and the theologian is to elucidate.[49] "It is not," he explained, "the right human thoughts about God which form the content of the bible, but the right divine thoughts about men. The bible tells us not how we should talk with God but what he says to us. . . . It is this which is within the bible. The word of God is within the bible."[50] In an essay on "The Christian Understanding of Revelation" (first published in 1948), he summed up revelation as "the word that is spoken to us, that is given to us in the witness of Holy Scripture."[51]

5 Closely allied with the understanding of faith as hearing God's word was the conviction that the divine act of revelation cannot be authenticated by human arguments. "Man," Barth wrote, "is of himself unable to find access to the revelation of God."[52] If Christian faith tries to produce evidence to establish its position, it ceases to be faith. As Brunner put the matter: "With the 'I believe' is expressed the renunciation of every kind of proof, the recognition of the impossibility of every proof."[53] To seek to ground faith by objective demonstration would be to lapse into a particular form of illusory justification by human work, namely justification by the works of the intellect. Revelation was acknowledged in one way or another to impose itself on man as a self-authenticating reality. To quote Barth: "Revelation in the Christian sense is the revelation of God. For the Christian there is no need of a special enquiry and a special proof to know and to declare who and what God is. For the Christian the revelation is itself the

proof, the proof furnished by God himself."[54] Bultmann's position was the same: "God's word has no authentication; it demands recognition"; it "is subject to no human criterion and is in itself authoritative."[55]

6 In particular faith's grasp of revelation was acknowledged to be independent of the findings of critical historical investigation. Wilhelm Herrmann, Barth's and Bultmann's teacher at Marburg, had made this point: "It is a fatal error to wish to settle the ground of faith through historical research. The ground of faith should be firm; the results of historical work are in constant flux. . . . The historical work on the New Testament cannot bring us a bit nearer to what concerns the grounding of faith."[56] Neither Barth nor Bultmann shifted from the view that the certitude of faith is independent of the probabilities of historians' conclusions. Barth's assertion was typically and unashamedly sweeping: "In history as such there is nothing, so far as the eye reaches, which could ground faith."[57] Bultmann put the same point, if with less zest: "Historical research can never lead to any result which could serve as a basis for faith, for all its results have only relative validity."[58]

7 Associated with the notion of revelation evading ordinary critical verification was the motif of its hiddenness. "God's word to men" Bultmann described as a "hidden word"; "the revelation present in scripture is a veiled revelation."[59] Jesus is "the concealed revealer, because he cannot legitimate himself to them [sc. the Jews]; for the right of his claim is visible only to the man who makes the decision of faith."[60] Barth revelled in insisting on the paradox of a hidden disclosure: "Even where he reveals himself, God continues to dwell in darkness."[61] The "deus absconditus" is "precisely as such the deus revelatus."[62] In defiance of all logic Barth asserted: "Revelation in the bible means the self-unveiling, imparted to men, of the God, who according to his nature cannot be unveiled to man."[63]

8 It was a further item in the consensus that revelation is essentially salvific in its origin and scope. It transcends human possibilities and is wholly due to the divine initiative. "My personal relation with God," Bultmann wrote, "can be made real by God only, by the acting God who meets me in his word."[64] The divine revelation comes to sinful man who of himself is closed against it.[65] It is not man's own powers but the grace of God through the Holy Spirit which lets him hear the divine word.[66] The meaning of revelation is the justification of the sinner; "revelation and forgiveness are the same."[67] In short revelation is "salvation-revelation (Heilsoffenbarung)."[68]

9 When Barth, Bultmann, and other dialectic theologians explained in detail the effect of saving revelation, we meet the recurrent theme of man's return to his true status as a creature. If sin is a false turning away from one's origin, [69] revelation means recovering a consciousness of creaturehood. "Man's eyes," Bultmann declared, "are opened concerning his own existence and he is once again able to understand himself."[70] Barth had something similar to say: "Our souls have awakened to the consciousness of their immediacy to God. And this means an immediacy of all things, relations, orders and forms to God, an immediacy lost and needing to be won again. . . . The soul remembers that its origin is in God."[71] Moltmann draws attention to the way this platonizing theme appears in the foreword to the second edition of Barth's Romans and indicates where it is to be found in the writings of Brunner, Gogarten, and Heinrich Barth.[72] Brunner gave classic expression to this theme: "The idea of origin is the identical meaning of all true philosophy and religion."[73]

10 The notion of man's return to his origin did not mean, however, that all the works of creation or the whole history of man were understood as the revelation of God. The "place" of revelation was taken to be Christ; here man encounters God's unique revealing and saving act. In an essay first published in 1931 Bultmann maintained: "Only in Jesus, that is, only in the event of revelation, only in the word which God speaks in Jesus and which proclaims Jesus, is God accessible to men."[74] In his John commentary he expressly insisted on Jesus' role as revealer being "exclusive" and "absolute": "The revealer represents God not in the legal sense, but it is in him and only in him that God comes to encounter."[75] Brunner shared this Christo-centric view of revelation.[76] Tillich, however, argued that even though revelation took place preeminently through Jesus of Nazareth, its occurrence was not limited by him. In criticism of Bultmann and Gogarten he propounded the view that faith "has grown up on the ground of the imperceptible history of revelation, which passes in hidden manner through history and has found in Christ its complete expression."[77] He was ready to acknowledge revelation wherever there was a "breakthrough of the unconditioned in its unconditionedness."[78] At least in his Romans Barth was somewhat ambiguous on this issue. Although he described the years A.D. 1-30 as "the era of revelation and disclosure," his account of revelation as the divine negation of all human self-assertion indicated that revelation was possible without any involvement with Jesus of Nazareth. The decisive function of Christ consisted in the fact that in him "we

have discovered and recognized the truth that God is found everywhere and that, both before and after Jesus, men have been discovered by him." "Every epoch" is then "a potential field of revelation and disclosure."[79] At a later date Barth clearly maintained
that revelation occurs uniquely in Christ, "the one and only light."[80]
This shift was part of the movement towards and unqualified dominance of Christology in Barth's thought which he described as follows: "In these years [1928-1938] I had to learn that Christian
doctrine . . . has to be exclusively and conclusively the doctrine
of Jesus Christ--of Jesus Christ as the living word of God spoken
to us men."[81] In his mature essay on "The Christian Understanding of Revelation" Barth wrote: "When the Christian language speaks
of revelation and God . . . it speaks of Jesus Christ." Here--but
only here Christianity sees revelation.[82]

   11 In understanding the revelation brought by Christ, his death
and resurrection were acknowledged to be of paramount importance.
"In his death," Barth wrote, "the invisible God becomes for us
visible."[83] Here human aspirations and self-righteousness are
exposed in the light of the divine act of judgment and renewal.
"The only source for the real, the immediate revelation of God is
death. Christ unlocked its gates. He brought life to light out of
death."[84] His resurrection is "the transformation," "the revelation," "the disclosing of Jesus as the Christ, the appearing of God,
and the apprehending of God in Jesus."[85] For Brunner too the resurrection was the climactic moment of revelation. It was then that
Christ's "divine glory broke through the concealing veil of his
human 'form of a servant.' The incognito is lifted, and only when
this happens does there arise in the disciples the full perception
of the truth that he is the Son of God."[86]

Bultmann's theology of revelation

   The major aim of this chapter has been to delineate the general
consensus on revelation which obtained in dialectic theology. In
doing that we have given particular attention to Karl Barth. At this
point we leave Barth, who developed the implications of revelation
as being one of the three forms of the word of God. Barth gave
his theology of revelation a Trinitarian style in which the triune
God is portrayed as revealing himself as Lord, that is, as the
revealer, the revelation and the revealedness.[87] Another development was Barth's debate against Brunner's defense of revelation
in creation.[88] To fill out the historical background we need to
delineate the specific views of Bultmann who has proved at least

as important as Barth in creating the context for the contemporary discussion of revelation.

$\underline{a}$ The salvific nature of revelation is strongly to the fore in Bultmann's account. "Man," he writes, "has always already missed the existence that at heart he seeks; his intent is basically perverse, evil."[89] It is not this or that particular moral failing which characterizes man as a sinner, but the fundamental attitude of self-affirmation in which man seeks to live autonomously, using the world to find security for his existence.[90] This is the primal sin, namely that "man does not honour God as God."[91] "The ultimate sin reveals itself to be the false assumption of receiving life not as a gift of the Creator but procuring it by one's own power, of living from one's self rather than from God."[92] Out of man's situation of "fallenness" there is "no possibility of escape as a human undertaking."[93] The New Testament "affirms the total incapacity of man to release himself from his fallen state."[94]

$\underline{b}$ But if it is correct that "prior to the encounter with the revealer the life of all men moves in the darkness, in sin,"[95] what can there be in fallen man to which the revealer speaks? Will Bultmann be compelled to admit that through revelation and faith the old man is completely annihilated and a new man who had no continuity with the old steps into his place?[96] In fact Bultmann agrees that without a certain "pre-understanding" man cannot grasp God's revelation, the preaching of God's saving deed in Christ. He detects in man precisely such a "pre-understanding of revelation which consists in a knowledge that asks about his own situation."[97] Human life is characterized as a self-questioning which arises from a consciousness of limited possibilities in a concrete existence structured by concern (Sorge), dread (Angst) and "being-towards-death."[98] "Before the encounter with the revealer human life has no unambiguous meaning. . . . Man's life is pervaded by the quest for reality."[99] This inescapable questioning about oneself is simultaneously a questioning about God. "The pre-understanding is grounded in the question which moves human life, namely the question about God."[100] This questioning about God is contained in or rather is to be identified with the questioning about one's own existence. Man "has a relation to God in his search for God, conscious and unconscious. Man's life is moved by the search for God because it is always moved, consciously or unconsciously, by the question about his own personal existence. The question of God and the question of myself are identical."[101] To be human is to search for both authentic self-understanding and the saving revelation of God. Left to himself man is incapable of achieving the goals of this search.[102] Yet it is precisely because his existence is moved by the quest that he can receive God in revelation.

c We have been looking at Bultmann's account of "man prior to the revelation of faith," the title of his first chapter on Paul's theology.[103] He acknowledges an extensive agreement between this New Testament understanding of man and the existential analysis of Martin Heidegger. The concepts which Heidegger has developed may be suitably applied in the work of elucidating the existence of man to whom God's gift of revelation comes. Questioning and seeking for understanding as features of man's being in the world, one's consciousness of limitation, concrete human existence being structured by concern, dread and "being-towards-death," authenticity and inauthenticity as two basic ways man can exist--these are some of the notions already touched on where Bultmann is in contact with the thought of Heidegger, at least the Heidegger of Being and Time.[104] "Instructed by this book," Bultmann writes, "I attained a deeper understanding of the historical character of human existence, and thereby at the same time the conceptual framework in which theology too can operate in order to bring faith to appropriate expression as an existential attitude."[105] In "Heidegger's existentialist analysis of the ontological structure of being" he sees "a secularized, philosophical version of the New Testament view of human life."[106] There remain, however, essential differences between Bultmann's theology and Heidegger's philosophical standpoint, above all with respect to the fallenness of man (understood by Heidegger as an absorbed concern with the world of things). For Heidegger man is called in the face of death to the decision of self-realization; his own powers can enable man to emerge from his lost state back into an authentic existence. But Bultmann, as we have seen, is insistent on the New Testament truth that man unaided cannot free himself from his fallen state; it is only God's act in Christ which can set man free to realize his authentic nature. The philosophers can analyze human existence, but are wrong in confidently expecting that man is able by himself to recover his true selfhood.[107]

d In Bultmann's view revelation appears as an address to the individual, a call to decision which offers the possibility of new being in faith.[108] Man is placed in the situation in which he must choose "for good or evil, for or against God."[109] By involving man in a decision for faith or unfaith revelation sets him "before the possibility of coming to his authentic existence."[110] The Heideggerian notions of authenticity and inauthenticity correspond, in Bultmann's judgment, to a description of human existence with or without faith.[111] The knowledge of God's revelation means true self-knowledge, the only right reply to the questioning which characterizes man's existence.[112]

e For the transition to faith and authentic self-understanding the relationship to Christ is essentially constitutive. "Faith is not an act that can be consummated by man on his own initiative, as if Jesus were only the 'impulse' toward it. Rather, it is exactly Jesus toward whom faith is directed: he who is the way, the truth and the life, and without whom no one comes to the Father."[113] Two things are being asserted about the role of Christ. First, it is God's act in Christ and the kerygma that proclaims Christ which alone make faith and true human existence de facto possible. "It is only in the relation which takes place in Jesus that one is given the genuine self-understanding of existence (Dasein) which is repeatedly looked for and missed."[114] Second, man's answer to Jesus' word is faith in Jesus himself.[115] "'Faith' is 'faith in . . .' That is, it always has reference to its object, God's saving deed in Christ."[116] We shall see later how a number of his former students dissent from Bultmann over this by interpreting faith to mean believing (in God) like Jesus rather than believing in Jesus himself. For Bultmann God and Christ are not two different objects of faith in competition with one another or with one in subordination to the other. "God meets him [the believer] only in Christ. . . . To put it another way, Christ is God's eschatological deed, beside which there is no room for any other deed claiming or promoting faith."[117]

f The object of faith is not accessible through rational argument and proof. "There are no criteria to establish the legitimacy of revelation's claim, be it the trustworthy witness of others, be it rational or ethical standards, be it inner experiences. It is only to faith that the object of faith discloses itself; faith is the only way of approach."[118] Hence "the man who wishes to believe in God as his God must know . . . that he cannot demand a proof for the truth of the word which addresses him."[119] Faith is grounded in nothing else than the "object" in which we believe. As Bultmann expresses the matter in Jesus Christ and Mythology, "the ground and the object of faith are identical."[120] If we believe in Jesus as the eschatological saving event, this object of our faith is also that which supports our faith and from which the power of faith comes to us.

g For Bultmann faith and revelation are events which occur, not realities which endure and are possessed. Revelation can be real only "actually,"[121] and the act in question is the present act of proclamation which affects the existential decision of the individual. Through preaching the New Testament kerygma becomes a personal address of God to me, a call to decision now which constitutes the saving and revealing event. Faith is the decision precipitated ever anew by the kerygma and legitimated by the revelation of God's grace in Christ. It is the "repeated answer to the word of God which is repeatedly encountered and which so proclaims God's saving deed in Christ that it [this saving deed] is repeatedly present in it [the word proclaimed]."[122] The preaching of God's decisive act in the death of Christ makes possible the movement from unfaith to faith, from inauthentic to authentic existence. Bultmann is maintaining: (a) that the proclamation here and now of the significance of Jesus Christ's death for us is not a preaching about revelation, but is revelation;[123] and (b) that it is the only "place" of revelation. "It is only in the word, as the one who is preached, that he [Christ] encounters us."[124] If the reality of God is manifested only through Christian proclamation, outside this proclamation there will be no genuine revelation, no genuine faith and no salvation.

h His Christocentric view of revelation causes Bultmann to devalue the Old Testament dispensation and scripture. Since he sees man's relation to God as bound to the person of Jesus in the sense that "Jesus Christ alone, as God's eschatological deed of forgiveness, is God's word to man,"[125] it is not altogether surprising to find him looking at the Old Testament "chiefly as an historical document" and interpreting it "as a paradigm of human existence,"[126] a story of "miscarriage."[127] His attitude involves him in drawing some far-reaching contrasts between Old Testament faith and New Testament faith,[128] an exaggeration which draws criticism even from Gotthold Hasenhüttl, a writer who interprets Bultmann's thought with dedicated friendliness.[129]

i Bultmann's conviction that it is proclamation of Christ's death and resurrection which alone actualize the divine-human encounter drives him to assess non-Christian faith in God as illusory. Outside the Christian kerygma there is no genuine knowledge of God, but only that "pre-understanding" which inescapably raises the question of God. Here lies "the intolerance of revelation"; apart from the proclaimed word which is revelation, "all men are seekers."[130] The natural man knows in his existence about God, but he finds a true knowledge of God only in a believing response to the kerygma.[131] John Macquarrie queries the absolute claim that "there can be no genuine knowledge of God apart from the Christian gospel." He charitably adds that Bultmann's thought is ambiguous here, and asks for a statement from Bultmann to the effect "that he does not share the preposterous view of some kerygmatic theologians that outside of the Christian revelation there can be no genuine knowledge of God but only idolatrous imaginings."[132] In his reply, however, Bultmann rejects the invitation to qualify his position. Outside of Christian faith there is "an understanding" of what God is; that is to say, "in all men, explicitly or implicitly, the question concerning God is a living one. The exclusiveness of the kerygma consists in the fact that it provides the answer to this question by offering the right to say 'God is my God.'"[133]

An evaluation

From the composite picture I have sketched of the views on revelation held by Bultmann, Barth, and other dialectic theologians the following points recommend themselves as valuable contributions: the central importance of one's doctrine of revelation (1), the notion of self-revelation (2), the critical significance of Jesus' death and resurrection in our appreciation of revelation (11), and the salvific nature of revelation [(8) and (a)] which addresses man (d) and elicits his faith (3). Faith and revelation are mutually defining--one profiles the other. Hence the theology of faith is the theology of revelation and vice versa. One could interchange the titles of Vatican I's Decree on Catholic Faith and Vatican II's Constitution on Revelation without seriously misrepresenting the contents of the documents. In Roman Catholic theology it was no coincidence that the recovery of a personal approach to faith went hand in hand with the recovery of a personal approach to revelation. The recent attempt on the part of Wolfhart Pannenberg to define revelation in terms of knowledge which (at least logically) precedes faith is startling and unacceptable. In a later chapter I will present and criticize Pannenberg's theology of revelation.

The characterization of revelation as divine word (4) is a summarizing account, open to a rich variety of explanations. We will shortly focus on difficulties in Bultmann's "word-theology." In a later chapter we meet Rahner's use of "word-revelation" to elucidate the meaning of salvation history. Two general comments are pertinent. First, any particular explanation of revelation as "the word of God" needs detailed scrutiny before one should decide to offer support or express dissent. Second, it would be inaccurate to imagine that such theologies of revelation are confined to

Protestant writers. Besides Rahner we can point to Latourelle as
a Catholic theologian who assures us that "seen in its totality,
revelation is a phenomenon of word (speaking)." Hence "to outline
the history of the word of God" is "at the same time to outline the
history of revelation."[134] The Constitution on Revelation from
Vatican II expresses the divine supremacy over all activity of the
Church and even the finest human eloquence by its opening phrase,
"Hearing the word of God. . . ."

To the bearing of history on revelation (6) and the role of the
Old Testament (h) we return later. Elsewhere I have discussed
Moltmann's justified strictures on the view that God's saving
revelation means a return to man's origins (9).[135] The young
Barth initiated a necessary theological revolution by taking revelation and not religion as his organizing center. But there is hardly
need now to dwell on the difficulties created by his conviction of
the otherness of God who is separated from man by the "infinite
qualitative distinction between time and eternity"(1). Barth himself later modified this view of God as the "utterly other," a
view which makes it very difficult to see how such a God might
reveal himself to men, let alone become man.[136] It is curious
to see that as late as 1966 Ronald Gregor Smith could argue that
"without a God who is utterly other" the way remains open for
pantheism.[137] And yet Gregor Smith proceeds to explain how this
absolutely other God gives himself to man in personal encounter,
a self-giving which can only be described as "paradoxical."[138]

Let us turn for a moment to points (5), (7), and (f) which express the conviction that revelation is a hidden revelation, closed
to proof. These important issues will recur in greater detail
when we meet the problems of faith, history, and salvation history.
(In recent years the opposite thesis, the demonstrability of revelation, has been argued vigorously by Pannenberg. I challenge his
view in a later chapter.) Behind the repudiation of arguments for
revelation there often lies the belief that our choice is either faith
or reason. Either we accept in faith the God who discloses himself to us or we prove by rational proof that God so discloses himself. If that were the choice, we would naturally elect faith rather
than reason. But, as I have argued in my Theology and Revelation,
the alternative is not a real one.[139] The extreme position on the
undemonstrability of revelation is expressed by Gregor Smith's
assertion: "You cannot prove faith by its fruit. Nor can you dis-
prove it."[140] In these terms nothing could ever in principle
count against the claim that God has revealed himself to a group
of persons--not even the most horrible crimes to which the alleged
revelation might lead them.

Lastly, we come to the claim that Christ is the unique revealer, the only "place" of God's self-manifestation [(10), (a) and (i)]. In a sense Bultmann takes a harder line here than Barth. Where Barth maintains that <u>outside</u> <u>Christ</u> there is no revelation, Bultmann holds that <u>outside</u> <u>the</u> <u>proclamation</u> of <u>Christ</u> there is no revelation. If Christ encounters man only as the one who is preached, then outside the kerygma there will be no revelation (g). The negative side of Barth's position was his vehement opposition to so-called "natural theology," which he defined as "the doctrine of a union of man with God existing outside God's revelation in Jesus Christ."[141]

Bultmann and Barth insist that Christ is the only revealer and that consequently a relationship to Christ is essential to faith in the self-disclosing God. How then should we assess the claims of those who do not accept (or even know) Christian faith and yet lay claim to some genuine knowledge of God? The solution of Barth and Bultmann is clear: we must simply deny these claims. "Are not all ideas of God without belief false? Are they not illusory notions which are destroyed by the word of the real God?"[142] These rhetorical questions result from a theological position which simply decrees the way revelation must reach man. They are not based on an investigation of non-Christian ideas of God. Carl Braaten suggests one solution by arguing that "Christ is the sole Savior, not the sole revealer."[143] Hence some men could enjoy a true knowledge of God outside Christ, even if all men are to be saved through Christ. However, salvation and revelation are too intimately related for this solution to be effective.[144] The whole of a man's life is the sphere of God's saving activity. Hence man's thought and knowledge should be included. If in the process of salvation God affects human understanding, the result must be something in the order of knowledge. For Christ to be savior for all men he must also be revealer for all men.

John Macquarrie argues that we ought to admit the case for true non-Christian ideas of God. The view of Barth is an "arrogantly exclusive claim" which "ignores completely the finding of anthropology, of comparative religion, and of the historical researches of scholars like Troeltsch." As they have not personally shared in these experiences, Christians are not in the position to deny the revelatory experiences which non-Christians report. The Christian ought to make a charitable judgment here, as well as respect the fact that the claims to encounter with the true God can be supported by admirable ethical consequences.[145] Macquarrie's argument encourages us to admit the <u>fact</u> of such encounters, but fails to elucidate their relationship to the revelation in Christ. Let me conclude by suggesting briefly the nature of this relationship.

Outside Christ there is no revelation. Outside official Christianity there can be revelation, but it is always a divine disclosure which comes from and leads to Christ. In reality there are no such things as the (merely) natural man, nor (merely) natural revelation, nor for that matter (merely) natural theology. Whenever sinful man finds some true knowledge of God, this is not the product of his own unaided efforts but due to God's grace mediated through Christ. Whether explicitly recognized or not, Christ constitutes the only true light which enlightens every man.[146]

The "Constitution on Divine Revelation" is not a very noteworthy statement.

James Tunstead Burtchaell

The revelation made to us in this life does not tell us what God is, and so our union with him is like union with an unknown Being.

Thomas Aquinas

Chapter III

Theology of Revelation
Out of Vatican II

The last chapter began with some general reflections on revelation and then offered a critical account of dialectic theology's contribution in this area. Contemporary Protestant and Catholic theologies of revelation remain in explicit or implicit counterpoint with the earlier consensus. Where the last chapter moved from general considerations to historical evaluations, I find it desirable in this chapter to shift in the reverse direction. After discussing the nature and implications of Vatican II's statements on God's self-disclosure to man, I plan to set out some essential requirements for theological work on revelation.

Vatican II on revelation

History takes time to evaluate the significance of Church Councils and Vatican II will be no exception to this universal law. But

certain lines of judgment have already emerged clearly, in particular with regard to the basic theological category of revelation.
Here significant contributions are found in the Council's documents
on the liturgy, the Church, ecumenism, religious freedom, non-
Christian religions, and the Church in the modern world, as well
as in the "Dogmatic Constitution on Divine Revelation" (Dei Verbum)
itself.[1] Anyone interested in the Catholic Church and its current
effort at self-renewal must attach importance to the Council's
refurbished account of revelation which can serve as a presupposition affecting any thorough theological reconstruction.

1 Two principles characterize the entire text of Dei Verbum,
those of personalism and scriptural orientation. Chapter I opens
with a clear statement that revelation is to be specified as the
personal self-disclosure of the triune God: "God chose to reveal
himself and to make known to us the hidden purpose of his will
(cf. Ephesians 1:9) by which through Christ, the Word made flesh,
man has access to the Father in the Holy Spirit." The personal
nature of revelation is expressed and clarified in various ways.
Revelation forms a dialogue in which God "out of the abundance of
his love speaks to men as friends" and "uninterruptedly converses"
with the Church. As a "covenant" it implies the meeting of and
agreement between the personal God and human persons. In the
face of the divine self-manifestation man ought to conduct himself
by "entrusting his whole self freely to God."[2]

Equally important is the deeply biblical definition given to
revelation. This is reflected in the fact that four out of the six
chapters of Dei Verbum are explicitly directed towards scripture.
By way of contrast Vatican I's constitution on Catholic faith (Dei
Filius) is notably less biblical--a fact suggested by the titles of
its four chapters ("God the Creator of All Things," "Revelation,"
"Faith," "Faith and Reason"). Small touches in Dei Verbum highlight that advance towards a deeper scriptural understanding which
has taken place since 1870. In place of the nonbiblical affirmation
that God chose "to reveal the eternal decrees of his will,"[3] Vatican
II speaks of the divine choice "to make known to us the hidden purpose (sacramentum) of his will" and refers in this connection to
Ephesians 1:9. A shift in the order of treatment offers what is
perhaps the most striking witness to this difference between the
two Councils. Vatican I considers the "supernatural," biblical
revelation only after recalling the so-called natural knowledge
available through ordinary created realities.[4] Vatican II elaborates
at length the divine revelatory activity in the salvation history
(which encompasses both Old and New Testaments), before it re-

affirms in a brief conclusion the teaching of Vatican I on the revelation mediated through created reality.[5]

Those who wish to contrast the two Councils' treatment of revelation make much of the personal color of Dei Verbum. Here again the difference is reflected even through quite minor touches. Where Vatican I affirmed that "it pleased his [God's] goodness and wisdom" (placuisse eius sapientiae et bonitati) to communicate revelation, we read in Dei Verbum: "In his goodness and wisdom God chose" (placuit Deo in sua bonitate et sapientia) to do so.[6] While allowing that the Holy Spirit's role might have been more fully acknowledged, we ought to note in Dei Verbum a deeply Trinitarian orientation. Despite its title, Dei Filius is theocentric rather than Trinitarian and Christocentric. The tone is set by the opening paragraph of the first chapter which lists (mainly time-less) attributes of the one God.[7] The richer personalism of Dei Verbum affects both sides of the revelatory transaction. Limitations are observable in the picture of man offered by Dei Filius. Faith is represented as believing those things to be true which God reveals.[8] It has become a commonplace to register the strongly intellectual tone which is here given to faith and to contrast this with the treatment of Vatican II. Dei Verbum understands the intellectual component of faith within the wider context of man's total submission to God: "'The obedience of faith' . . . must be given to God who reveals, an obedience by which man entrusts his whole self freely to God, offering 'the full submission of intellect and will to God who reveals,' and freely assenting to the truth revealed by him."[9]

What commentators can miss, however, is that Vatican I's intellectualist bias belonged to the nineteenth-century Zeitgeist which, despite its evident romantic and traditionalist elements, worshipped proof and revelled in the manufacture of vast systems of ideas. Pre-Freudian man understood himself as a creature of clear intellect and noble will. Contemporary anthropology made its appearance as much as anything else when Vatican I confidently rehearsed the external "arguments of revelation," the miracles and prophecies of both Old Testament and New,[10] and pointed with pride to the convincing sign offered by the Church itself: "The Church by itself, with its marvellous extension, its eminent holiness, and its inexhaustible fruitfulness in every good thing, with its Catholic unity and its invincible stability, is a great and perpetual motive of credibility and an irrefutable witness of its own divine mission."[11] A modification of nineteenth-century intellectual optimism would come later when the ambiguities, irrationality and experimental nature of human existence received more adequate recognition--not to mention the discovery of the role of the unconscious.

No great difficulty exists for those who wish to establish the biblical and personalist emphases of Dei Verbum and to introduce in this regard comparisons unfavorable to Vatican I. But we should not succumb to anachronism. In 1870 the work of Buber, Ebner, Freud, Heidegger, Camus, Sartre, and Marcel still lay ahead-- to say nothing of the revival of interest in Kierkegaard and many other forces working toward that richer grasp of human complexities on which we pride ourselves. Furthermore, would Vatican I's account of revelation have proved more successful in its own day, if the Council had been more scriptural and more personal in its approach? Probably not. Anticipation of coming trends might, of course, have made Dei Filius a greater aid and comfort to twentieth-century Christians than it has proved to be. But it is hardly fair play, unhampered by any statute of limitations, to put the bishops of Vatican I on trial a century later as if they were theological war criminals.

2 The perspective of salvation history and the role of the community in the acceptance and transmission of revelation form manifest characteristics of Dei Verbum. Revelation is interpreted as a salvific process of divine self-disclosure in history which reached its climax in the events of Jesus' death and resurrection. All took place according to God's "careful plan" for "the salvation of the whole human race."[12] To recognize how revelation is mediated through salvation history involves acknowledging the function of the community which experiences (and helps to make) this common history. Commentators have good reason to be satisfied with the respect for the social dimension of revelation shown in Dei Verbum where "the word of God" is described as having been committed to "the entire holy people."[13]

It makes sense to contrast the two Vatican Councils over these two features of Dei Verbum. But here again it is easy to do less than justice to Dei Filius and the theological accounts of revelation which it encouraged. Vatican I may not be arraigned for totally neglecting salvation history as the matrix for revelation.[14] In its own way Dei Filius makes much of the Church's role in accepting and transmitting revelation, albeit that "the Church" is mostly taken as identical with the teaching officers within the Church. In fact the Church's function as the great sign of divine revelation bulks so large that Ratzinger speaks of an "ecclesiomonism" which Vatican II leaves behind in proclaiming Christ as the definitive

50

divine witness to God's self-manifestation. The Church can be a sign of revelation only insofar as it lives from the great sign which is Christ.[15] To oppose Dei Filius to Dei Verbum on the grounds that the former has an individualistic and the latter a social view of revelation would be a misleading appraisal.

3 What makes the two Councils decisively different with respect to their teaching on revelation (and in other areas also) are their respective views on (a) their relationship to the past and (b) their tasks in the present. Vatican I formulates its continuity with the Tridentine view of scripture and revelation as a "renewal" of a previous "decree."[16] Vatican II is far from endorsing the same kind of Conciliar policy when Dei Verbum speaks of "following in the footsteps of the Councils of Trent and of First Vatican (Conciliorum Tridentini et Vaticani I inhaerens vestigiis)."[17] Karl Barth's paraphrase "moving forward from the footsteps of those councils" catches the sense which the statement conveys in its context.[18] The bishops at Vatican II, when explaining what they understood by revelation, declined to put their feet precisely where the prints of their predecessors were plain to see. Today we look askance at the Tridentine-style anathemas which the bishops at Vatican I issued in Dei Filius (as in other documents). Their self-imposed task was to preserve the true teaching on revelation and faith which they saw as threatened by contemporary errors. "The saving doctrine of Christ" was to be "professed and declared," while "opposing errors" were "proscribed and condemned."[19] The long standing Conciliar function of anathematizing heresy and error did not prove congenial to Vatican II, which both in the area of revelation and beyond understood its task as that of "hearing the word of God with reverence and proclaiming it confidently" (Dei Verbum, no. 1).[20] Striking expression is given to this fresh appreciation of a Council's purpose when the new notions of "listening" and "serving" are introduced alongside traditional descriptions of what constitutes the function of authoritative teachers within the Church: "This teaching office is not above the word of God, but serves it, teaching only what has been handed on, listening to it devoutly, guarding it scrupulously, and explaining it faithfully" (Dei Verbum, no. 10).[21]

4 Some unease has been caused by two features of Dei Verbum. Central to any adequate exposition of revelation is the analysis of man's status and role in receiving revelation. Where is even the need for such analysis recognized in Dei Verbum? There is in fact little said about the "anthropological" side of revelation and, as Ratzinger complains, the whole theme of man's sinfulness is

gathered in one little word, a reference to the "fall" of our first parents (no. 3).[22] Yet it would falsify the achievement of Vatican II to register this complaint without a glance beyond Dei Verbum. Elsewhere the Council works out its view of man, notably in the Pastoral Constitution on the Church in the Modern World (Gaudium et Spes) which takes as "the pivotal point" of its presentation "man himself" (no. 3).[23] This document goes at least some distance towards supplying what is required to supplement the content of Dei Verbum.[24]

A second cause of theological discomfort is located in the account offered by Dei Verbum of the transmission of revelation. Endorsing a dynamic viewpoint, the Council affirms a steady growth in the understanding of revelation. The result is that "as the centuries succeed one another, the Church constantly moves forward toward the fullness of divine truth" (no. 8).[25] This optimistic statement, as Ratzinger rightly comments, remains silent about the fact that the traditional understanding of revelation which one generation in the Church transmits to another can be faulty in some aspects and calls for responsible scrutiny and reformation.[26] Ratzinger points out that in Dei Verbum Vatican II has even less to offer than the Council of Trent with regard to criteria for such a critical examination of tradition.[27] It is, however, only fair to add that such criteria are in fact implied by the constitution on revelation (and other documents) adopted by Vatican II. Almost at every stage such documents involve a review and critical reassessment of traditional understanding.

Requirements for a theology of revelation

1 Against the background of these comments on Vatican II let me now suggest some essential guidelines for theological work in the field of revelation. The first is a warning against succumbing to the kind of "pan-revelationism" which has surfaced in some Catholic circles. In Protestant theology Barth's rediscovery of revelation led to the use of this category reaching inflationary proportions.[28] Gerald Downing's Has Christianity a Revelation?[29] emerged as a belated protest against such exaggerations. This book first appeared in 1964 when the trickle of Catholic writing on revelation was about to become a flood. It is ironic that Downing's work (which for all its deficiencies embodied a healthy reaction against the excesses of revelation theology) should have been published just then. "Revelation" is a general concept, open to the kind of wide application which "salvation history" and "the

word of God" enjoy. But like these other categories it falls short, even in its refurbished form, of becoming a panacea to cure all our theological ills. The "pan-revelationism" which I have in mind is the kind of over-application exemplified by aspects of Gabriel Moran's writings. "Catechetics," he assures us, "is on the verge of its greatest breakthrough . . . The only thing which can save the catechetical movement from self-strangulation is to prepare teachers who have a theological understanding of Christian revelation."30 "Revelation" (rightly understood, of course) becomes the focus of excessive expectation. To claim that it is the only thing which can save catechetics and so effect the "greatest breakthrough" recalls the exaggerated claims made by Oscar Cullmann for the category of salvation history. Only slightly more restrained is Moran's appeal for a correct view of revelation as the key to the renewal of religious life.

> The old theological notion of revelation . . . can easily be the obstacle to reform and progress. One finds that . . . there remains a notion of revelation that is impersonal and objectified. The result of this deficiency is that creativity and autonomy are not wholeheartedly endorsed. They are judged at the bar of an impersonal system out of the past. A properly developed theology of revelation would tend to converge with the findings of contemporary sciences. It is imperative, therefore, that we begin to understand Christian religion as personal rather than impersonal and social rather than individualistic.31

Moran's persistent recourse to the category of revelation and re-lentless application of it as a principle of explanation bears com-parison with the thoroughgoing revelation theology practised by Barth, Brunner, and Gogarten in the heyday of dialectic theology.32

2 A quest for "the" theology of revelation would exemplify the "Platonic" fallacy. The illusory nature of such a quest is also sug-gested by the critical analysis (which I offer in this book and else-where) of the views on revelation advanced by Barth, Bultmann, Downing, Fuchs, Moltmann, and Pannenberg. The fact that cer-tain contemporary statements on revelation leave much to be desired does not, of course, mean that some other scheme is left in possession of the field. What is called for is an integral approach that is ready to preserve a diversity of insights. The absence of any single dominant figure among the successors to Barth and Bultmann is in its own way a help. There is less danger of becoming dazzled by some brilliant account and thinking that at

last we have met the definitive theology of revelation. Let me illustrate an "integral" approach with reference to Fuchs and Moltmann.[33]

Fuchs' view incorporates the values of love, the individual and the present moment. In Moltmann's account we meet the complementary values of hope, the community, and the future. Behind these differences lies the plurality of scriptural witness. Fuchs seizes on the Gospels;[34] Moltmann turns rather to Romans, I Corinthians and the Epistle to the Hebrews.[35] The Christ of Fuchs' theology is the Master whose word invites us to a discipleship of love. Moltmann's Christ is the coming Lord of the world. There is room for a theology of revelation which takes "Follow me" as its motif, as well as for one which is inspired by the prayer "Come, Lord Jesus."

3 My third requirement is that the theologian of revelation needs to be keenly conscious of the fact that his reflections are intimately connected with anthropological data. I am not suggesting a return to some kind of Roman Catholic modernism or Liberal Protestantism which would subordinate God to man and reduce revelation to being the mere (if finest) product of man's religious experience. I am asking rather for an acknowledgment that revelation is mediated through human thinking, speaking, hoping, loving, and acting. We have come a sufficient distance from the liberal theology which was so severely castigated by the early Barth. Today we are hopefully in a better position to face the fact that revelation is inevitably conditioned by man, without thereby treating it simply as a human phenomenon and degrading God to being the projection of man's needs and demands.

Bultmann rightly feels the need to clarify the situation of man who receives revelation, the faith in which he appropriates revelation and the self-understanding which the revelation-event effects.[36] Bultmann is deeply concerned with the role of revelation as an occurrence that puts "me" in a new situation as a self. In fact, at times the human involvement is so accentuated that the term "revelation" operates as the word "faith" does for other theologians.[37]

We can put the task of anthropological reflection this way. Revelation occurs as an encounter, a kind of "big boom" situation which can leave man asking who or what was encountered. How is the "big boom" to be read off? It is not by ignoring the human subject that we can adequately discern the divine subject who comes to encounter. We appreciate the Creator precisely in appreciating our creaturehood.

54

Whatever particular forms our description of man takes, integral thinking will keep in mind the individual as well as the social dimensions of human existence. God addresses himself to man who lives together with other men and yet must believe and die alone. Where an individualistic anthropology dominates, a theology of revelation and faith can deteriorate into a private, esoteric doctrine. Where the community aspect of man is made paramount, that secret divine coming to the individual can be passed over: "If a man loves me, he will keep my word, and my Father will love him, and we will come to him and make our home with him" (John 14:23). An integral approach will try to keep in view both the pilgrim people of Hebrews and the fourth Gospel's picture of one-by-one salvation as individuals hear Jesus and come to believe in him.

Where Bultmann's anthropology falls down is through a preoccupation with the individual and solitary traits of human existence such that he can affirm: "Only in radical loneliness does man find himself."[38] An anthropology of revelation will remain impoverished so long as it omits to recognize adequately that it is only in community, through intersubjectivity, that man develops his own subjectivity. Revelation must be related to the community of language and knowledge which essentially shapes man's existence. His understanding does not exist separately from the language with which he is addressed and with which in his turn he addresses others. Thought and word are completely interwoven with one another.

4 The theologian who deals with revelation has to take seriously his belief that it is to twentieth-century man that God makes himself known. In seeking to describe and explain the experience of divine revelation eliciting human faith, the theologian should be attuned to contemporary man's knowledge of himself and talk in terms that make a meaningful communication in the present day. Here, as elsewhere, theological expression must not fall behind human self-understanding at this point in history, if it is not to sound incredible or simply unintelligible. To make this demand is not, however, to suppose that there is such a thing as some single way of self-understanding enjoyed by "the" twentieth-century man. Contemporary experience remains obviously manifold and this diversity is reflected in the four theologians we mentioned above. Fuchs speaks in terms of language and man's involvement with language. He also expresses his theology in the context of love, differing here from Downing. Fuchs looks characteristically to the situation of family love; Downing's

interest is rather with the Christian community of love. For his part Moltmann wishes to make himself heard by those preoccupied with hopes and fears for the future of the Church and the world. Pannenberg mirrors man's quest for intellectual certainty and the support of known truth. In one way or another the theological articulation of revelation should enjoy a meaningful connection with present forms of human experience.

Through Gabriel Moran's many (incidental) remarks about twentieth-century men and their understanding of themselves runs the implication that all is sweetness, light and clarity. To change the image, no chinks are allowed to appear in Moran's armour. He seems just a shade too sure that we know today what man is. Twentieth century science in its many fields has taken good care of that. But one feature of contemporary human experience--as evidenced on university campuses, in films, plays, novels, and by research reports of all kinds--is surely that men and women of the late twentieth century commonly exhibit acute problems of puzzlement and self-questioning. Despite (or perhaps partly because of?) Freud, Durkheim, and Weber, many remain unsure of who they are. If man is a sick animal, this sickness discloses itself partly in a deep insecurity about the answers available on human nature and destiny. It is little more than a platitude to observe that "man" seems to have become almost as great a problem as has "God." This state of affairs has obvious consequences for any theology of revelation which wishes to unfold theology as a person-to-person encounter between God and man.

5 We maintained above (in no. 4) that an anthropology of revelation inspires little confidence when it neglects the social dimension of human existence. Man's personal response to God's self-revelation takes place in a collective situation. As Luther remarked, "he who wants to find Christ must first find the Church." Hence a fifth requirement for a theology of revelation is the adequate acknowledgment of the ecclesial nature of revelation. Faith in a God who discloses himself takes the form of submission to a social regime. Faith's secret communion with God does not merely coexist with an ecclesial relationship, let alone show incompatibility with it. Human faith in the revelation mediated by Christ as the climax of Israel's history presupposes the preaching of the Church (Romans 10:14-17). This faith brings with it baptism into the Church (Romans 6:1-11; I Corinthians 12:13). Over and over again Paul indicates this intimate relationship between man's faith, divine revelation, and the Church (Galatians 3:23 ff.). As it is within the community that revelation

occurs, revelation will enjoy a history and a tradition--themes to which we will return.

6 The ecclesial nature of revelation should not, however, be misconstrued. It is one thing to acknowledge it and quite another to act as if there were not (or even could not be) revelation outside the Church. Latourelle falls into such ecclesiocentrism when he writes: "The encounter with Christ and his mystery is effected only through hearing the apostolic witness, handed down through the Church and consigned as Scripture" (italics mine).[39] This exclusiveness ought to be discarded along with such principles as Bultmann's denial of any revelation outside the kerygma. Both as regards its ecclesial nature and in other ways there appears to be an uncommonly strong temptation to encapsulate revelation in some simple formula. Hence I propose as a sixth requirement that theologies of revelation shun exclusiveness and respect the complexity of the facts. A further example of such exclusiveness is Pannenberg's attempt to interpret revelation simply as God's indirect self-revelation through the facts of history. As we will argue, this formulation is too narrow to account even for the biblical evidence.

In the preceding chapter I drew attention to the narrowness involved in Bultmann's affirmation that revelation is confined to the proclamation of Christ. Bultmann provides yet another instance of an oversimplified formulation when he explains that, as a decision between yes and no, faith occurs either entirely or not at all. There can be no such thing as different degrees of man's believing recognition of God's self-revelation nor a deepening of faith. If the event of revelation takes place, it does so as an indivisible whole which brings total illumination: "Everything has been revealed, insofar as man's eyes are opened concerning his own existence and he is once again able to understand himself. . . . All questioning ceases and everything is understood."[40] It is hardly quibbling to point out that Christians (a) do not normally experience revelation as total illumination and (b) commonly express their conviction that there exist degrees of faith. For very many Christians it makes excellent sense to speak of stronger and weaker faith. The logic of Bultmann's simplifying account of revelation as the event of being called to the decision of faith leads him to conclusions which fail to fit the facts.[41]

7 Closely allied with the last point is my seventh requirement that theologies of revelation eschew thinking in alternatives. Here again Bultmann ought to be mentioned as a major offender. He presents us with the choice of interpreting revelation either

as an address calling for the new self-understanding of faith or as the communication of doctrine. His own position is clearly stated: "God's revelation in Christ is not the communication of knowledge as such, but rather an occurrence for man and in man that . . . opens up to him a new understanding of himself."[42] Such antithetical formulation is a general feature of Bultmann's theological style. A powerful example of this is provided by his discussion of the New Testament account of faith, a theme intimately linked to the theology of revelation.

> "Faith" . . . has . . . "undogmatic" character insofar as the word of proclamation is no mere report about historical incidents: it is no teaching about external matters which could simply be regarded as true without any transformation of the hearer's own existence. For the word is kerygma, personal address, demand, and promise; it is the very act of divine grace . . . its acceptance--faith--is obedience, acknowledgment, confession.[43]

Objective structures form the antithesis to the individual life when Bultmann argues against any "history of religion": "If the religious life is to be found not in objective formulations, but in individual life, there cannot be a history of religion."[44] Theologizing in alternatives assumes an "adjectival" form in Moran's writings where such antitheses as "personal" versus "impersonal" and "social" versus "individualistic" recur.

This style of theology can generate more problems than it solves. To oppose "the communication of knowledge as such" to "a new self-understanding," as Bultmann does, appears quite unreal. In the sphere of revelation (and elsewhere) growth in knowledge of things (and persons) other than oneself involves at least a minimal growth in knowledge of oneself. To characterize the older view of revelation (as found in Vatican I) as "individualistic" and the newer view (as found in Vatican II) as "social" has strictly limited value. In a very real sense the older view is social and the newer view individualistic. The creedal approach of Vatican I highlights the function of those with teaching authority to set forth dogmas to be affirmed by all members of the Church. Whatever else we say about the close relationship proposed between revelation and orthodoxy, it enjoys heavy social overtones. On the other hand, Vatican II's stress on the personal nature of revelation (rightly) acts as an encouragement for the individual Christian to scrutinize his own life situation for the signs of God's self-manifestation.

8 A further requirement is that theologies of revelation ought to exhibit due respect for the fact that the divine self-disclosure in Christ remains limited and is grasped only in the free act of faith. St. Paul would encourage us to speak of revelation's limited nature rather than of its hiddenness or obscurity. The Qumran literature along with apocalyptic and Gnostic writings highlights the theme of hiddenness. This theme emerges also in some New Testament passages in which revelation is represented as the disclosure of something previously hidden. "At that time Jesus declared, 'I thank thee, Father, Lord of heaven and earth, that thou hast hidden these things from the wise and understanding and revealed them to babes'" (Matthew 11:25; cf. Mark 4:22; I Corinthians 2:6ff.). In Paul's letters--or at least in those letters which are generally agreed to come from Paul himself--the antithesis between hiddenness and disclosure is lacking. The time "before" revelation is characterized rather by law, sin, and death.[45]

Being limited, revelation does not enjoy compelling force. Within the New Testament the fourth gospel challenges any attempt to take even striking miracles as an objective proof of revelation which forces itself upon men. Faith based only upon miracles does not count as genuine faith (2:23ff.; 6:14f.; 6:26f.). Today we apprehend revelation in reliance on the word of many witnesses and subject to the limitations which that reliance implies. If we recall the resurrection as crucial in the whole history of revelation, here we run up against the limitation imposed by the lack of any public manifestation of the risen Christ. He discloses himself only to a closed group of chosen followers. Furthermore, the Christian gospel, as Paul recognizes clearly, can look like an affront to human ideas (I Corinthians 1:18--2:8). The consequence of the various limitations in revelation is that human assent can be withheld. Faith in the divine self-disclosure remains free; otherwise, of course, it would not be faith.[46] At the same time, this divine manifestation is sufficiently clear for man to be held blameworthy if he fails to respond.[47]

The acceptance of personal relationships and of truths on which human life can be based always involves the exercise of freedom and an element of risk. Robert Frost wisely remarked: "What a man needs is the courage to take a chance on his own discriminations." In the matter of Christian faith we do not find a special exemption from that insecurity which derives from the absence of any tangible, innerworldly guarantee. The problem is only superficially solved by pointing to present religious experience as con-

59

veying a direct knowledge which is immune from the kind of question that faces claims about past and present religious facts. That Christians claim certain kinds of religious experience is patently obvious. But the question arises: What is it that they experience? Christians know their experiences to constitute various disclosures of God. Such knowledge affecting the depth of man's existence comes about only through the active intervention of man's free choices.

The New Testament implies an essential relationship between human decisions and human knowledge of God (Philippians 1:9). The "spiritual" man and the "unspiritual" man are not equally endowed with a capacity for grasping the things of God.[48] The free decision to believe involves cognition; new knowledge inheres in faith.[49]

9 What I have just stated about the role of free faith should not be taken to imply that we may dispense with grounds for the acknowledgment of revelation. My ninth requirement is that a theology of revelation respect the reasonableness inherent in faith's recognition of God's self-manifestation. For Paul faith denotes a total personal submission to God, an obedience which incorporates two essential elements. Alongside the trusting self-surrender there is the willingness to recognize certain things as true.[50] This second element touches on the reasonableness of faith. Revelation stops short of being strictly demonstrable, but it does not suppress the question of evidence for its truth. In this respect Bultmann's position manifests a one-sided voluntarism: "We cannot demonstrate to anyone that God's revelation is there in Jesus Christ. The New Testament and the word of preaching proclaim God's forgiving grace in Christ, and man is asked whether he is willing to understand himself in the light of this word--whether he will believe" (italics mine).[51] Confronted with the divine revelation in Christ man faces a question of truth (Is this claim true?), as well as a question of decision (Is he willing to believe?). The willingness to accept a self-understanding in the light of God's grace partly depends on the recognition that the grounds for this change are true.

10 An obvious requirement (which was clearly noted in the last chapter) is that theologians show a thoroughgoing regard for the Christological nature of revelation. The incarnation is no simple quantitative increase in man's knowledge of God, as if the coming of Christ enjoyed only epistemological importance. Jesus' message transcends mere information about God; it is the word of power which effects divine life in the receptive hearer (John 5:24). Jesus is the uniquely perfect revealer who is full of grace and truth and

in whom the divine reality encounters men as a gracious gift.
There is no going beyond him. In Christ God has "said himself."
Wherever revelation occurs, it has a Christological orientation.
Nothing may be played off against Christ, not even the Holy Spirit.
The Holy Spirit's presence in manifesting God's reality never be-
comes an experience independent of the history of Jesus, but in
one way or another effects the recognition that in that history God's
saving activity was manifested.

11 Closely connected with the preceding requirement is the need
to respect the unique and irrepeatable role of the apostles in revelation. "The apostles" should, of course, be taken to include St. Paul
and not be restricted to "the twelve," as in Latourelle's account.
"If revelation," he writes, "is effected by an encounter with the
living God, in Jesus Christ, only those can be the authentic medi-
ators of revelation who were then the witnesses of His life, who
have been initiated into the mystery of His person. . . . Now the
apostles were the only ones who had living and direct experience
of Christ."[52] The apostles' function in revelation is implied by an
account of faith which surfaces here and there in later writings
of the New Testament. In place of being a total submission to God,
"faith" appears transmuted into a readiness to accept as true certain (apostolic) doctrines which are handed on as orthodox teaching
(Jude 3; Colossians 2:6f.; II Thessalonians 2:14f.). To come to
belief means passing through a learning process and assenting to the
"holy commandment delivered" to the community (II Peter 2:21; cf.
1:12). Käsemann comments that in II Peter "revelation has come
to the community in the manner of an object which is handed over;
further, it is now available within the community on the same
basis."[53] To join Käsemann in preferring the understanding of faith
and revelation set out in Paul's major epistles should not, however,
lead us to overlook an important feature of Christian revelation
acknowledged in later writings of the New Testament. Although they
knew God in their present experience, these later Christians recognized that they remained dependent upon the original revelation
enjoyed by the apostles and were "guarding" the apostolic truth
(I Timothy 6:20; II Timothy 1:13f.). The so-called Apostolic
Fathers likewise considered themselves different from the apostles
and based what they said upon apostolic doctrine to which "nothing
might be added" and from which "nothing might be taken away."[54]

12 In respecting the apostolic nature of revelation the theologian
is concerned with the past. He ought also to be concerned with the
presentness of revelation and perceptively investigate how people
appropriate revelation now. In his The Historian and the Believer

Van Harvey sets a good example by insisting on the need to examine the ways in which historians do as a matter of fact carry on their work. He fails, however, to make the required complementary investigation into the ways in which believers come to faith and continue to believe. More light could be shed on the various problems concerning divine revelation and man's responding faith, if the facts were investigated and theologians refrained from fastening onto formulas by which they wish to account for the mediation of divine revelation. We need to ask how revelation does reach men, not how we think it should reach them.

Through being conscious of the importance of investigating the human experiences in which revelation is (or could be) embodied, the theologian runs up against a major problem. How is he to distinguish between human experience which is simply human experience and human experience which is also the experience of receiving revelation? Primarily it is not so much a question of what man receives in revelation (or how he receives revelation), but that he actually does receive revelation. We can never detect revelation by itself. God's self-disclosure is not simply "there," like some static thing or some independent process which could be isolated and become the object of our attention. Christ the revealer, God the revealed and man as the one to whom revelation is given belong together in an inseparable unity. Paul writes of God revealing his Son (Galatians 1:16) and then speaks equivalently of the coming of faith (Galatians 3:23 ff.). The divine revelation and the emergence of human faith are the two sides of the same event. We cannot separate them in order to discriminate the religious experience which is faith responding to revelation from the experience which lacks a corresponding revelation.

These remarks are not intended as a challenge to the theologian's right (and duty) to construct a coherent account of revelation in the spirit of "fides quaerens intellectum." They are meant as a reminder that this work carries with it the role of an "intellectus dubitans de fide." The theologian must be ready to question and may not simply assume, as Ernst Fuchs seems to assume, that he can begin with the phenomenon of faith.[55] To do that is to suppose that some particular phenomenon is faith and hence that divine revelation (to which this faith responds) is found there. But the "intellectus dubitans de fide" to which I have drawn attention is equivalently an "intellectus dubitans de revelatione." Some words of Vatican II may be aptly applied in this context. The Church "labors to decipher authentic signs of God's presence and purpose in the happenings, needs, and desires in which his people [the mem-

bers of the Church] has a part along with other men of our age."[56]
The revelatory action of God in the present needs to be deciphered
through careful scrutiny. The presence of revelation may not be
lightly assumed.

13 Finally, revelation's relationship to the future ought to be
insistently recalled. A systematic account of revelation rightly
centers on that unfolding history of divine promise which gives
new direction to man's hopes. By word and event God communicates
his promise, and--first provisionally in the Old Testament and
then definitively in the New Testament--summons into a new
future those who respond with trusting hope.

In such a view of revelation our knowledge of God, far from
being a collection of static "facts," stands or falls with the recognition of the divine fidelity. By acknowledging that God has proved
faithful to his promises, man shows himself ready to face with
trust that future which will finally disclose the "God before us."
Through hope man "knows" in anticipation that new future which
has not yet come to pass. To ignore this future-orientation of
present revelation would be to misrepresent its essentially antic-
ipatory structure.[57]

Every age is immediately related to God.
Leopold von Ranke

No one is saved merely by believing that certain events happened a long time ago.
Bishop Stephen Neill

Chapter IV

Faith and History

The truth of Christian revelation remains irreducible to any set of abstract, timeless ideals. This sweeping denial makes no exception even for such lofty notions as that a truly human life is possible only through worshipful obedience of God and that man's loving service towards his fellowman forms the indispensable proof of a love for God. Christian faith is tied to history in being connected with a series of specific historical events and a specific set of persons, in particular with Jesus of Nazareth and events in which he was involved. Christians see their own history as in some way founded in Jesus' history. The recurring acts of preaching, administration of the sacraments, and other ritual actions within the present Christian community convey an historical message by including recitations of past events. The mediation of the divine saving activity to "my" life through the sacraments and the preached word is believed to be essentially linked with our acceptance of authoritative witness about certain past acts of God on man's behalf. The past becomes contemporary so that--in one and the same moment--information is communicated and man's decision is invited in response to the present offer of divine grace. Despite the many divergences which separate the various theological explanations of the link between Christian present and historical past, every theologian makes some connection between faith (and revelation) and past history.

Within the New Testament the Acts of the Apostles and the epistles could suggest that the outlook of the first Christians focuses on present and future history. We do not find much in those books to suggest the importance of reminiscence about the life and teaching of Jesus, although we ought at once to add that the memory of Jesus' death and resurrection and--in its degree--the story of Israel are highlighted in the Acts and the epistles. What the gospels disclose is that the first-century Christians maintain a link with a person of the past who enjoys the greatest significance for them. Christian faith affects man's present and future history, but its historical nature cannot be reduced to these present and future dimensions. However we articulate this in detail, the New Testament makes it clear that faith arises as a consequence of certain events in past history which at least in some measure determine the shape and content of faith.

Christianity is professedly an historical religion. The link with history forms an inner dimension of Christian faith. But with that said we are left with a host of questions. How does Christianity's connection with its origins work? What is the way that this connection is known? What role does the historical Jesus play? (By "the historical Jesus" we can mean, of course, either (a) Jesus of Nazareth as he existed in his particular place and time in history or (b) Jesus as his life can be reconstructed by critical historical methods, that is to say, the Jesus of the historians. The context should make it clear which of the two senses is intended.) In this chapter I wish to offer first some generalizing remarks about the relation of faith to Jesus of Nazareth and then elaborate some principles about the link between faith and history.

The universal and the particular in faith's
relation to Jesus

It is necessary but clearly insufficient to point out that Christian faith looks to a particular historical person. Reverence for heroes, both in its simpler forms and in the kind of full-blown personality cult which attaches to a Mahatma Gandhi, a John F. Kennedy, or a Che Guevara, relates itself to an historical person. Christians, however, find Christ significant in a way that transcends the relationship to Guevarists to Che Guevara, Marxists to Karl Marx, and Lutherans to Martin Luther. If Christians were no more than "Nazarists," they could look back to Jesus of Nazareth as their hero, the founder of their movement, the object of a lasting personality cult. The fact that they are "Christians" and that Jesus of Nazareth is "the Christ" draws attention to that absolute function as revealer and savior which gives this historical person a definitive, unsurpassable role such as cannot attach to a Gandhi, a Marx, or a Luther. Jesus' concrete historical existence enjoys a universal value before God for all human lives. Faith in God may not be de-historicized but retains an essential link with the man from Nazareth.

What Paul says about his apostolic work in I Corinthians 3:5 ff. does not bear application to Jesus, as if Jesus' contribution were ultimately no more than to bring to birth a faith which then concerned itself only with God. Jesus could never echo what Paul, Peter, and other apostles rightly confess: "What then is Apollos? What is Paul? Servants through whom you believed, as the Lord assigned to each. I planted, Apollos watered, but God gave the growth. So neither he who plants nor he who waters is anything, but only God who gives the growth" (I Corinthians 3:5-7).

Two dangers are to be avoided in assessing the connection of our faith with Jesus. The first is the danger of a Kierkegaardian abstraction which trivializes the historical existence of Jesus. Kierkegaard himself maintained: "If the contemporary generation [of Jesus] had left nothing behind them but these words: 'We have believed that in such and such a year the God appeared among us in the humble figure of a servant, that he lived and taught in our community, and finally died,' it would be more than enough."[1] In our own century Bultmann has escalated this position to the point that he decrees: "It is the Christ of the kerygma and not the person of the historical Jesus who is the object of faith." This faith in the kerygmatic Christ emerges as faith in the (present) Church: "It [the Church] is not the guarantor of faith but is itself the object of faith."[2] His position leads Bultmann to identify the Church and Christ in a degree to which even Catholic theology never dared to go. The second danger is the trend to make Jesus' message rather than his person the definitive, unsurpassable fact. Jesus may not be reduced to the status of a higher kind of Socrates

who teaches his disciples and then leaves them to the truth itself
as something to which he does not himself belong.

The link between the concrete and the universal factors may be
made, as it were, in either direction. We can confess the historical
person and so share in his universal value. Thus the criterion of
the "last" judgment is not love in general but the Son of Man identified with the hungry, the prisoners and all whose need forms a call
on our compassionate help (Matthew 25:31 ff.). Concrete attitudes
towards Jesus rather than adherence to general rules will determine man's status in the coming judgment (Mark 8:38; Matthew
10:32 f.; Luke 9:26). The reverse direction is indicated by the
prologue to the Fourth Gospel where the Word of universal significance becomes incarnated and is visibly "there" in the human
life of Jesus of Nazareth.

Another way of approaching this problem of the concrete and
the universal is to examine what we can call "the boundaries" of
Jesus' history. It is, of course, puzzling to know how we may fix
the boundaries for the history of any human life and even for a
single human event. If we may not pass judgment until we have
heard the whole story, how far does the whole story extend?
What, for example, is the history of Karl Marx? Should his history
be understood as his actual life together with his total subsequent
effect on human history? In that case, attempts to set down the
history of Marx in 1883, 1914, 1939, and even 1970 could only
purport to be provisional. Or should we rather try to discriminate
between the subsequent effects which an historical person deserved
to enjoy and those which were adventitious and became associated
with his name? To make such distinctions we need to scrutinize
the life of the person in question and reach some conclusions about
the forces which his efforts set in motion or helped to set in motion.
Such an examination could, for example, lead us to maintain that
many of the effects attributed to Marx's influence lacked any intrinsic causal connection with his real life's work.

To illustrate some facets of the problems we face in setting
"boundaries" for the history of Jesus, it may help to examine the
following passage from Dr. Stephen Neill.

What we have to explain is the Christian Church. In history
consequences cannot be greater than causes. Here is a great
spiritual movement, which has withstood the changes and
chances of nineteen centuries. How are we to account for it?
The Roman Empire would be inexplicable without Julius Caesar

and Augustus; what was the corresponding factor in that other movement in the first century A.D., which led to the birth and growth of the Christian Church?[3]

We can leave to one side a number of other points in this passage which need challenging or qualification. The feature which concerns our argument particularly is Dr. Neill's use of the principle that "in history consequences cannot be greater than causes." He invokes the analogy of the Roman Empire and, tacitly assuming that there was one single personal factor behind the birth and growth of the Christian Church, enquires what this factor might be. A critic of this procedure, even if he agreed that there was such a personal factor behind the birth and early growth of the Church, could point out that it is at least conceivable that other causes intervened subsequently and by sheer good luck to effect the full growth and the lasting preservation of the Church. These later causes, if they lacked any intrinsic link with the life of Jesus, hardly belong to his "history" or at any rate to the history he deserved to enjoy.

A further method of approaching the problem of the concrete and the universal is to distinguish Jesus as he was in himself from what Jesus was and came to be for others. Is it legitimate to consider Jesus simply as an historical individual belonging to the first half of the first century A.D.? Or are we missing the whole point if we prescind from his function in "the whole divine plan," that is to say, if we fail to allow the boundaries of his history to coincide with the boundaries of universal human history? In short, should we take a soteriological or a "strictly historical" approach to Jesus?[4] To echo Melancthon's classic statement, do we really know Jesus at all, so long as we fall short of acknowledging what he has done to save all mankind?

Still another way of expressing the problem of the concrete and the universal in faith's relation to Jesus is to contrast the causality and the content of faith. Let me explain this contrast by commenting on the work of Bultmann and John Knox. We find there that interest is focused on present causality to the detriment of the (historical) content of belief. For Bultmann the historical Jesus remains in the past and as such lacks significance for salvation.[5] Knox interprets sharing in the Church's life as by definition identical with knowing the risen Lord communally, so that the so-called "Christ-event" is nothing other than the coming into existence of the Church.[6] Bultmann explains the genesis of faith through the kerygma,[7] Knox through the contemporary Church. There is a

69

minimal historical aspect to both explanations. Bultmann makes the "that," the sheer existence of the historical Jesus, a necessary presupposition for the kerygma. This link between the historical Jesus and the contemporary kerygma seems almost purely formal. Knox describes the Church as the community of those who remember Jesus. For both theologians it is enough that the gospel message now presented to me derives somehow or another from the historical Jesus and his circle. Whether or not the content of the message now proclaimed actually comes (and can be shown to come) from that historical origin is not reckoned important. The center of interest has shifted to the present. History is subjectivized, becomes a matter of the here and now, and is transmuted into the "existential-historical" element. Hence the "arena of history" emerges as ultimately equated with "the sphere of the individual" who can find faith in his (recurrent) present encounter with the kerygma.[8] By associating both history and faith with the present time the tension between the universality of faith and the concreteness of (past) history is relaxed. Preoccupation with the way in which faith today is (repeatedly) caused leads here to the question of faith's (historical) content being devalued. However, a more realistic appraisal of Christian faith recognizes that the substantial content of the preached message is essentially bound to its origins. This message loses force to the extent that its derivation from those origins is minimized and neglected.

The distinction between Historie and Geschichte serves to express a separation between the causality and the content of faith. The so-called Historie an sich ("history in itself") is the mere factuality of the objective happening, the past events in their pastness which are open to investigation by the methods of critical history. The Geschichte für mich ("history for me") is the history as significant happening encountered existentially for the meaning it conveys. I am challenged by the past events in their presentness and subjective meaning for me. The upshot of this distinction is that the event as Historie is theologically neutralized. The Geschichte as significant for my faith is removed from the objectively controlled area of historical events. At play here we find an unwarranted subjectification of historical events. So long as some significance comes home forcibly to me and claims my decision of faith, this significance remains immune from challenge through the scrutiny of past events in their concrete reality. Interest in present causality edges out concern for the content of past history. Faith becomes independent of Historie, of the events as they actually happened in the past. It remains historical only in the sense of being geschichtlich. But it is now high time we moved on to propose some principles for dealing with the link between faith and history.

Statements of the problem

Various statements of belief such as the Apostles Creed appear to commit the Christian to certain historical propositions in such a way that if these propositions were proved untrue, the believer would be shown to have believed falsely. One must grant that a great many historical affirmations to which all Christians once unquestioningly subscribed are now acknowledged to be non-contributory to the structure of faith. (Think, for instance, of the authorship of various biblical books.) At the same time, however, faith seems to remain dependent upon some matters of past history. If it were demonstrated that Jesus never lived or that he preached a message which was quite opposed to the accounts given in the gospels, Christian faith would be shown to be falsely based. The fact that possible historical discoveries could falsify grounds for Christian faith indicates a certain dependence of faith upon history.

Here we run up against the question: How can the absolute, unconditional assurance of Christian faith now depend upon matters of past history? To put the problem in the classic terms in which Gotthold Lessing (1729-1781) expressed it: "Accidental truths of history can never become the proof of necessary truths of reason." By "necessary truths of reason" Lessing intended various truths about God. His problem, as he saw it, was his failure to make a leap across "the ugly, broad ditch" which separated the absolute truths of reason from the contingent truths of history.[9] This problem requires to be broken up into three problems which we can label those of (a) contingency, (b) probability, and (c) particularity. By the problem of contingency I have in mind the (ontological) possibility that the events alleged to be vital for faith did not happen. In themselves these events need not have taken place. How then can the unconditioned faith of the Christian depend on such contingent happenings? By the problem of probability I refer to the lack of (absolute) certainty in our knowledge of historical events. To this problem which has assumed such formidable proportions I will return in a moment. The problem of the particularity of historical events which was Hegel's special legacy to theology poses the issue: Even supposing that we enjoy an assured knowledge of some particular historical event (or set of events), how can such particular events reveal the infinite God?

Nothing less than history as a whole can reveal God, and history as a whole is not yet available.[10]

Let me elaborate now the problem of probability which in one form or another is what most theologians understand by the problem of faith and history. If we agree that faith depends on our knowledge of history, we appear to give an unfair advantage to the historian and place an unreasonable burden on the simple. "Not only the theologian," John Macquarrie writes, "but the ordinary Christian believer would be at the mercy of the historian." And this he considers "intolerable."[11] Even in the case of the historian, it is argued, faith cannot and ought not to depend on the results of his critical investigations. He cannot build his faith on these results because they enjoy merely relative value and remain open to revision and further qualification, not to mention falsification. The certainty of faith cannot be supported by findings which never rise above the level of high probability. Thus Wilhelm Herrmann wrote: "What is available for the learned, what is an historical problem and despite a great deal of trouble can be made only probable--this lacks the power to ground faith."[12] Brunner put the same point in biblical terms: "When a thoughtful person refuses to build his relation to the eternal on anything so unsafe as historical science, he is acting rightly: for such building is indeed a glaring example of building one's house upon the sand."[13] This case against supporting faith by history is further strengthened the more we incline to take a "subjective" view of historical explanations and agree with some scholars that "since all historical judgments involve persons and points of view, one is as good as another and there is no 'objective' historical truth."[14] Further, once faith is erected on the basis of historical findings, the historian seems to abdicate his professional freedom in research. To call these findings into question would be tantamount to calling into question the faith which they support and which ex hypothesi is unquestionably certain. In any case we ought not to build our faith upon such findings. Such an attempt would constitute a search for (false) justification through the works of the intellect, for security in human assurances rather than in God's word alone. It would, in Bultmann's opinion, form an attempt to take faith as a possession under man's control rather than accept--what it is-- a recurring decision in the face of the recurring moment of grace. "The question which has to be decided for or against belief--one which is never a question of knowledge gained by research and preservable as a possession, but is always one of the will and of responsiveness to the 'moment,' which cannot therefore be decided by any science."[15]

Although one must be careful of sweeping generalizations here, it seems fair to bring Barth, Bultmann, Herrmann, and Brunner together as maintaining that faith does not depend upon history (understood as our critically acquired knowledge of what actually happened in the past). The Historie, the factuality of the objective, past events which are susceptible to the scholarly scrutiny of historians, was taken to be theologically irrelevant. Faith was portrayed as an extra-historical perception (Barth and Brunner) or as an obedient response to the word of the kerygma (Bultmann). History as connected with faith appeared only in the guise of such notions as "supra-history," "meta-history," or "primal history" or else under the rubric of an authentic, "historical" existence now (Geschichtlichkeit).

But ultimately none of these accounts enjoy a true invulnerability vis-à-vis historical research. Herrmann looked for something absolutely certain on which to base faith and he found this in the inner life of Jesus. Today his confident assertions about Jesus' inner life suggest that Herrmann was projecting his own ethical convictions onto Jesus. Far from being immune from the results of historical enquiry, these assertions seem unwarrantably arbitrary when laid alongside the very cautious conclusions which the evidence is now commonly recognized to tolerate. In Bultmann's view the fact that Jesus lived and was crucified is a necessary presupposition for the kerygma. Hence, in principle, the kerygma would be undermined if it were shown that the real Jesus disappeared at the end of his ministry and through a case of mistaken identity someone else had been crucified in his stead.

To deny that Christian faith enjoys a special immunity against the findings of historical enquiry does not, of course, entail that one must automatically express allegiance to some particular theological school, let alone become a camp-follower of a particular theologian. Ethelbert Stauffer, Joachim Jeremias, Pannenberg and the so-called "new questers" of the historical Jesus (Käsemann, Fuchs, Ebeling, Conzelmann, and others) are some of those who-- either explicitly or implicitly--interpret faith to be at least in principle vulnerable to the results of historians' investigations. For all understand knowledge of Jesus in his past actuality to contribute to my faith now. Stauffer is convinced that faith must rest upon objective, historically verifiable facts and that such facts are available. God's revelation, in Jeremias' view, is properly mediated only by the assured words of Jesus rather than by the expressions of Christian faith recorded in the New Testament epistles. Faith depends upon and in principle is preceded by an historical investigation which can put us in secure contact with the vox ipsissima of Jesus. Thus we may establish that the subsequent Church kerygma incorporates nothing essentially new.

Let me hold over to later chapters further discussion of these views and those of the "new questers" and of Pannenberg. I want now to conclude this chapter by setting out two basic convictions relating to the problem of faith and history.

Two convictions

My first conviction may sound trivial but, given the way so much discussion has gone, it must be highlighted. From history alone Christian faith derives neither its structure nor the kind of certainty it enjoys. If faith is to remain Christian faith, it must retain, of course, its historical "ingredients." Yet one may become preoccupied with the problem of history at the risk of neglecting prayer, the Church, the influence of other people, educational experience, and many other factors which can help to effect and preserve faith. Faith is neither based simply on historical knowledge nor is it a mere prolongation of historical knowledge, as though historical investigation alone would suffice to establish and vindicate--either with probability or certainty-- the claims of Christianity. Christian faith may not exist independently of historical knowledge, but it cannot be reduced to it. In the matter of faith history fails to have the only word, or even necessarily the last word. There is not a single Christian, I guarantee, whose faith (rightly or wrongly) is founded on nothing more nor less than his knowledge of history.

Whatever shape their particular explanations take, many theologians are at one in assuming that to solve to their own satisfaction the problem of history's connection with faith is to explain how faith arises or at least to point to the precise area where faith can come into being. Even such a fine work as Van Harvey's The Historian and the Believer suffers from this defect. Its presupposition consists in the conviction that to analyse the work of the historian and his function vis-à-vis Christianity is to clear up the issue of faith. For his part Hugo Meynell rightly warns us against lapsing into an indifference to history which assumes that "since absolute certainty is unattainable about matters of historical fact, one cannot to any degree validate or invalidate Christian belief by historical enquiry."[16] But it should be added that in the validation (or invalidation) of Christian belief much more than historical enquiry is at stake.

What I am asking for is that we should investigate how faith does as a matter of fact arise, not how we think it should arise. Van Harvey's book here sets a good example by examining both what recognized historians do when they go about their work and what they think they are doing. Unfortunately Van Harvey does not pursue the same kind of empirical enquiry as regards faith, failing to ask how in fact people come to believe. Over this issue it is little help to argue a priori from the implications of the dogma of the incarnation, as Pannenberg does, to the effect that faith must be wholly derived from the history of God's revealing and saving activity.[17] Pannenberg is anxious that the truth of faith should exhibit a concrete relationship to the world. He is convinced that such a relationship will be eliminated if faith is separated from historical truth. But how do we know this? Perhaps the truth of faith, while isolated from historical truth, manifests a concrete connection with the world in other ways. The only method for deciding such a question is to examine faith in the concrete.

The faith of rank and file Christians would appear to be much less affected by the work of historians than theologians sometimes fondly imagine. The ordinary believer's knowledge of Jesus seems to be hardly dependent upon historians' researches. The fact that he sits a good deal lighter to history than many theologians would permit makes the following three problems less troubling for him. There is only a little that we can know about Jesus of Nazareth with any kind of normal historical certainty, if we adopt strict standards of investigation. Secondly, when they invoke the New Testament Christians seem to be founding their faith at least partially upon things that are not historical facts but the results of faith. Thirdly, there is an astonishing variety of responses when we ask Christians to list the historical facts which they regard as crucial for faith. At this point, as elsewhere, there exists no standard pattern of facts which serve as prerequisites for faith. In the making of his faith the Christian can draw on a complexity of factors which go far beyond the findings of historical science. For the historical ingredients of his faith he may accept some common consensus or perhaps carry through some examination of the evidence for himself. But in neither case is his faith wholly dependent on the findings of history, let alone at the mercy of the latest historical theory. Further, the ordinary nontheological believer, in particular the educated one, may in some ways be better placed than the professional theologian to recognize that there does exist a reasonable consensus in the historical knowledge of

75

faith. It is a consensus which the progress of historical-biblical studies promises to corroborate rather than destroy. The scholar struggling to find his place in the theological sun remains prone to highlight divergences and problems, since there is little advantage in merely relating a set of established conclusions.

In asserting above that Christian faith does not derive from history "the kind of certainty it enjoys," I had in mind my dissatisfaction with statements of the history-faith problem which speak in an exaggerated fashion of the "absolute" certainty of faith. Such statements can fabricate a greater gap between faith and the allegedly relative and probable results of historical research. Despite its firm commitment, faith remains always provisionally given. The only style of life open to man is one that can be no more than tentative and experimental. There is nothing especially shocking about the fact that with respect to his Christian faith man is always trying things on for size, as he must do in "other" areas. In this endless process of trying things on for size the Christian is at the mercy of history in much the same way as he lives at the mercy of reality itself, above all the human reality of other men. The social dimension of faith means that in a large variety of ways we are relying on other men. One of these ways touches our knowledge of the Jewish-Christian history and in particular the life, death, and resurrection of Jesus. If we trust that the progress of historical science will not destroy our contact with what we have accepted as the historical ingredients of our faith, we are no more giving way to a reckless confidence than when we trust that other changes will not show us that we have been relating to domestic, economic, and other sectors of life in an utterly mistaken fashion. Life would be intolerable if we had to live under the persistent fear that we could be confronted with the startling news that reality is not what we have taken it to be. We admit that it may be logically possible that we have been deluded, but we are confident that it is not so.

Ultimately what I am arguing for is the view that faith entails an historical risk. One important rider must be added. Faith does not depend upon history alone. And the historical risk is part of the general risk of reality as the believer understands reality.

My second conviction is that if theologians who concern themselves with the problem of faith and history neglect the study of the way historians actually go about their work and use their terminology, they do this at the peril of creating a private world and a private language of their own. Theologians can lightly take it upon themselves to prescribe the rules, limits, and objectives of historical enquiry. Thus Bultmann maintains that the proper goal of historical understanding is that decision by which the historian finds true "historicity" (<u>Geschichtlichkeit</u>) of existence. The "historical" describes the historian's life now rather than the past events then. Historicity arises from the fact that man exists only in encounters and consists in the responsibility which recurring moments of decision manifest in the face of the future.[18] Bultmann quotes with approval the remark of J. G. Droysen that "every man is indeed a historian. But the man who makes <u>historein</u> his vocation has something to do which is of human concern to a special degree."[19] In effect, in Bultmann's opinion, "the historian cannot see history from a neutral stand-point outside history." He finds history's meaning in the present when he ceases to remain a spectator and looks for this meaning in his own responsible decisions now.[20] What is being called for here transcends that kind of open willingness to deal imaginatively and sympathetically with the subject matter which is commonly reckoned a required quality for historians. In these terms, the historian's understanding of the matter in question seems precluded if it proves totally alien to his previous experience. To a degree he must be subjectively engaged, if the yield is to be objective. To that extent Bultmann is saying something which is widely acceptable (if not very startling) in maintaining that "the presupposition for understanding is the interpreter's relationship in his life to the subject which is directly or indirectly expressed in the text."[21] But Bultmann goes beyond this point to demand effectively that historians should be outstanding in their quest for such meaningful encounter as would enable them to see the meaning of history in their recurring and responsible decisions. There is an astonishing disparity between this picture of historians as the most authentic men and what historians actually appear to be, no better and no worse humanly speaking than any other class of academics. It would be open to someone to decree that only those who measured up to Bultmann's requirements would count as historians. But this artificial denial of the name to masses of historians, if it were noticed outside theological circles, would confirm the worst suspicions of those who regard theologians as either having their own peculiar vocabulary or else imposing peculiar limits on ordinary words like "historian."

Another example of the way theologians try to manipulate history and historical terminology is the frequent assertion from Bultmann's school that Christ is "the end of history."[22] Bultmann explains that in the encounter with Christ "the world and its history comes to its end and the believer becomes free from the world by becoming a new creature."[23] Ernst Fuchs elaborates this concept of history on the basis of Paul's teaching that Christ is the end of the law (Romans 10:4). In Fuchs' view "the truth of revelation annuls history" (Geschichte). For history is "the product of the efforts" which "sinners make in order to be able to live." Not only Israel's history but all history shows this impulse of sinful man to found his life on his own works. Through the grace of God in Christ man can be delivered from his past. History as "the product of sinful man's hunger for life" ends when the individual answers obediently revelation's call to love and joy and finds his true historical existence (Geschichtlichkeit) by being relieved of the burden of the past, taking responsibility for the present and becoming free for God who is his future.[24] But this transmutation of Christ the end of the Old Testament law into Christ the end of history looks a strange operation. Literally the world and its history have not come to an end. The Christian may experience that through his encounter with Christ he is no longer enslaved by sin and controlled by earthly engagements. But far from being free from the world and its history, the believer ought to be free for the world and its history. His faith and hope impose on him a deep responsibility for changing the world and directing its history. [25] In any fully meaningful sense the world and its history come to an end for him only at death.

The remembered past is deeply significant for the Christian community's grasp of revelation. As an historical religion Christianity focuses on certain points in space and time, on a "then" and a "there," on particular persons and groups of people from the past. While this preliminary expedition into the problem of faith and history has been brief, it will be followed up in later chapters, in particular in those dealing with salvation history and with the historical Jesus.

Yahweh says, "I act, as the one who acts, i.e., in salvation history; I am the God of salvation history."
Oscar Cullmann

This view of Heilsgeschichte, ignoring history, goes on to assume many different forms of self-explanation: it becomes super-history, or transhistorical, or it points to a timeless truth, or it takes refuge in sheer miracle: the reality is God in his dramatic interventions, and everything else is reduced to unreality.
Ronald Gregor Smith

Chapter V

Salvation History

At the centre of much debate about the relationship between history and faith lies the issue of Heilsgeschichte or salvation history.[1] Those who argue for the elimination of this notion, no less than those who are theologically comfortable with it, agree that it is possible to trace a salvation history approach to the Jewish-Christian religion from its earliest periods. In the scriptures, Irenaeus, Augustine, various creedal and conciliar statements, liturgical texts, the writings of many theologians of different traditions, sacred art, and other theological material we encounter many indications that God's self-communicating activity is to be understood in the context of a history of salvation. In the nineteenth century J. C. K. von Hofmann systematically elaborated the idea of salvation history as the biblical record of God's self-revelation in history. Oscar Cullmann has been outstanding among the contemporary writers who champion a theology of salvation history.

His Christ and Time and Salvation in History represent this category
as the key to a correct understanding of the Christian message.[2]
Due to the work of Gottlieb Söhngen, Jean Daniélou, Urs von Balt-
hasar, and others, a salvation history approach gained ground in
Catholic theology.[3] A measure of official endorsement of this
development emerged in the documents of Vatican II which spoke
explicitly of salvation history.[4] The Council described "the whole
history of the human race"[5] as a history which finds its "key,
focal point and goal" in Christ.[6] As it evolves, human history is
open to scrutiny for signs of divine activity directed towards man's
salvation. The Church "labors to decipher the authentic signs of
God's presence and purpose in the happenings, needs, and desires in which this people [of God] has a part along with other men
of our age."[7]

One possible procedure would be to write a chapter in the
history of theological ideas by tracing the way in which Heilsgeschichte and related categories have been employed by twentieth-
century theologians. Our investigation would in that case need
also to cover such terms as "suprahistory," "metahistory,"
"history of promise," "primal history," "history of revelation,"
"history of the transmission of traditions," "redemptive history,"
and "facts of salvation." We would review the contributions of
Martin Kähler, Karl Barth, Gerhard von Rad, Alan Richardson,
Karl Rahner, Jürgen Moltmann, various contributors to Mysterium
Salutis, Wolfhart Pannenberg, and others.[8] An alternative procedure would be to confine ourselves to one notable proponent of a
salvation history theology, for example Oscar Cullmann, and
engage in a critical discussion of his work. It would be easy to
evoke a clamor of applause from some quarters by reiterating
the kind of criticisms which Bultmann, Barr, Steck, and others
have made and adding further objections.[9] I prefer, however, to
offer a contribution by indicating the major possibilities, limitations and problems in the use of salvation history as a theological
category. The kind of questions to be faced are the following:
What precisely is intended by the term "salvation history"? What
is the relationship of salvation history to profane history? If we
take seriously the "history" element in salvation history, will
we require the historian to recognize that it lies within his com-
petence qua historian to investigate God's salvific activity in
history? Is salvation history properly so-called co-terminous
with biblical history, so that it ends with the conclusion of the
apostolic age? Or does it include also the history of the Christian
Church or even the whole history of mankind? Should we distinguish

different kinds of salvation history, for example, "special" and "general" salvation history?

Some German views

Among German Protestant theologians there exists an astonishing disparity between Old Testament scholars and their New Testament counterparts with respect to judgments on salvation history. Such Old Testament scholars as Gerhard von Rad, Claus Westermann, Walther Eichrodt, Walther Zimmerli, and Rolf Rendtorff take in various ways a positive stand towards a theology of salvation history. Many New Testament theologians, however, view such a theology with disfavor, if not angry disgust. A brief account of their interpretations and assessments of Luke, Paul, and John may usefully introduce the later discussion about the possibilities and problems in the use of salvation history as a theological category.

Among New Testament writers Luke is commonly portrayed as the theologian of salvation history both by those who approve of this theology and by those who disparage it. The redactional criticism of Hans Conzelmann established that a triple division in the plan of God (Acts 2:23) provides the structure for Luke's two-part work on Christian origins. The three phases of salvation history that Luke recognizes are the period of the law and the prophets, the period of Jesus, and the period of the Church (which stretches from Jesus' ascension to his parousia).[10] The different epochs are distinguished by varied workings of the Holy Spirit. In Israel the Spirit produced particular inspirations. In the middle period Jesus is the sole bearer of the Spirit. During the epoch of the Church God bestows the Spirit on all believers, even if their enjoyment of the Spirit is qualitatively inferior to that of Jesus.

For the Bultmann school Luke's portrayal of the gospel in the context of a salvation history scheme forms an attempt to solve the problem created by the delay of the expected parousia. It represents an "interim solution between Mark and John,"[11] a falling away from the "heights of Pauline theology (maintained by Mark and recovered by John)."[12] It is a deterioration in that the temporal framework which is a secondary, detachable element in Jesus' preaching,[13] which appears marginally in Paul and which is (legitimately) eliminated by John has been adopted as if it were the heart of the matter. The true gospel message, the call to the decision of faith, has been largely concealed and forgotten. In fact the perspective of the third gospel betrays the beginning of apostasy

83

from the proper eschatological attitude of the primitive Church and from the true existential self-understanding of the original kerygma. It reveals the onset of so-called "early Catholicism." By this latter phenomenon is understood the emergence of a structured Church which dispenses salvation and in which the sense of eschatological urgency has given way to a belief in a continuous, institutionalized covenant-history of God with man.[14] In place of Luke, Bultmann proposes Paul and John as authentic interpreters of the gospel. Paul's teaching on the justification of the sinner and the Johannine realized eschatology present the true essence of Christianity. Bultmann finds the fourth gospel poles apart from the Lucan scheme. "The history-of-salvation perspective as a whole," he writes, is lacking in John."[15] Ph. Vielhauer maintains that Paul does not betray any consideration of salvation history.[16]

Bultmann's interpretation of the New Testament message, on the one hand, plays down the significance of past events in their (past) historical reality. As we shall see, he acknowledges only the mere "that" of the historical Jesus as being relevant for faith. In the next chapter we take up Bultmann's interpretation of the Old Testament as a paradigm of human failure which lacks positive continuity with the New Testament and has no intrinsic bearing on Christian faith. On the other hand, eschatology is de-temporalized; the truly futurist elements are dismissed as mythology. The eschaton should be understood existentially as referring not to some "last things" in the world process, but to the end of worldliness for the individual believer and his entering now into an authentic existence. The "end-time" (Endzeit) is the present moment of decision (Entscheidungszeit).[17] In place of the continuity of a Lucan salvation-historical scheme Bultmann highlights the present actuality of the recurring word-event which elicits man's religious decision. Reports about past events and the anticipation of future events cannot constitute the saving occurrence here and now. Only the word of proclamation does that by linking together Christ's cross and resurrection and making them present "eschatologically" for the decision of faith. "Christ meets us in the preaching as one crucified and risen. He meets us in the word of preaching and nowhere else. The faith of Easter is just this-faith in the word of preaching."[18] "In the eschatological event," he explains, "there is no preparation and development; there is only the decisive 'now,' no 'then,' no 'later.'"[19] As an alternative to any theologies of salvation history Bultmann proposes a theology of the salvation event (Heilsereignis, Heilsgeschehen). This salvation event occurs when the proclaimed Christ of faith meets me in the kerygma and calls me to decision.

No other writer has done more to destroy Bultmann's position than has Ernst Käsemann, even if he disdains to join Cullmann in proposing a theology of salvation history and continues to regard Lucan writings as representing a deterioration into "early Catholicism." We will see later how he initiated a return among Bultmann's former students to the recognition that the detail of the historical Jesus' life is relevant to our faith. Käsemann also struck at the foundations of Bultmann's version of the New Testament message by his criticism of the fourth gospel. Even if one disagrees with Käsemann's final judgment that this gospel was accepted into the canon "by human error and divine providence," nevertheless, his Testament of Jesus presents forcibly the case against making John's gospel and its realized eschatology the norm by which to assess the rest of the New Testament.[20] Thirdly, Käsemann has argued that a truly futurist eschatology lies at the heart of Paul's theology and is not to be belittled as a mere remnant from his Jewish past.[21] Hence we cannot maintain that the Pauline view is specifically oriented towards the individual and his private justification here and now.[22] With respect to the world and its history Paul envisages the perfect dominion of God through Christ which is yet to be achieved. Our present enjoyment of the Spirit must be understood with reference to the future reality of God's rule and man's coming participation in the resurrection. "To God's divinity there corresponds only a new world in which death has been defeated and brought to nothing."[23] History remains "the realm in which men suffer and hope, groaning and travailing in expectation of Christ's future for the world."[24] It is not yet the "end-time," but rather the beginning of the end. The impact of Käsemann's work has been to open up the perspective in which salvation is viewed. On the one hand he looks back at least as far as the historical Jesus and on the other hand he looks forward to the parousia. Käsemann has effectively required that our account of salvation give proper recognition to the Synoptic account of Jesus, as well as to Paul's hope for the future completion of present salvation.

At this point it may be as well to elaborate some further relevant data from Paul's letters. The first thing to note is that the distinctions which the apostle recognizes in history are not rigidly fixed. In chapters 3 and 4 of Galatians he distinguishes two periods of history--from Abraham to Moses and from Moses to Christ. The first period antedates, the second succeeds the communication of the law. Abraham receives the promise, Moses the law. In Galatians the history from Adam to Abraham is omitted. Paul is intent on proving the preeminence of the promise. In Romans chapter 5, however, where he covers the period from Adam to Moses, he omits any reference to Abraham. But at the same time he affirms, as he does in Galatians, that with Christ a new epoch in salvation history begins: "Christ is the end of the law, that every one who has faith may be justified" (10:4). In Romans Paul is concerned to establish that the history of God's salvific activity supposes a history of human ignorance and sin (chapters 1-3). The revelation of divine justice implies man's judgment. To be sure Israel in her history enjoyed advantages over the gentiles. But ultimately "there is no distinction; since all have sinned and fall short of the glory of God" (3:22 f.).

In Romans (chapters 9-11) Paul ponders the Israelites' choice in the face of the divine call to faith, offering us "a salvation-historical interpretation of events in the mission field."[25] In their case God's free choice (9:16) was answered by man's free rejection (9:18). The manifestation of God's justice in Christ means both discontinuity and continuity in salvation history. Paul distinguishes the gentiles as the new and true people of God (Galatians 6:16) from the Israel of public history. At the same time Paul secures continuity in salvation history by means of the category of the "remnant" (Romans 9:27; 11:5). In the former dispensation there were those who did not "bow the knee to Baal" (Romans 11:4). This "remnant," the true Israel, is now apparent in the Church. As for the other Israelites, Paul predicts that the imminent end of history will see their conversion (Romans 11:11-32).

What the apostle provides is no systematic theology of salvation history, but a fragmentary treatment which yields the following points: (1) Paul's view covers human history from Adam to the parousia (I Corinthians 15; Romans 5 and 8). It does not extend merely from the crucifixion to the parousia (I Corinthians 11:26). (2) History is for him a saving or a damming history, an Unheils-geschichte as well as a Heilsgeschichte, according to whether man accepts or rejects God's free choice (Romans 3:2 ff.). At the same time, human unbelief and sin can be turned to good use by God (Romans 9-11). (3) Despite its discontinuity this history exhibits continuity in that God remains faithful to his promises and gifts (Romans 11, 29) and a "remnant" of the historical Israel has not rejected the divine choice. (4) Salvation history appears simultaneously as revelation history and the history of faith. In Romans 3:21 f. Paul draws together in a classic synthesis the notions of God's saving righteousness: "Now the righteousness of God has been manifested apart from law . . . , the righteousness of God through faith in Jesus Christ for all who believe." In Galatians the sending of the Son to effect our sonship (4:4 ff.) is equivalently the revelation of that Son (1:16) and the coming of saving faith (3:23 ff.). This salvation history is correctly appraised as a history in which God discloses himself to mankind and makes the obedience of faith possible.

Word and event in salvation history

In the most straightforward terms salvation history can be described as God's activity for human salvation in history. From the outset one ought to notice the distinction which is normally introduced between general (or universal) salvation history and special (or official) salvation history. The whole of human history viewed from a salvific perspective forms general salvation history. Special salvation history is God's activity for human salvation in that history recorded by the books of the Old and New Testament. Used in either sense, salvation history is acknowledged to find its focal point in Jesus Christ who is the meaning and goal of all history, no less than of that particular history recorded in scripture.

Now there are obviously a number of formidable problems thrown up by the assertions made in the last paragraph. A helpful way into the discussion is to raise a question about special salvation history: In what "special" way is God active in the biblical events disclosing himself and calling forth man's faith? One might decline the attempt to answer this question and rest content with asserting that salvation history is that kind of history which as a matter of fact gives rise to faith. Thus Hugh Anderson writes: "The significance of 'sacred history' would then be seen not to lie in the idea that this tiny fragment of history furnishes a ready-made explanation of the whole of history or of the whole cosmic process. Its significance would lie rather in its power to beget faith."[26] I find it difficult to remain theologically comfortable with this position. It is hardly enough to decree that the history which can produce faith will count as "sacred history." Why should this history produce faith? Why should nonsacred history fail to produce faith? The alternative view which Anderson rejects is not in fact a position held by any theologian. No one asserts that the events of Israel and the New Testament "explain" in any proper sense of the word the whole of human history. At best they provide the warrant for such very general assertions as that Jesus is (and will be seen to be) the meaning of all history.

Two widely divergent accounts of the "special element" in salvation history are offered by Karl Rahner (who aligns himself with the theology of salvation history) and the late Ronald Gregor Smith (who rejects a salvation-historical view of Christianity). It is only where "profane history is clearly interpreted by the word of God in history as to its saving or damning character" that Rahner recognizes "the special, official history of salvation and revelation, immediately differentiated and standing out in relief from profane history." On this basis even "a miracle would be merely an extraordinary and inexplicable event," so long as "it did not occur in connection with a word-revelation." "The word-revelation makes the miracle logically comprehensible and gives point to its role as a sign indicating something." Profane history becomes transparent here and there through the presence of the prophetic word in the Old Testament and the Word become flesh in the New Testament. The saving (or damning) character of Heilsgeschichte (or Unheilsgeschichte) is conferred precisely because God by his word has interpreted particular events in profane history.[27] Rahner puts full weight on the side of the interpreter rather than on the side of the actions which are interpreted. Many others would join Rahner in highlighting the significance of reflection, interpretation, perspective--in short, the word--as the key to salvation history. In a review of Robert Dentan's The Knowledge of God in Ancient Israel James Burtchaell remarks that Dentan asserts "too facilely that God has acted in Israel's history. Nothing in Israel's history is that peculiar. Israel was a people that knew the same ups and downs which befell other nations. What made her peculiar was not her history, but her historical reflection, and one suspects that the same theological understanding could have been provoked by the history of Ilium or of Media."[28] Dr. Stephen Neill declines to admit anything special about the events which constitute salvation history. The point of divergence from profane history is found in one's point of view: "Heilsgeschichte and secular history are the same history: each from a different point of view is the story of God's providential government of the nations."[29] In these terms to hear the prophetic word or to accept the apostolic interpretation enables a man to see a particular stretch of history as saving or damning. A new perspective has been supplied. This explanation of salvation history, however, leaves unanswered the question: Why is the special word of interpretation available for these historical events and not for those?

On the other hand, Gregor Smith explains salvation history in a way which attributes a decisive importance to the role of (miraculous) divine actions.

Thus the theory of Heilsgeschichte is that God intervenes, against reason and against the historicity of man, with a miracle that compels obedience; and that in the sequence of miraculous acts preceding and consequent upon the life of Jesus, as well as in the similarly outlined life of Jesus, we have the real story of mankind--in other words, a story of supreme arbitrariness, of sovereign indifference to the whole sweep of human history, and of a sublime reduction of all that man has done to a handful of selected "moments," objectifiably certifiable, in the peculiar story of Israel.[30]

In this account "the sequence of miraculous acts" dominates; word-revelation does not rate a mention.

There are difficulties with both versions of salvation history. Rahner makes the word-revelation so preeminent over the saving and revealing events (which it interprets) that these events lapse into subordinate significance. It is hardly sufficient to observe that "the interpreting and revealing word of God, which constitutes the official and special revelation- and salvation-history as distinct from the general salvation- and revelation-history, does not occur always and everywhere but has its special place in time and space within history."[31] This revealing word of God has its special place in time and space within history precisely because it is associated with "special" persons and "special" events. On the basis of what Rahner says official revelation and salvation history could have occurred in fifth century B.C. Athens, provided that the revealing word of God had been available to interpret the particular events of profane history which occurred in that place at that time. Burtchaell's comment is the logical consequence of Rahner's position. Certainly the revealing word, inasmuch as it is not given through creation nor the ordinary events of profane history, enjoys its particular importance in salvation and revelation history. But at the same time the word remains ultimately subordinate to the event and the central person involved in this history. God's supreme act in salvation history was to raise Jesus from the dead. Here the action has priority over the word, the reality over the gospel interpretation.

Against Gregor Smith's account of salvation history there are some important objections to be made over and above the fact that he neglects the role of the revealing word in salvation history. The "miraculous acts" to which he refers--whether one accepts them as having actually taken place or not--hardly form "a story of supreme arbitrariness, of supreme indifference to the whole sweep of human history." As a disciple of Bultmann, Gregor Smith naturally finds in the Johannine writings an acceptable view of "the relation of salvation to time and to history."[32] Now it should be remarked that in the so-called "book of the signs" from the fourth gospel (1:19--12:50) various miraculous events are portrayed as counting among the signs which characterized the life of Jesus. The aftermath of this sequence of signs is clearly stated: these miracles do not compel obedience (12:37 ff.). After elucidating "the theory of Heilsgeschichte" in terms of a "sequence of miraculous acts," Gregor Smith goes on to speak of "a sublime reduction of all that man has done to a handful of selected 'moments.'" There is a jump in logic here which evades me. The point of miraculous acts is surely that they are done by God and not by man.

It is crucial to a fair appreciation of a theology of salvation history that we draw attention to a misconception which is hinted at when Gregor Smith refers to a handful of "objectifiably certifiable" moments in Israel's story. Elsewhere he explains that a Heilsgeschichte view holds "that in the whole of human history we may see certain selected moments, as the dramatic, observable, and demonstrable intervention of God in man's history" (italics mine).[33] Later he recalls that he has discarded this "attempt to point to objectively available moments in the course of history as proof of meaning in history" (italics mine).[34] Gregor Smith's misgivings at this point seem justified in some cases. In Pannenberg's theology of revelation, for example, we meet the claim that the divine reality has so manifested itself that this self-revelation can be critically authenticated on the basis of reason and historical investigation. The historian qua historian can provide "the burden of proof that in Jesus of Nazareth God has revealed himself."[35] Thus for Pannenberg God's intervention in man's history is truly demonstrable and open to proof. Against this view we can build a strong scriptural case from John and Paul. In the fourth gospel the incredulous see in Christ's work (his miracles and discourses) the extraordinary element (6:2; 11:47; 12:18). But the mere seeing--eventually the seeing of all Christ's works--did not as such lead to an acknowledgment of his identity as the divine Revealer who had entered man's history (12:37). Only those "drawn" by the Father see the works as signs revealing the presence and personal action of the Son of God (2:11; 6:63 f.; 6:68 f.; 9:38 f.; 11:25 ff., 40; 20:3 ff.). For the others these works are not clear proof or open demonstration (7:3 ff.; 10:24 f.). Pannenberg's view seems no less irreconcilable with

Paul's message. The word of the apostle proclaiming Christ is identified as "the word of God" which "is at work" in those who believe (I Thessalonians 2:13). When through Paul's proclamation men come to "the knowledge of the glory of God in the face of Christ," this is the work of God who once said: "Let light shine out of darkness," and is now illuminating men's hearts to give them this knowledge by--as it were--a new act of creation (II Corinthians 4:6). Both Paul and John imply that God's salvific action in history is not something open to demonstration and "objective" proof.

However, a salvation history theology does not necessarily imply that God's intervention in human history becomes observable and susceptible of proof. If Vatican II invoked the divine "plan of revelation" and the "history of salvation," it reiterated the scriptural and traditional conviction that the faith which recognizes this divine intervention is the work of God and not the product of human argument. "If this faith is to be shown, the grace of God and the interior help of the Holy Spirit must precede and assist, moving the heart and turning it to God, opening the eyes of the mind, and giving 'joy and ease to everyone in assenting to the truth and believing it.'"36 The history of salvation is, in these terms, recognizable only through the perspective of a divinely given faith which enables me to experience events as God communicating himself, revealing his "plan" and saving me. Salvation history remains indemonstrable qua salvation history from the point of view of the so-called neutral, uncommitted observer.

In a sense it seems strange to find Gregor Smith making the charge that a theology of Heilsgeschichte must claim to be based on demonstration and objective proof. To criticize such a theology for embodying a subjective, uncritical, "religious" view of human history would be a much more understandable reaction. In fact we find Gregor Smith elsewhere pressing such an objection. "It [Heilsgeschichte] is like a ghostly imposition upon the rest of history, a selective spiritualizing of history which is in the last analysis dependent on the subjective whim of the 'Christian' historian."37 We will return to this point shortly.

Yet another difficulty raised by Gregor Smith is one that has frequently been brought forward by the Bultmann school. A salvation history view undercuts personal responsibility. It proposes to us "an observable drama of which we are mere spectators" (italics mine).38 From outside the Bultmann school we meet what amounts to the same objection being put by Moltmann: "The traditional theology of saving history . . . has aesthetic and poetic

91

categories of its own, but none by which the reality of history today could be grasped and altered" (italics mine).[39] In his Salvation in History Cullmann shows that he is very conscious of this objection. His answer commands respect. A salvation history theology should not be interpreted as if it were opposed to Bultmann's key conviction that the kerygma calls us to find true self-understanding and authentic existence through the ever-recurring decision of faith. Such a theology is far from alleging a kind of fixed divine plan which excludes contingent human decisions and reduces man to the status of a nonparticipating onlooker. Salvation history creates the basis for existential decision by calling man to align himself with God's saving activity which comprehends past, present, and future. For Cullmann the call to decision is subordinate to Heilsgeschichte; it is not in conflict with it.[40]

A genuinely futurist, cosmic eschatology (which forms part of a salvation history theology) meets with Bultmann's disapproval in terms that are closely related to Gregor Smith's ethical objection just mentioned. Such an eschatology is alleged to endanger the proper exercise of human freedom. However, as I have argued elsewhere, there is no real alternative here. We are not compelled to choose between such a cosmic eschatology and personal responsibility. Indeed it is precisely that hope for the world's future which arises from a cosmological eschatology which can be the source of energetic obedience towards God. Furthermore, one can rightly have serious misgivings about the ethical consequences of Bultmann's own existentialist view of eschatological existence.[41]

A final feature of Gregor Smith's case against Heilsgeschichte is the observation that such a view smuggles in an illicit Hegelianism. It must be granted that there are points of contact between Hegel's thought and a theology of salvation history. The link, however, is hardly provided by the notion of "steady progress towards a given goal."[42] Heilsgeschichte remains inseparable from Unheilsgeschichte the story of human disaster and sin. In the words of the Portuguese proverb quoted by Cullmann, "God writes straight, but with crooked lines."[43] The major point of contact concerns the Hegelian doctrine of the unity of history. Only the end of all history will reveal publicly the divine salvific plan which has been at work in hidden fashion through the whole of history. In this respect we find a link with Hegel's view that the truth of the whole becomes visible only at the end.[44] Of course, the fact that some theological conviction (or at least something like it) is to be found in German idealism does not mean that it is automatically wrong. Bultmann himself agrees with the Hegelian principle that it is "only from the end of history" that "the meaning of historical occurrence" can be "finally intelligible," even if he adds at once: "But since such a view from the end is impossible for human eyes, a philosophy that seeks to understand the meaning of history is not possible."45

Features of salvation history theology

Although one must be careful of sweeping generalizations, it seems fair to suggest that six major constitutive elements will be involved in a Heilsgeschichte theology. (1) Such a theology commits us to the view that God acts and reveals himself in history. Faith recognizes that God is active in the world and in certain specific events was active in a special way. We will return shortly to a discussion of what it means to speak of an "act of God." Theologies which invoke "acts of God" are not necessarily salvation history theologies. But all salvation history theologies must invoke "acts of God." (2) A theology of salvation history makes a positive assessment of the Old Testament's function for Christian faith. The history of Israel constitutes a history of salvation which stands in some kind of continuity with the New Testament dispensation and is not merely its negative foil. To the question of the connection between the two Testaments we return in the following chapter. (3) The life, death, and resurrection of Jesus form the heart of salvation history. A theology of Heilsgeschichte necessarily excludes any "liberal" appraisal of Jesus' role as the initiator and model of human faith. Whether it invokes his divinity, the definitiveness of the covenant between God and man established through his death and resurrection, the function of his resurrection as the real anticipation of the final end of all history or some other principle, a salvation-historical approach refuses to tolerate the reduction of Jesus to the status of a great man who would differ in degree but not in kind when compared with an Isaiah, a Buddha, or a Socrates. Jesus' saving acts are with us now in a way that Socrates' virtuous acts are not.

(4) A salvation-historical view stands committed to a genuinely futurist eschatology which involves both man and his world. In other words, a Heilsgeschichte theology implies an Endgeschichte (a final history) still to come. (5) Salvation history is opposed to an individualizing of the gospel. The Christian remembers a common past and hopes for a common future which he appropriates for himself by his present decision. Earlier we noted the salvation-

historical perspective characteristic of Paul's letters to the Romans and Galatians. It is hardly a coincidence that these letters are strongly social documents concerned with that justification by faith to be found in (ecclesial) community with our fellowmen. By bringing them into the ambit of salvation history, justification establishes a solidarity between those formerly estranged and creates one people, "the Israel of God" (Galatians 6:16).

> In Christ Jesus you are all sons of God, through faith. For as many of you as were baptized into Christ have put on Christ. There is neither slave nor free, there is neither male nor female; for you are all one in Christ Jesus (Galatians 3:26-28).

Pace Cullmann, the lack of a full salvation-historical perspective in the fourth gospel entails a relatively diminished concern for the world, its history, and the Church.[46] John's attention is directed towards the individual's experience of faith. (6) A Heilsgeschichte approach clearly safeguards the fact that the saving events are independent of our faith. While truly redemptive for us, they serve as a "given" which exists prior to our faith. Salvation history guarantees that redemption is no hidden form of self-redemption.

To give up the category of salvation history would be a quite unnecessary piece of intellectual self-sacrifice. Yet the fairly widespread objection to a Heilsgeschichte theology could not have arisen unless there were justification for it. I suspect that the two most acute problems for such a theology are the need to explain what is involved in talking of "acts of God" and the need to clarify the link between salvation history and so-called ordinary history.

Acts of God

Talk about "acts of God" can claim excellent scriptural backing. The profession of faith at the offering of first-fruits (Deuteronomy 26:5-10) and at the renewal of the covenant at Shechem (Joshua 24: 2-13) express the conviction that various events are attributable to the special intervention of God, the Lord of history.[47] The Christians inherited from Israel this conviction (Acts 7:2-53; 13: 17-23) and extended it to the events of Jesus' life, death, and resurrection. These they interpreted as historical acts of God:

Men of Israel, hear these words: Jesus of Nazareth, a man
attested to you by God with mighty works and wonders and signs
which God did through him in your midst, as you yourselves
know--this Jesus, delivered up according to the definite plan
and foreknowledge of God, you crucified and killed by the hands
of lawless men. But God raised him up, having loosed the pangs
of death, because it was not possible for him to be held by it
(Acts 2:22-24).

When we come to modern theological accounts of what constitutes
an "act of God," we meet an astonishing variety of views. Hugh
Anderson is unwilling to say more about "God's acts" than that they
are historical occurrences which "pass into language," in the sense
that "faith arises from the proclamation of what God has done."
In this view an act of God would be any event of (biblical?) history
which has the power to "beget faith" when it is proclaimed.[48]
    For John Knox we know the action of God only in the coming in-
to being of the Church. The "Church-event" alone properly counts
as an--or rather as the--act of God. What God "did" was to
"create" the Church.[49] But in which sense did God create the
Church? Knox explains that to say "God acted" is "the simplest,
most general, way of affirming the divine character of an experience," but he warns us against imagining that we can speak
of God "acting" in "any literal sense" of the term. It is a "story"
which is "mythological in character," but which remains the
only form that "the Church's attempts to realize and convey the
divine meaning of its own existence" could conceivably take.[50]
Ultimately, in Knox's opinion, "an act of God" is no more than
the kind of language which--so he maintains--the Church must
necessarily use in describing her own existence.
    Yet another explanation is offered by Pannenberg. An act of
God is an event which can be judged not only "in its concrete
relationship to events of its immediate and its broader context,"
but also in its relationship "to history as a whole." This last
relationship makes itself visible only in some events, preeminently in Jesus' resurrection, an event which really anticipates
the end of all history. It is "only through their contact with this
particular event" that other events acquire a relationship "to the
whole of reality" (which for Pannenberg is identical with "universal history").[51]
    Even though these views command respect, they provoke dis-
sent primarily because none of them goes anything like far enough
in teasing out the elements involved in labelling some event as an

"act of God." It seems undesirable to turn aside into an enormous parenthesis for the purpose of collecting and examining minutely the many explanations of this term. But some account of the term must be offered if this chapter on salvation history is not to remain essentially incomplete. I suggest that an adequate explanation should embody the following six points. (1) To characterize some event as an "act of God" is to allege a special presence and a particular activity of God. We assume that there are various degrees of engagement on the part of God. Some events or series of events reveal more of the divine concerns and interests than others. In this sense not all ages have an equally immediate relationship to eternity. To deny that there exists such various degrees of divine engagement with the world and its history should logically lead one to deism. (2) The particular divine activity denoted by an "act of God" remains at least in some measure recognizably independent of the world and created causality. Thus the resurrection of Jesus as an act of God manifests a special divine causality. Other happenings designed as "acts of God" may involve a finely meshed array of human causality. We could cite the events leading up to the Babylonian captivity or those which brought about the execution of Jesus. Even in such events a certain degree of independent divine creativity is postulated when we describe them as "acts of God."

(3) Such situations are understood to imply a religious claim and convey a moral significance. Thus the ministry and resurrection of Jesus require that men acknowledge a divine claim being made, take certain decisions, and adopt a particular pattern of action. Peter's Pentecost proclamation of God's activity in the life, death, and resurrection of Jesus concludes with the call to repent and be baptized (Acts 2:38). (4) The special freedom and unpredictability of an act of God implies an element of mystery. Acts of God are never unambiguously so. They remain concealed to the extent that men may see or fail to see these events as acts of God. Recognition is uncompelled. The factor of relative concealment allows cognitive freedom to persist.

(5) When we postulate "a particular activity of God" and "a special divine creativity," this should not be taken to imply that the divine causality involved is measurable. The effects of the so-called "acts of God" may be visible and spatial. But we are not asserting that something occurs "out there" or "back there" to which we can point as God's causal contribution. The divine activity is no more susceptible to spatial attributes than is God himself. (6) To maintain "a certain degree of independent divine creativity" is not

intended to exclude the fact that some events may be experienced both as (a) acts of God and (b) as acts of man. The Babylonian captivity would be a case in point. The events which made up that historical episode were understood to embody two values. Experiencing them as (a) not only presupposed experiencing them also as (b), but also went beyond experiencing them as (b).

History and salvation history

Sooner or later we ought to raise the issue of the relation between history and salvation history. Does Heilsgeschichte merit the name of history? Or does the element of salvation predominate at the expense of history? If Heilsgeschichte embodies "the idea of a non-historical history,"[52] surely it would be preferable to drop the category as unnecessarily confusing and misleading. To begin with, it is as well to admit that we might decide to avoid the term "salvation history" on account of the particular way we plan to use "history" and related words. We might wish to restrict the term to merely human achievements and experiences and withhold it from acts (both miraculous and providential) that are attributed to God. In that case the work of an historian would entail the reconstruction of the past by scientific methodology with the aim of establishing the nexus of innerworldly causes and effects. In offering his explanation and reconstruction of the causal connections, the historian would not take it as his task to admit or invoke the activity of God, special or otherwise. Such an approach need not mean that we would deny God's causality, let alone his existence. But it would simply indicate that we intended to restrict "history" and related terms to this-worldly phenomena, human causality and all that is open in principle to public inspection. The historian would not profess to examine whether God "acts" in history. God would not be for him an historical category.

Others maintain, however, that the historian should hold himself open to all possibilities, even the possibility of special divine (miraculous) causality being at work.[53] In this view the faith account of some event as an act of God could rate as a true historical judgment. God's involvement in what is understood by "history" can be taken astonishingly far. Ronald Gregor Smith goes to the point of defining history by reference to God: "History is constituted by the personal decisions which arise out of the confrontation in faith of the personal demand of God to each single person."[54] Behind such a statement lies, of course, a Bultmannian view of history. My point here is simply to demonstrate that we

97

can find a resolute opponent of Heilsgeschichte interpreting history
in a highly theological fashion. One could imagine the astonished
reaction of A. J. P. Taylor, the contributors to the Cambridge
Modern History or Daniel Boorstin, if Gregor Smith's account of
what constitutes history happened to fall into their hands. It seems
worthwhile to remind ourselves, however, that a healthy tolerance
is needed here. There are many ways of "doing" what we wish to
call "history." There are no eternally prescribed limits or a
priori rules imposed on the historian. European historians, for
instance, have to accept the fact that their Anglo-Saxon colleagues
fail to interpret the historian's task in exact accord with their own
procedures. If Gregor Smith wished to attach a theological meaning to the word "history," we may not deny his right to do so,
simply on the grounds that this meaning fails to conform to ordinary
usage. What we may demand, however, is that a writer follow out
the rules he has set himself and give some consistent account of
how he understands history and also salvation history, if he decides
to adopt the latter term.

Before I offer my own opinion, it may help to illustrate what is
required by examining Cullmann's usage and drawing attention to
some deficiencies. Cullmann is convinced that what he calls
Heilsgeschichte is entitled to the name for three reasons: (1) it
leaves room for human freedom, and (2) it deals with a connected
series of events which (3) belong also to ordinary history. Salvation history is set apart from ordinary history in that the latter
implies an unbroken sequence of events, whereas the former is a
history that shows remarkable and apparently arbitrary gaps.

> Whereas events of history unfold as a general chronological,
> historical sequence without interruption, and the record of
> them is accordingly set down without any gaps, it is essential
> to biblical salvation history that it shows gaps which are quite
> remarkable from an historical standpoint, and which unfold
> entirely by leaps. Isolated events appear differentiated and
> sorted out of the total historical process, historically speak-
> ing, in an arbitrary way. . . . There are great chronological
> gaps within this process, completely inexplicable for history
> and philosophies of history. These gaps do not exist merely
> within one and the same period. Whole periods as such are
> "bypassed."[55]

As regards reason (1), probably by accident rather than by
design Cullmann succumbs to pessimism in his explanation of the

role of human freedom in salvation history. "Within the divine plan," he explains, "a place is left for historical contingency, for human resistance, sin, and the mysterious 'detours' taken because of this resistance and sin--in other words, salvation history also includes a history of disaster."[56] Human freedom surely includes also a freely given obedience to God and an ac- quiescence in the divine plan. I have serious trouble with (3). The difference which is indicated here between history and salva- tion history lies on the side of our knowledge, not on the side of what takes place. Events of human history occur in continuous sequence without interruption, even as the divine activity at work in the world is uninterruptedly there. There are no ontological "gaps" or "leaps" in what God does for man. But in what touches our knowledge of events, it does not necessarily hold true that the record of historical events is or must be set down without any gaps. In given periods of history there exist notorious gaps, great stretches of human history from which only the knowledge of isolated events has survived. Cullmann instances "a large gap" between the birth and the baptism of Jesus, explaining that salva- tion history in this case, as elsewhere, "rests upon the divine selection of events within the whole of history."[57] I detect a cer- tain confusion here between the order of reality and the order of knowledge. There were no ontological gaps between the birth and baptism of Jesus. The gaps concern rather what is known or at least reported to us.

With respect to reason (2), I find it surprising that Cullmann fails to grapple seriously with the problem that the so-called series of events which make up salvation history includes a wide variety of episodes in which God is represented as acting. The series covers such things as the creation story, man's fall into sin, the flood, the events of the end-time, as well as such straightforward occurrences in profane history as the Israelites' deportation to Babylon, the crucifixion of Jesus, and the destruc- tion of Jerusalem. The problem has faced Cullmann ever since he enumerated in Christ and Time the elements which he as- sociates in the "Christ-line" of biblical history.

Primitive Christianity places both the divine creation "in the beginning" and the divine goal of all becoming "at the end of the days" in precisely the same Christocentric perspective of Biblical history, that is, in precisely the same temporal Christ-line which it uses to view the historical events in which figure the people of Israel and the activity of Jesus and the apostles and the Primitive Church.[58]

99

Cullmann proposes that we ought to recognize that there exists an analogy between history and salvation history.[59] What I badly miss in his discussion is a frank admission of the difficulty created by the fact that the various kinds of events which make up salvation history bear sometimes only a remote analogy to each other. The dissimilarities in factual status between the crucifixion of Jesus and the Genesis flood-story are startling.

What convinces me of the legitimacy of continuing to use the term "salvation history" is ultimately the fact that salvation history encompasses such genuinely historical components as the death of Jesus and the fall of Jerusalem. I would decline to adopt the category, if salvation history were to be applied only to the events of creation and the end-time, the so-called Urgeschichte and Endgeschichte, or if it included only events which were doubtfully real. A measure of historical factuality is essential. At the heart of salvation history lies a set of events open to human observation and accessible to historical investigation, even if the Heilsgeschichte perspective on these events embodies a specifically theological understanding which is not susceptible to ordinary verification. Faith sees the deportation of the Israelites as a judgment of God and the birth of Jesus as the incarnation. The historian and the believer may share a common interest in a particular set of events, but I would not ask the historian qua historian to recognize such events as God communicating himself in a special salvific presence and activity. It lies beyond the work of the historian either to use or to demonstrate the conviction that man's salvation constitutes the inner meaning of world history. Only the special judgment of faith acknowledges that God is the Lord of History and that, despite the apparent contingency, there exists an inner continuity in the whole human story.

Salvation history and post-biblical times

After instancing some episodes from the exodus story, Paul declares: "Now these things happened to them as a warning, but they were written down for our instruction, upon whom the end of the ages has come" (I Corinthians 10:11). Here the Christian community is seen as the end and goal of salvation history. This raises the question of the continuation of salvation history in post-biblical times. How can we know when and where we are to acknowledge some special salvific act of God? Are such episodes as the discovery of North America, the defeat of Hitler, the canonization of saints, the holding of Church Councils, the liturgical movement, the formation of the biblical canon, and all the events which constitute the history of the Church rightly taken as occurrences of salvation history? Gregor Smith's general complaint about Heilsgeschichte can act as a salutary warning at least with respect to the post-biblical period. Salvation history, he objects, "is like a ghostly imposition upon the rest of history, a selective spiritualizing of history which is in the last analysis dependent on the subjective whim of the Christian historian."60 The remedy against such indulgence of subjective whims is to begin from the biblical events and look for the salvific meaning of subsequent events in the light of Jesus' history and the foundation of the Church. If the divine plan of salvation is unitary, there exists at least the possibility of seeking some criteria for assessing post-biblical events as episodes in salvation history. I suggest that two principles can guide us here. (1) Where the activity of the Christian community is clearly an attempt "to bring about the obedience of faith" (Romans 1:5), we may legitimately view such episodes as part of salvation history. "The power of God for salvation" (Romans 1:16) will be at work where the Gospel is proclaimed, the Eucharist celebrated, and the sacraments administered. Beyond that we should acknowledge the acceptance of the canon of scripture as belonging to salvation history. We may also want to add other particular episodes and movements in Church history. But our decision ought to be guided by the degree of our conviction that at these points we are truly confronted with the power of God effecting the obedience of faith. (2) The post-biblical history of the Jewish people forms part of Heilsgeschichte. No matter how difficult or perhaps impossible it may be to plot a pattern in the particular episodes of Jewish history, nevertheless, the Apostle Paul (Romans 11) obliges us to acknowledge that a special form of divine engagement is at work in this history.

What conception of God and the world enabled men not only to place the Old and New Testaments side by side, but even to understand one in the light of the other?

Karl Barth

The Old Testament (as against the New) might be conceived in many respects as a divinely interpreted model of pre-Christian religion rather than as an absolutely and in every respect unique and incomparable quantity.

Karl Rahner

Chapter VI

The Relation of the Two Testaments

In the last chapter a positive assessment of the Old Testament's
function for Christian faith was noted among the characteristics
of a salvation history theology. It was no mere coincidence that
Catholic theology recaptured a sense of the Old Testament's importance at a time that it developed the themes of salvation history.
Fittingly the divine plan of salvation unfolding through history
formed the leitmotif of Vatican II's treatment of the Old Testament
in Dei Verbum (nos. 14-16).[1]

Yet it may seem far from obvious that the Old Testament should
be read in Church as part of canonical scripture or that Christian
theologians should use it as a basis for argument. The Old Testament consists of a collection of pre-Christian books recording a
pre-Christian religion. Surely this imperfect revelation is to be
left aside now that the definitive revelation has come with Christ.
Do Christians really lose something essential by neglecting the Old
Testament?

As an initial answer to such questioning it is worth recalling that fundamental relationship expressed by the early confession "Jesus (is the) Christ"--a confession which quickly became a name for the person on whom the interest of the New Testament was uniquely concentrated. The Old Testament with its manifold Messianic expectations was retained and now focused on the central figure of Jesus. The self-understanding of the first Christians emerged as a product of Israel's hope and faith in Jesus. The debate between Judaism and the early Church concerned the right use of the Old Testament almost as much as it concerned the figure of Jesus himself. The temptation narratives in Matthew and Luke (which reflect this debate over the understanding of the Old Testament) portray both Christ and the devil as offering warrant for their positions by citing the words of scripture. But mere citation from the Old Testament does not decide the legitimacy of one's case. The Jewish interpretation of Israel's hope forms a Satanic temptation. The Christians claim access to the true sense of the Old Testament, an access which the risen Christ confers (Luke 24:25-27, 44 f.). The meaning of his life, death, and resurrection are grasped by entering into the Old Testament dynamic.

Although one must be careful of any sweeping categorizations concerning the relation of the Old Testament to the New, it seems fair to suggest that all theological interpretations of this relationship highlight either discontinuity or continuity. This division holds true, despite many divergences concerning the way in which this continuity and discontinuity are explained by particular theologians. In the term "Old Testament" either "Old" or "Testament" will be emphasized.

Discontinuity

The conviction of discontinuity may be expressed by presenting the Old Testament as the time of religion and the New Testament as the time of faith, or by contrasting an impossibility (of justification through faith) with a possibility (of justification through faith). It is a trite observation to remark that we can expect theologians preoccupied with the classic Lutheran distinction of law and gospel to elaborate the thesis of discontinuity between the two Testaments. Thus Bultmann interprets the Old Testament history as a story of miscarriage, in particular the collapse of the notions of covenant, kingdom of God, and people of God. The only fulfillment conceded to the Old Testament finds expression in the paradoxical assertion that it "is fulfilled in its inner contradiction,

its miscarriage."[2] On the basis of collapse the situation of justification arises. For the Christian "the Old Testament is no longer
revelation" and "the history of Israel is not history of revelation."[3]
Yet the link between the two Testaments is not reduced to the case
of a mere substitution of something unrelated. If the Old Testament
fails to prove revelatory for Christian faith, nevertheless, it evokes
the preunderstanding which contributes to our hearing the New
Testament. It offers a "basic possibility" for understanding human
existence under the law.[4] Hence "man must stand under the Old
Testament if he wants to understand the New."[5] Both testaments
share a common understanding of existence. Beyond this admission Bultmann resolutely refuses to go. The Old Testament is not
God's word for me now. Israel's history falls short of forming a
history of revelation for the Christian. It is part of our Christian
history only in the sense that we might say that "the Spartans fell
at Thermopylae for us and that Socrates drank hemlock for us."
Hence "Jerusalem is not a holier city for us than Athens or Rome."[6]

If one adopts the thesis of discontinuity, the requirements of
consistency will shape the interpretation of the passages from Paul
which were cited in the previous chapter as indicating a salvation
history approach. One would then explain Paul's argument as
being dictated by his polemic. To confute opponents who demand
that the Gentiles observe the Mosaic law, Paul shows himself
quick to make good debating points. The law can hardly be indispensable for justification, if even in the Old Testament we find
justification by faith (Romans 4). The law must be assessed as
inferior to the promise (which is now fulfilled in Christ), because the promise existed prior to the law (Galatians 3:15 ff.).
To buttress the discontinuity thesis with the apostle's authority
we will need to argue with Ernst Fuchs that, no matter how Paul
uses the scriptures for apologetical ends, intrinsic continuity
with the Old Testament enjoys no significance for him whatever.[7]

The Christological consequences of Bultmann's position should
not be glossed over. His underplaying the positive function of the
Old Testament links up with his conviction that detail about the life
of the earthly Jesus (including his historical background) remains
irrelevant for faith. To interpret the Old Testament as a story of
collapse helps Bultmann to detach the gospel of Christ from history
and offer a nonhistorical interpretation of Christ. Further, the
assertion that Israel's history and hopes are merely destroyed
calls for dissent. Is nothing at all fulfilled? Do the Old Testament
notions of covenant, kingdom, and people of God fail to find any
kind of (positive) fulfillment in the kingdom which Jesus proclaimed,

in the (new) covenant which his death and resurrection effected and in the new Israel which formed about the apostles in the aftermath of Pentecost? Finally, how are we to interpret the claim of Christians who on reading (or hearing) the Old Testament experience in various ways God's self-disclosure? Bultmann argues that in this context the Christian is reading the Old Testament existentially and not as part of the history of his own people. But at least some Christians will insist that they appropriate the Old Testament revelation in the consciousness that they stand in continuity with the history of Israel, that Abraham is their father in faith, and that Jerusalem remains a holy city for them. In the face of such insistence Bultmann's only recourse would be to declare them deluded or decree that such experiences fail to count as revelation.

Continuity

In various views which affirm the continuity between the two Testaments two points stand out as foci of attention, the person of Jesus and the ongoing process of salvation history. The affirmation of the relevance of the Old Testament for Christian faith involves attributing to divine fidelity a continuity between the Testaments. A unity in salvation history emerges due to the action of God. Such an assertion of continuity can coexist with a frank acknowledgment of the discontinuity that arises from the fact that the divinely given law has been superseded as a way of salvation, to say nothing of the discontinuity due to Israel's large-scale and repeated failures towards God.[8] Stephen's speech in Acts (chapter 7) summarizes salvation history as a history of the divine failure with men. The other focus of attention is found in the principal figure of salvation history, Jesus himself. Here some remain content to argue the thesis of continuity on the grounds that Jesus cannot be adequately understood except in the context of the Old Testament. Others go further to introduce the self-consciousness of Jesus himself. Thus for Cullmann it is essential to maintain that Jesus understood himself against the background of the Old Testament, being conscious that in his person he was the Son of Man and the Servant of Yahweh.[9]

The theme of continuity between the Testaments may be proposed in a qualified fashion. Thus Moltmann insists that within the history of promise the New Testament goes beyond a mere cancelling of what has been promised in that it lifts the Old Testament expectations to a new level.[10] Other interpretations of this

continuity--particularly in the past--have not merely expounded
the New Testament as the natural development of the Old but have
maintained a prior presence of the New Testament. Thus Augustine
understood the New Testament reality as being already given in
the Old Testament, even if this presence remained as yet un-
disclosed: "The New Testament lay hidden in the Old: the Old
Testament is now revealed in the New."[11] Many of the Church
Fathers escalated the continuity between the Testaments out of
all proportion, running wild in their interpretations of the Old
Testament as one extensive prediction of the New.[12]

Some principles of continuity

By arguing in the last chapter for the possibility of making an
honest woman of salvation history, I have committed myself in
some measure to the view of continuity between the Testaments
and equivalently to the view that the Old Testament remains
relevant for Christian faith today. Let me now set out some principles for assessing this continuity, first pointing out some qualifications which should be kept in mind. The fact that we assert a
relationship of continuity should not lead us to minimize the independent value of the Old Testament. Even if per impossibile
there had never been a New Testament, the Old Testament would
have enjoyed its own importance as a period of special divine
self-disclosure. Those who acknowledge only the books of the Old
Testament do genuinely profit by this record of God's special
dealings with his chosen people. Secondly, the interrelationship
may not be specified as simply Messianism. It is broader than
that. Thirdly, the simple argument that all is held together by the
one salvific plan of God requires to be qualified by the recognition
of those elements--both on God's side and on man's side--which
work for discontinuity.[13]

The Same Religious Tradition   The ultimate value of a religious
tradition rests in its doctrine of God. Both Testaments are concerned with the same God.[14] When Jesus spoke of his Father,
he meant the God whom all Jews knew, the Yahweh whose encounters with Israel are related in the Old Testament. The God
of the creation story was identified as the God who had disclosed
himself to man in Christ: "It is the God who said, 'Let light shine
out of darkness,' who has shone in our hearts to give the light of
the knowledge of the glory of God in the face of Christ" (II Corinthians 4:6). The God who brought Israel out of Egypt was acknowledged as the God who had raised Jesus from the dead.

The New Testament writers interpret Jesus and what had happened through his life, death, and resurrection by means of the thought-patterns which they had inherited from their past. The new situation which arose through the events connected with Jesus brought fresh insights and radical reinterpretations, but this growth took place within the framework of Israel's traditional piety. The first Christians were not particularly inventive in composing new prayers. They retained the psalms and other Old Testament prayer-forms, bringing to them fresh meanings in the light of Jesus Christ. As a way of expressing ethical forms Old Testament commandments were preserved. Moral practice received, of course, a changed context and new motivation through the events of Christ's coming. Almost every important theological concept in the New Testament was derived from some Hebrew term which had already enjoyed a long history of use and development in the Old Testament. These concepts were enriched --usually by acquiring a deeper spiritual meaning and a more universal area of application.

The Same People   The continuity between the people of Israel and those of the New Testament goes much deeper than the merely external link involved in the fact that the first Christians happened to be Jews. (The early Church experienced that kind of continuity with the worshippers of Diana when some Ephesians accepted the Christian Gospel.) The one Israel continued in the New Testament with the Gentiles now "grafted in" to make the new Israel of God (Romans 11:37 ff.; Galatians 6:16). For Paul "the acceptance of the Gospel was . . . the recognition of the advent of the true and final form of Judaism."15 Luke too represents Christianity as true Judaism, not as a new creation substituted for the former people of God. As Luke tells the story, it was entirely the fault of Jews that the Christians had to organize themselves apart from the synagogue (Acts 13:42 ff.).

The Person of Jesus   It was essential to Jesus' person and mission that he appeared as a descendant of Old Testament families. Dissatisfied with the fact that Mark's account of Jesus opens with his baptism, Matthew and Luke trace his origins from Abraham (Matthew) and from Adam (Luke). As one who arose from the Old Testament Jesus effected the situation in which the new Israel came into being. By acclaiming him as the Messiah the first Christians were affirming his key function in the one divine plan of salvation which spanned both Testaments. In the strict sense the Messiah was expected as the anointed king of Davidic dynasty who would establish in the world the definitive reign of Yahweh.

The Christian description of Jesus unified various Old Testament salvific figures by amalgamating with the Messiah such figures as the Suffering Servant and the Son of Man. Whether such amalgamation happened in pre-Christian Judaism remains quite uncertain. No pre-Christian work seems, for instance, to have a suffering Messiah. In his person Jesus was believed to unify many Old Testament ideas (the element of continuity), while transforming them profoundly (the element of discontinuity).

The Contribution of New Testament Writers   The history which the New Testament writers invoke and the text which they cite are the pre-Christian history of Israel and the pre-Christian scriptures. It is clearly insufficient to allow no more than a contingent connection, as if these writers simply draw on a history with which they are familiar and quote a sacred literature which is conveniently at hand. Rather they take for granted the authority of the literature and the revelatory significance of the events to which they constantly appeal.

In general we can safely assert that in their exegesis of the Old Testament the New Testament writers are both Christo-centric and to an extent discriminating. There is a reciprocal process at work in their Christocentrism. If Christ is the key to the Old Testament, the Old Testament is the key to Christ (Luke 24:55 ff.). In particular they relate the two Testaments by seizing onto Old Testament predictions. Thus the author of Psalm 22 is credited with foreseeing in detail the passion of Jesus (Matthew 27:35, 39, 43, 46). In fairness to them we ought also to observe that the New Testament writers decline to use the Old Testament indiscriminately. There are some prophecies which they ignore and others which they modify. For instance, Matthew 11:4-6 draws on Isaiah 35:5, 6, omitting 35:4 which is a prediction of vengeance.

Certainly, the Old Testament forms an essential element in St. Paul's Christianity. Importance is not gauged here merely by citing quantitative reports: the apostle in fact quotes the Old Testament ninety-three times. We need to call attention to the firm statement of continuity which shapes Paul's understanding: "Whatever was written in former days was written for our instruction, that by steadfastness and by the encouragement of the scriptures we might have hope" (Romans 15:4). If Paul explores Christianity and buttresses its teaching in the light of the Old Testament (I Corinthians 9:9f.), he lays claim to a new freedom in the interpretation of his Jewish tradition: "God . . . has qualified us to be ministers of a new covenant, not in a written code but in the Spirit; for the written code kills, but the Spirit gives life" (II Corinthians 3:5f.).

One theme of continuity to be drawn from the apostle's reflections is that of Old Testament promise finding New Testament fulfillment. Passages such as I Corinthians 15:3 f. could encourage
us to scour the Old Testament for texts predicting Christ's death
for our sins and his resurrection for our justification. Certainly
we will be able to turn up texts which promise "the descent from
David according to the flesh" (Romans 1:3), a promise which
Paul acknowledges as fulfilled in Jesus. But rather than concentrate
on detecting isolated promises which achieve fulfillment it is
preferable to evaluate the New Testament as completing a whole
history of promise. Paul calls attention to the broad scope of fulfillment in Christ: "All the promises of God find their Yes in
him" (II Corinthians 1:20).

Closely allied to these themes of promise and fulfillment is
Paul's appeal to typology. Within the matrix of salvation history
Old Testament realities (the types) emerge as divinely established
models foreshadowing the New Testament realities (the antitypes).
The antitype gives the type its real meaning. The correspondence
can be constituted by difference as well as by resemblance. Thus
Christ comes to reverse the work of Adam who brought sin and
death (Romans 5:12-14; I Corinthians 15:22).

One formula?

Ultimately, the relationship between the two Testaments resists
any kind of satisfying encapsulation in a single formula. The Old
Testament is not merely a period of preparation for the New Testament fulfillment. To affirm that Christ forms the answer to man's
antecedent hopes leaves much unaccounted for. Promise is not
uniformly prominent in the Old Testament. Typology is even less
prominent. Besides, insistence on the unity of typology as the
key to the interrelationship of the Testaments would make the
Old Testament largely useful only for illustrative purposes. A
more successful formula for interpreting the relationship is
found in the saving role of Christ for men who need the redemptive
realities. The story of the Old Testament records in varied
fashion the weakness, absurdity, and guilty failure of men. Human sinfulness in the face of divine love and man's powerlessness
to cope alone with the futile, puzzling, and oppressively evil
features of existence--these are themes which sum up much of
what the psalmists, historians, prophets, and wise men of the Old
Testament have to say. If one were forced to provide a single
formula, it would be human need for redemption. However, the

110

relationship between Old Testament and New remains as complex as salvation history itself. No one formulation does justice to its manifold phenomena of continuity and discontinuity.

Some practical implications

Let me conclude by sketching some important consequences that result from one's understanding of the Old Testament. (1) On the negative side, neglect of the Old Testament constitutes con-crete evidence of a weakened Christianity. A Docetic tendency must be numbered among the most unfortunate implications. Where we fail to accord proper recognition to Jesus' background in Jewish history, to that extent we are effectively setting Jesus in a void and refusing to acknowledge the full human background which the Incarnation entails. As true man he entered the history of his nation at a precise stage in the development of their religious traditions and political achievements. Their total history formed the "given" against which and within which his work was done.

(2) A proper sense of the Old Testament carries with it the recognition that Christ was limited by history. He did not reveal everything nor did his apostles do just that. In comparison with the centuries of developing revelation recorded in the Old Testa-ment, the New Testament period was severely limited. Let me mention some areas in which the Old Testament enjoys a supe-riority in disclosing God and man. If we were restricted to the New Testament, it would be difficult to escape the impression that Christian faith implies indifference or at least resignation towards various forms of political oppression. Reflection on the progress of salvation in the Old Testament, however, reveals no lack of divine concern for the temporal liberation of the op-pressed. Through the exodus and other military and political episodes God and his intentions are disclosed. Secondly, the New Testament lacks any extended treatment of man being faced by God and reacting to the manifestation of the divine will. Through a rich variety of historical, prophetic, sapiential, legal, and liturgical writings the Old Testament answers the question: Who is man? Job and the wisdom literature in general show us men facing such problems as innocent suffering, the brevity of man's life, and the vanity of human wishes and wrestling with them in a satisfying, "existentialist" fashion. The New Testament has nothing comparable to offer. Thirdly, the story of Israel reveals God's people undergoing a history marked by religious decline as well as religious progress. Events carry not only God's grace

111

to but also his judgment on his people. The New Testament, on the other hand, records little more than the coming into existence of the new Israel. It contains nothing like the extended history of the Old Testament in which we see how the developing story of God's people is far from necessarily immune from sinful practices, corrupt leadership, and other communal failures before God.

(3) A robust absorption of the Old Testament dynamic of progress in religious thinking could be immensely helpful. The Old Testament does not constitute a closed system of doctrine about God and man. In changing historical situations new inter-pretations of a basic creed are evoked and fresh meaning given to God's promises. Within the New Testament we glimpse a similar wrestling for a new understanding of God's relations with men as the startling events connected with Jesus take place. There is a basic structural correspondence. In both Testaments the ongoing tension between tradition and new experiences yield fresh insights and fresh affirmations.

(4) Finally, where the Old Testament remains comparatively unimportant for Christians, there is no compelling necessity for them to enter into true dialogue with Judaism. So long as Chris-tians act as if the Old Testament was not really part of God's authentic revelation to his people, they will lack the motivation for that special relationship with those who remain before God "beloved for the sake of their forefathers" (Romans 11:28). In that case Christians will be content to look on Jews as a curious group of survivors. They will view them in much the same way that anthropologists regard primitive tribes who happen to be still with us in modern times.

PART TWO

Faith and Revelation in
Two Recent Theological Statements

The question concerning the revelation of God . . . is not seeking for some authoritarian court of appeal which suppresses critical questioning and individual judgment, but for a manifestation of divine reality which meets the test of man's matured understanding as such.

Wolfhart Pannenberg

Pannenberg's own road to Christianity had been more one of rational reflection than of Christian nurture or a conversion experience.

J. M. Robinson

Chapter VII

Wolfhart Pannenberg:
Revelation as Knowable History

When asked to explain what is meant by God's revelation in Christ I have no short or easy answer to give. In Part One of this book I discussed the divine self-disclosure both directly and through the related themes of theological procedure, history and faith, salvation history, and the link between the Old and the New Testament. The theologian of revelation has a good deal of explaining to do. Further, each Roman Catholic theologian speaks today more and more for himself, even though he may not be sure that his work is important enough to gain a serious hearing from his fellow Catholics and other Christians. A further way of conveying my own approach is to examine critically two contemporary state-ments on revelation, those by Wolfhart Pannenberg and Gerald Downing. The first believes that he can provide theology with a healthy, new understanding of revelation. The second wishes to phase out the category altogether. At this point confrontation with their views can serve to supplement what has already been argued in this book. I think it profitable to convey my own convictions through explicit (and precise) dialogue with two theologians, each of whom has won for himself from at least some of his coreligionists the reputation of being an enfant terrible.

At the heart of Pannenberg's theological thinking lies the certainty that reason and historical investigation can do for others what they did for him, namely establish the objective grounds of faith. In both Barth and Bultmann he found the same "authoritarian claims to revelation" which "exempt themselves from questions of critical rationality." He turned away, he explains, "from the 'theology of the Word of God' in its different present-day forms" to develop his own position.[1] Pannenberg's rejection of the prevailing (German) consensus is far-reaching. Knowledge, not faith, forms man's immediate response to the divine self-revelation, which is not a word to be heard but takes place through God's activity in history. The claims of revelation require authentication by rational argument and historical investigation. In principle man does not need special divine help to grasp revelation. The disclosing events are not ambiguously obscure but carry their own clear meaning in themselves. Far from being the unique "place" of revelation, the Christian proclamation simply constitutes a report which communicates the necessary information about the grounds of faith. -- Our fuller exposition of Pannenberg's view follows, after which we will give a critical assessment.

History and theology

To appreciate Pannenberg's position we must begin with his basic axiom that "history"--and not the word of God, the kerygma or anything else--forms "the most comprehensive horizon of Christian theology."[2] The concern of theology is to understand the truth of history. In this conviction he resembles Alan Richardson, for whom "Christian theology itself is a matter of the interpretation of history."[3] By "history" Pannenberg means history in in the ordinary sense. No basic divisions of history are to be admitted. The word is not to be used differently in sacred and secular contexts. Hence he writes with approval of the nineteenth-century theologian Richard Rothe for having refused to make "in principle" a division between Heilsgeschichte and profane history.[4] Here again Pannenberg agrees with Richardson, who argues that "there is only one history," "the history which historians are engaged upon in the ordinary course of their work." Pannenberg would accept his

116

claim that "the only question which really matters" is "the question whether God has or has not revealed himself in the history which historians talk about."[5] But Pannenberg goes further: the self-disclosing actions of God in history can as such be investigated by an historian. In fact the historian should provide "the burden of proof that in Jesus of Nazareth God has revealed himself." To that extent theological truth depends upon historical enquiry. In that sense God's self-revelation is "in principle historically verifiable."[6]

Pannenberg puts forward his basic notion of history in explicit opposition to the existentialist, "word" theology which dissolves "history into the historicity (Geschichtlichkeit) of existence," thus making the events of "my" history here and now--and not the objective, historically ascertainable facts of the past--the center of ultimate historical concern.[7] He will not tolerate such a reduction of historical significance to this one aspect. He finds it quite unsatisfactory to describe revelation as "historical" because it calls the individual to his authentic "historical" existence--whether we interpret this existence with Ebeling and Fuchs in terms of language[8] or with Bultmann in terms of a decision yielding a true self-understanding. There is no "historical" existence of the individual apart from the (past) history of the world.

Pannenberg is consciously opposed also to the particular Heilsgeschichte tradition which has evolved from Martin Kähler and which depreciates the value of history for theology. On the one hand, this tradition repudiates the notion that revelation can be verified historically. On the other hand, it holds that "the proper content of faith is suprahistorical."[9] In Richardson's words, this tradition proposes a "flight into a realm of Heilsgeschichte," "where the critics cease from troubling and the faithful are at rest."[10] In its privileged position faith remains sealed off from historical enquiry which could neither verify nor refute the divine revelation. As does Richardson,[11] Pannenberg assigns the same nontheological cause for this disengagement from history, whether it takes the form of an existentialist, kerygmatic theology, or of a Barthian flight to Heilsgeschichte. The methods of critical history

seemed no longer to leave room for the salvation-event. Hence the Heilsgeschichte theology fled before the rising tide of critical history into the supposedly safe harbour of a suprahistory, or--with Barth--of a primal history

117

(Urgeschichte). For the same reason existentialist theology withdrew from the same meaningless and hopeless "objective" course of events to the experience of the significance of history in the authentic existence of the individual.[12]

Scientific historical investigation seemed to threaten or refute faith in divine revelation rather than confirm it. Hence revelation was to be rescued by removing it from the sphere of ordinary history. Pannenberg, however, insists on "the historical quality (Geschichtshaftigkeit) of the salvation-event." This leads him to reject not only any talk of an authentic existence which remains ungrounded in the experience of "reality as history," but also any theories of "a Heilsgeschichte separated from ordinary history." He adds: "It belongs to the full meaning of the incarnation that God's saving deed took place within the universal interrelationships of mankind's history and not in a ghetto of Heilsgeschichte or in an Urgeschichte the dimension of which 'cuts across' ordinary history."[13]

Self-revelation

In putting forward his theology of God's self-revelation through history Pannenberg assumes that there is no need to labor the point that revelation is essentially God's self-disclosure. Despite the "confusing variety" of terms and theories, he is confident of an almost universal agreement on this issue.[14] Yet he acknowledges that talk of God's self-revelation "must somehow be confirmed on the basis of biblical evidence if it is to be theologically justifiable." Hence he argues as follows for God's "indirect self-revelation" as a "reflex of his activity in history."[15]

First thesis

Pannenberg presents his view of revelation in the form of seven theses. The first thesis runs: "The self-revelation of God in the biblical witnesses is not of a direct type in the sense of a theophany, but is indirect and brought about by means of the historical acts of God."[16] In his explanation of this and the other theses Pannenberg draws on the material provided in the earlier chapters of Revelation as History by R. Rendtorff (chapter II, "The Concept of Revelation in Ancient Israel") and U. Wilckens (chapter III, "The Understanding of Revelation within the History of Primitive Christianity"). It is important to note that for Pannenberg the basis of the distinction between direct and indirect revelation is not "the mediateness or immediateness of the act of communication." It is a matter rather "whether the content of a communication can be linked in a direct or indirect way with its intention." That is to say, a direct revelation would have God himself as its immediate content, whereas an indirect revelation communicates the truth of God only mediately. The facts of history are known in themselves; in the first "intention" they mean something other than the revelation of God. It is only indirectly, "as acts of God" that they "cast light back on God himself."[17]

What kind of arguments does Pannenberg bring forward in support of his first thesis? Negatively, he queries the scriptural justification for the notion of God's direct self-revelation maintained by various theologies of the word. If several New Testament passages (Hebrews 1:2; John 1:1 ff.; Colossians 1:25 ff.) do suggest such a direct self-communication, this is a Gnostic motif which exists on the fringes of the New Testament and should not be taken as the normative scriptural view. Besides, even this Gnostic idea of revelation is drastically altered by being related to the Jesus-tradition, thus receiving "an element of indirectness, which is totally foreign to Gnosticism."[18]

In providing positive grounds for his first thesis Pannenberg reminds us that the divine self-revelation is originally connected by the Israelites with God's saving acts in bringing his people out of Egypt. Around the time of the Babylonian exile, however, the prophets no longer understand the events of the Moses-Joshua period as the definitive self-revelation of Yahweh. They look forward to a decisive act of salvation by which he will disclose himself to all nations. The experience of history has made Israel realize that the final revelation of Yahweh remains still to come. This change of perspective, Pannenberg adds, becomes even clearer with the apocalyptic writers. Within the context of universal history they await the manifestation of Yahweh in connection with the eschatological events. In the light of the prophetic tradition and apocalyptic expectation the life, death, and resurrection of Jesus should be acknowledged as the eschatological self-revelation of God.[19]

Second thesis

Pannenberg's second thesis ("Revelation does not occur at the beginning but at the end of the revealing history") follows immediately, he maintains, "from the indirectness of the divine self-

vindication." The "revealing history" must be wholly there before
the self-communication of God which it contains can be properly
acknowledged. Hence--as the apocalyptic writers recognize--it
requires the eschaton, the end of all history, to reveal Yahweh
as the one, unique God of all mankind.[20] Hegel is correct in
maintaining that "what the truth of the whole is becomes visible
only at the end."[21]

Third thesis

Man's appropriation of revelation is the theme of Pannenberg's
next thesis: "In distinction from special manifestations of the
deity, the historical revelation is open to anyone who has eyes
to see. It has a universal character." He insists that the divine
self-manifestation ought not to be taken as a "secret or mysterious happening. An understanding that puts revelation into contrast
to, or even conflict with, natural knowledge is in danger of dis-
torting the historical revelation into a gnostic knowledge of se-
crets." In the Old Testament the accounts of the divine self-
disclosing activity frequently state that Yahweh manifested himself not merely to Israel but before the eyes of all nations. Likewise, the event to which Paul witnesses "took place totally within
the realm of that which is humanly visible." The truth is there
for all to see. To recognize it nothing more is required than the
application of man's normal powers of apprehension. The presence of the Holy Spirit does not constitute some special condition
"without which the event of Christ could not be known as revelation." When men fail to accept the reality of God's self-disclosure
through Christ, this is simply due to the fact that they are not
using "their reason in order to see correctly." Knowledge of the
divine self-manifestation demands only that men are confronted
either directly with "the events which reveal God" or with "the
message that reports" them. We have an obligation not to treat
these events as if they were "naked facts" and neglect their context in the history of the transmission of traditions. Strict attention
to this context shows how the events in question carry their own
intrinsic meaning which is in no way imposed on them subsequently.[22]

For Pannenberg faith is not required--either as a condition or
as a concurrent element--before one can recognize God's revelation in the history of Israel and Jesus Christ. Faith neither provides
access to some truth hidden in historical events nor adds some
"special," revelatory meaning to the events in question. On the

contrary, it is on the basis of the prior "open appropriation" of these revealing events that faith arises. Man's knowledge, not his faith, constitutes the precise correlative to God's self-revelation. As a trust directed towards the future, faith presupposes that one already knows the revelatory events precisely in their revelatory character.23

Fourth and fifth theses

Pannenberg's fourth thesis ("The universal revelation of the deity of God is not yet realized in the history of Israel, but first in the fate of Jesus of Nazareth, insofar as the end of all events is anticipated in his fate") and fifth thesis ("The Christ event does not reveal the deity of the God of Israel as an isolated event, but rather insofar as it is a part of the history of God with Israel") obviously go closely together. The self-revelation of Yahweh was marked at first by a provisional character. Hegel rightly maintained that nothing less than the whole of reality understood as history can disclose (indirectly) the divinity. Only the totality of history can supply the perspective from which we may grasp the whole course of history as the divine self-revelation. This possibility came with the Christ-event in which the end of world history has appeared proleptically. Within the context of apocalyptic expectation Christ's resurrection is known to be the real anticipation of the end of all history. With him there has already taken place what will come to other men only at the end. Hence the Christ-event, while retaining its historical particularity, enjoys a uniquely absolute value in revealing God. Here Israel's God has definitively manifested himself as the one God of all men.24

Sixth thesis

The eschatological character of the Christ-event implies the proclamation of the gospel to the whole world. Pannenberg's sixth thesis affirms: "In the formulation of the non-Jewish conceptions of revelation in the Gentile Christian Church, the universality of the eschatological self-vindication of God in the fate of Jesus comes to actual expression." God is finally revealed as the one true God of all mankind and no longer merely as the God of the Israelite race.25

Seventh thesis

The last thesis ("The word relates itself to revelation as fore-
telling, forthtelling and report") explains how the words authorized
by Israel's God or by Jesus of Nazareth relate to the historical
events by which God reveals himself. In the case of prophecy
only the fulfillment of promise makes the divine power truly manifest. Laws and commands do not enjoy a revealing function, but
presuppose that God's authority is already known. In the New
Testament the word of God has also a kerygmatic function, yet
as such it does not constitute revelation. The proclamation merely passes on information about the eschatological happening which
as the self-revelation of God to all men provided the impulse for
this kerygma.[26] After this outline of Pannenberg's understanding
of revelation, we turn to a critical assessment.

Need for verification

Clearly we are confronted here with a theology that enjoys
strong apologetic motivation. In an age of historical consciousness, Pannenberg wishes to show that Christian theology can take
history with utter seriousness. He looks with extreme dissatisfaction at the refusal on the part of many modern theologians to
seek objective grounds for faith. While thoughtful men suspect
that the Christian gospel may rest on illusion, preachers invite
their hearers to make the leap of faith.[27] This situation Pannenberg
regards as deplorable. Its consequence is that faith will either be
abandoned altogether or will decay into a "blind gullibility" and
"superstition" that calls for a "sacrificium intellectus."[28] His
own aim is to use history to verify Christian claims and show to
any sincere enquirer how certain the truth of revelation is.[29]
   In thus clarifying and recommending the gospel, Pannenberg
discloses something of the same vehement conviction which we
shall find in Gerald Downing's Has Christianity a Revelation?
Downing is persuaded that his position should be accepted by
"a realistic theologian," "the theologian who is at all aware of
the actualities of the Christian situation." Opposing views merit
dismissal as "nonsense, even pernicious nonsense." They involve a claim that is "absurd if it is not blasphemous."[30] Downing
and Pannenberg differ, of course, in that the former argues against
all doctrines of revelation, while the latter puts the case for a
particular theology of revelation. In detail their differences can
be striking, even curious. We shall see how Downing asks for a

believing commitment to a life of love in the Christian community, but does not regard this self-committing faith as man's response to some divine disclosure. Pannenberg argues for a particular view of God's self-revelation, but alleges that man's immediate response to this revelation is not faith, but knowledge. From the former we hear of faith without revelation, from the latter of revelation without faith. Downing apparently attributes an objective reality to the risen Lord's appearances, and yet wishes to deny that the resurrection brings any revelation. For Pannenberg, on the other hand, the resurrection not merely enjoys the kind of objectivity which Downing recognizes but constitutes the primary event of God's definitive, universal self-revelation.

Two basic queries

As we shall see, Downing aims to phase out revelation-talk in favor of the category of salvation. This theological program serves at least to alert us to the fact that salvific values are largely ignored in Pannenberg's scheme. In a footnote Pannenberg acknowledges that revelation and salvation belong together, so that divine revelation "in its deepest sense means salvation." But he professes himself content that this connection should remain "presupposed" to his discussion.[31] He puts off the evil day when the task of integrating the themes of revelation and salvation must be faced squarely.

A second basic query touches the place of the incarnation in Pannenberg's argument. This doctrine affects his claims (1) that the theologian ought to be concerned to understand history (taken in the normal sense of the word), and (2) that ordinary historical investigation can establish God's self-revelation. Pannenberg plays false to this view of theological dependence upon history when he writes:

It is not primarily on the basis of historical presuppositions but already on theological grounds that a salvation history separated from ordinary history . . . is hardly acceptable. It belongs to the full meaning of the incarnation that God's saving deed took place within the universal inter-relationships of mankind's history and not in a ghetto of Heilsgeschichte or in an Urgeschichte, the dimension of which "cuts across" ordinary history (italics mine).[32]

The "already" suggests that fidelity to traditional dogmas rather than an open examination of history controls Pannenberg's thinking here. He objects to talk about Heilsgeschichte and Urgeschichte on the grounds of their alleged incompatibility with the doctrine of the incarnation, and not because these categories are foreign to the ordinary historian's craft. In his Jesus--God and Man Pannenberg refuses to begin with the incarnation; this doctrine finds a place in his Christology only as one of the last statements to be made.[33] Yet at the very outset of his treatment of revelation he uses such an "ultimate" doctrine to exclude the notion of salvation history. He employs the dogma of the incarnation also to establish his conviction that the events by which God reveals himself enjoy this revelatory meaning as something inherent to them. "It is only if the revelatory meaning is itself enclosed in the data that we may here speak of an incarnation, an entering of God into our way of existence."[34] At this point Pannenberg is appealing to the incarnation to show that meaning must be intrinsic to the biblical events of revelation. Elsewhere it is precisely by arguing from the intrinsic meaning of these events that he aims to establish firstly that God is revealed in Christ and ultimately that talk of the incarnation is legitimate.

Pannenberg's first thesis

Let me take up Pannenberg's theses in detail. To begin with the first: "The self-revelation of God in the biblical witnesses is . . . indirect and brought about by means of the historical acts of God." The statable moral which Pannenberg wishes to drain off from his summary of the evidence is clear: the biblical writers recognized a significance which was already "there" in the historical events they recorded. What he wishes to eliminate is the suspicion that these men were reading this significance into history. But may it not have been that they acknowledged God's hand in history because in some prior, personal communication God had already revealed himself to them? In the light of this prior knowledge they could have interpreted the events before them. As James Barr has pointed out, the texts of Exodus place as much emphasis on God's personal self-communication as on any revelation through divine actions.

Far from representing the divine acts as the basis of all knowledge of God and all communication with him, they represent God as communicating freely with men, and particularly with Moses before, during and after these events. Far from the incident at the burning bush being an "interpretation" of the divine acts, it is a direct communication from God to Moses of his purposes and intentions. This conversation, instead of being represented as an interpretation of the divine act, is a precondition of it.[35]

Pannenberg does not wish to deny the place which such personal self-manifestations of God enjoy in the Old Testament record. But he pleads that "the modern problem of revelation" requires that we concentrate on the "idea of the self-confirmation of God through his action." "Other forms of self-manifestation are not able to convince us today of the divinity of what appeared at a time in the past; they can only be convincing for those who were the immediate recipients of such experiences."[36] This is, of course, a defensible position. But in that case it is misleading for Pannenberg to maintain that "the biblical witnesses" indicate the kind of indirect revelation he champions. His first thesis ought to be adjusted to read: "The only form of divine revelation which we find to be convincing in the biblical witnesses is an indirect self-revelation through the historical acts of God."

God's self-revelation in history reached its peak in the life, death, and resurrection of Christ. Here the apocalyptic expectation of a final resurrection proves indispensable for Pannenberg. "Why the man Jesus can be the ultimate revelation of God, why in him and only in him God is supposed to have appeared, remains incomprehensible apart from the horizon of the apocalyptic expectation."[37] When the disciples encountered the risen Jesus, they spontaneously recognized this event as "the beginning of the universal resurrection of the dead, as the beginning of the events of the end of history."[38] By really anticipating the end of all history, Christ's resurrection took on a universal significance and disclosed the ultimate reality, God.

Various criticisms have been levelled at the "apocalyptic" element in Pannenberg's argument.[39] The deepest problem arises from a failure in internal consistency. If the apocalyptic expectations are required to understand revelation through the history of Christ's resurrection, revelation through history is necessary to establish the truth of these expectations. Pannenberg's second thesis, however, rules out such a justification. This thesis asserts that revelation occurs "at the end of the revealing history." If that is so, revelation directly concerns the past. It is not clear how man's recognition of the revelation communicated by past events could have (legitimately) provided a context for interpreting the resurrection as the anticipation of the <u>future</u> end of all history. Personal communication from God would be one way to vindicate this expectation of final resurrection. But that is excluded for Pannenberg, who insists that we know revelation only indirectly, through the mirror of the divine activity in history.

The third thesis

Pannenberg's third thesis and its accompanying explanation run into some serious difficulties. To begin with, the claim that the event to which Paul witnessed took place "totally within the realm of that which is humanly visible" badly needs qualification. To comment only on Christ's resurrection. This was "humanly visible" in the sense that the risen Christ encountered a number of witnesses. However, Paul and the other apostles were far from claiming to have <u>seen</u> all that they proclaimed. Paul announced (but certainly did not see) that the Father raised Christ to be Lord of the living and the dead (Romans 10:9; 14:9; II Corinthians 4:14; Philippians 2:9-11).

In his preoccupation with the role of evidence Pannenberg affirms that both those who directly experience the Christ-event and those to whom they report these experiences require only their <u>natural powers</u> to appropriate the revelation communicated through Christ. As we have seen, this position fails to do justice to what Paul and John say about the special divine intervention necessary before men acknowledge the truth of revelation.[40] It also logically involves Pannenberg in maintaining that man's immediate response to God's self-revealing activity is knowledge, not faith.

I do not believe that the New Testament supports Pannenberg's two-stage scheme of <u>knowledge</u> (by which through our normal "equipment" for knowing we recognize revelation) and <u>faith</u> (by which we commit our future in trust to the self-revealing God). As described by Paul, knowledge constitutes part of (and not a presupposition to) man's believing commitment. In the one saving act God reveals himself in his Son and calls man to accept the grace of justifying faith: "The righteousness of God has been manifested" through "faith in Jesus Christ" for those who have accepted the invitation to believe (Romans 3:21 ff.). Men do not first recognize through their natural powers "the glory of God" manifested "in the face of Christ" (II Corinthians 4:6) and only then acquire through Christ "the righteousness of God." Rather

126

from the outset God "is making his appeal" (II Corinthians 5:20f.) through Paul's "open statement of the truth" (II Corinthians 4:2). The illuminating divine action brings "the knowledge of the glory of God in the face of Christ," which is equivalently "the spirit of faith" (II Corinthians 4:6, 13). When men fail to accept Paul's message, he describes them as those who do not see "the light of the gospel of the glory of Christ" or as "unbelievers" (II Corinthians 4:4). There is no suggestion that the recognition of revelation and the act of faith are to be separated as successive stages in one's submission to God. As I Corinthians 1:21 implies, to recognize the divine revelation is to believe: "For since, in the wisdom of God, the world did not know God through wisdom, it pleased God through the folly of what we preach to save those who believe."

A further difficulty with Pannenberg's third thesis concerns his claim that revealing events derive their intrinsic meaning from their context in the history of the transmission of traditions (Überlieferungsgeschichte). This is first of all a matter of his attitude towards the role of tradition in supplying the fundamental significance for events: "All political occurrences and even all events of nature" "derive point and meaning through their relation to the traditions in which the human society affected by them lives." This held true for the Israelites who "lived on the basis of certain events which in a selective tradition were handed on to the memory of later generations."41 Eventually tradition provided the setting which yielded the intrinsic significance of the Christ-event.

I can readily agree with Pannenberg that tradition constitutes a most influential element in human interpretation of new events. It not only determines the context within which the meaning of these events is read off but also suggests various possible interpretations. Tradition can even firmly indicate the correctness of one particular interpretation. Nevertheless, this interpretation may not be automatically justified. We cannot alter the fact that our predecessors have formed and handed down to us various traditions. But honesty demands that we get rid of the conviction that we must accept without demur the interpretations which tradition suggests.

What of the revelatory value which tradition actually gave to the events experienced by the Israelite society and the first Christians? The Israelites understood their acquisition and possession of Canaan within the framework of a traditional conviction. Yahweh had promised this land to them and faithful to his word had given Canaan to them, thus revealing himself as their mighty God. But the mere occupation of Canaan did not, as such, justify Israel's assertion that it owed the land to Yahweh and stood under his powerful protection. "Many peoples," Helmut Gollwitzer observes, "trace the acquiring of their land back to their god." For outsiders, however, such traditions are very far from being automatically convincing.[42] Pannenberg is hardly persuasive when he dismisses such questioning as the result of "a superficiality" which "would see all earthly developments as nothing but human arrangements and involvements."[43] I do not wish to defame tradition. Pannenberg is correct in maintaining that a traditional conviction can shape later interpretation. Nevertheless, we must ask: Did the earlier generation transmit a correct understanding? Was the later generation justified in accepting this traditional interpretation? It is quite true, as Pannenberg argues, that no later generation can simply escape from the context of tradition to make fresh evaluations from "the outside."[44] Yet it dare not accept tradition without raising the issue of its truth.

In his contribution to Theology as History Pannenberg introduces some qualifications which seriously jeopardize his original claim that the basic meaning of revealing events derives from the framework of tradition in which they occur. He recognizes that "human history always accomplishes itself as history of the transmission of traditions in dialogue with the heritage of a past which is either adopted as one's own or else rejected." What is handed down may not be treated as "self-evident" or "unalterably valid."[45] I can only wish that he would explain the criteria which could permit (or require) the rejection of "the heritage of a past." The more frequently such rejection is allowable, the less convincing it becomes to insist that tradition fixes the intrinsic meaning for the revealing events of Jewish-Christian history. Pannenberg admits generous possibilities for rejecting the meaning originally indicated by the Überlieferungsgeschichte when he writes: "Every interpretation of an event must be justified from the context in which it was experienced or from the context of new experiences which call forth new interpretations."[46] The history of Jesus can scarcely enjoy its true meaning from its contemporary setting, if our fresh experiences today can legitimately call forth quite different interpretations.

Finally, even if we agree to accept Überlieferungsgeschichte as a legitimate source of meaning for later events, a special problem arises with respect to those who first shaped the tradition. R. Rendtorff suggests this problem when he remarks that "the more recent investigations of Überlieferungsgeschichte which takes its enquiry back behind the literary form of the text cannot-- if it wishes to be consistent--stop at settling the oldest attainable form of the tradition. It must enquire further into the events which formed the occasion for the origin of the tradition."[47] The man (or men) who began the Israelite traditions lacked what Pannenberg alleges is the prime source for history's intrinsic meaning, Überlieferungsgeschichte itself. They interpreted the significance of events without this significance being thrust upon them by some antecedent tradition. They gave the initial shape and impulse to that later history of the transmission of traditions which eventually formed the context in which the Christ-event was understood. But--on Pannenberg's principles--how can we justify the original form of this Überlieferungsgeschichte?

The seventh thesis

Before we conclude our examination of Pannenberg's position something must be said about his seventh thesis, which forms the negative consequence of his attempt to explain revelation totally in terms of God's activity in history. This thesis denies a revelatory function to the word, whether it is a matter of the words of prophets, the preaching of Jesus, or the apostolic proclamation. Let us look briefly at Paul and John to see whether in fact the chief theologians of the New Testament support an explanation of revelation exclusively in terms of action.

A particularly helpful passage is Romans 10:20: "Then Isaiah is so bold as to say, 'I have been found by those who did not seek me; I have shown myself to those who did not ask for me.'" Citing these words of Isaiah which were originally concerned with Israel, Paul applies them to the revelation which had reached the gentiles. The context (10:14 ff.) shows clearly that this revelation occurs through the word of apostolic proclamation. This proclamation is no simple, disinterested account of past events. The word here transcends mere narration. It creates a situation, carrying the present action of divine disclosure to the hearers.

Elsewhere I have analyzed these and other key passages from Paul which seem to justify the following conclusions.[48] For the apostle revelation is a contemporary communication by God to the community here and now. It takes place through word and event, that is to say, through the preaching and (suffering) exis- tence of the apostle. Rather than think of revelation exclusively or even predominantly as some past event or action "back there" which legitimizes the later apostolic proclamation, Paul emphasizes the presentness of revelation. God's self-manifestation takes the form of a saving action through word and event for those who know and acknowledge the death and resurrection of Christ. The revelatory function of word emerges as essential to Paul's thought.

No less than the Pauline letters, St. John's gospel tells against Pannenberg's attempt to reduce revelation to God's deeds alone. The fourth gospel, even if it fails to describe Jesus explicitly as the divine revealer, clearly understands him as such and intends his words, as well as his actions, to be acknowledged as revelatory. His words are not merely about God, but from God. Jesus discloses himself and his Father by speaking of what he knows and bearing witness to what he has seen (3:11). What he says is not subordinated to, but is equated with what he does in his role as revealer: "When you have lifted up the Son of man, then you will know that I am he, and I do nothing of my own authority but speak thus as the Father taught me" (8:28). His words are "spirit and life" (6:63), creating knowledge and faith in those who receive them: "I have given them the words which thou gavest me, and they have received them and know in truth that I came from thee; and they have believed that thou didst send me" (17:8). The value of Jesus' words in revealing God goes to the point that in the prologue John can call him without qualification the Word who is God. As we have seen, Pannenberg agrees that the prologue suggests that God communicates himself in the word, but argues that this is a Gnostic notion existing on the margin of the New Testament. Gnostic notion or not, the idea of revelation through the word belongs not only to the prologue but to the body of the gospel as well.[49]

The scriptural warrant for speaking of revelation in terms of "word" is strong. Pannenberg acknowledges this by recently proposing a program of "depositivization." "Authoritarian forms of tradition," he admits, "play a significant role in the Old and New Testaments," "documents from a period in which the entire social and intellectual life was stamped by authoritarianism." It "belongs to the authoritarian features" that "the prophets received and presented their words directly as words of God, and that the early Christian apostles, such as Paul, proclaimed their message as the 'Word of God' . . . with the claim to represent the authority of God himself to their hearers and readers." Pannenberg considers it "reasonable for Christian theology" to strip away these "authoritarian forms." "The question concerning the revelation of God" must be reformulated to meet "the test of man's matured understanding as such."[50] This in fact means putting aside Paul's affirmation that the divine revelation takes place through his apostolic preaching. In brief, Pannenberg wishes to argue on the basis of what he finds convincing in the biblical testimony and this involves him in eliminating much scriptural evidence.

Pannenberg's elucidation of revelation suggests a healthy concern with the demands of rationality and with the ascertainable events of past history. But unfortunately he cannot be taken as a wholly reliable guide. His theology of revelation remains essentially impoverished by two omissions. It fails to incorporate the function of God's grace in man's appropriation of revelation and drastically underplays the role of the divine and human word in the communication of revelation. Perhaps future writings by Pannenberg on the subject of faith and reason will supply what has been missing from his view of revelation. So far his search for adequate objectivity has led him to underplay the subjective conditions under which man's faith responds to God's revelation.

God remains quite hidden in his saving activity, until
the end.

Gerald Downing

Faith is surprising to the believer, indeed more surprising
to him than to anyone else. Yet were it nothing but a kind
of transcendental deed, the leap not only into the dark but
as it were of the legless, it would be amazing but not
surprising.

Peter Steele

Chapter VIII

Gerald Downing:
Christianity without Revelation

Late twentieth-century man is frequently afflicted by anger and desperation when he comes to realize how problematical are the structures of consciousness he has inherited. The meaning and order which have been put into life by his fathers may be easily and obviously taken out again. Among the many complaints about our predecessors, some of the best argued, if not always the loudest, have occurred in the area of Christian theology.

In Gerald Downing's Has Christianity a Revelation? we meet a severe case of disillusionment with the language of divine revelation which he inherited from Barth, Bultmann, and other theologians of the immediate past. Revelation-talk has lost credibility for him. It is not simply that he quarrels with his predecessors on terminological grounds and wishes to avoid their language which strikes him as highly unsuitable. He goes further to question whether Christians can meaningfully be said to know God.

This is a startling case which so far has been either ignored or discussed in a superficial manner. In a book which explores revelation and basic notions closely connected with it theological integrity demands that Downing's vigorously argued denial of revelation should be faced. A critical confrontation with his thesis can also serve to clarify further my own position on revelation.

Summary

Despite the detailed argument with which Downing's case is supported, it can be summarized briefly. Christian theologians have maintained that God has revealed himself in such a way that we can truly be said to know him. They explained this as happening either through propositional revelation or by way of personal encounter. Downing rules out propositional revelation; it would be incompatible with the widespread, bewildering disagreement among those who purport to possess and understand revealed truth. Nor does he allow the claim that we can enter into an I-Thou relationship with God in which we genuinely know him. Such an encounter in which God would stand revealed is not open to proof in the way that the claim to have encountered a particular human being can be established. Finally, talk of divine revelation is neither justified by current linguistic usage nor sufficiently supported by scripture and traditional Christian writings.

This three-pronged argument is developed in great detail. First, Downing contends that neither the Old Testament nor the New Testament writers imply that there was (or is) a revelation of God. Words or passages which appear to suggest a revealed knowledge of God should be understood otherwise. Such Hebrew terms as yada, when applied to man's relations toward God, find their best English equivalent in "obey God." This holds true of eidenai, ginōskein, and cognate words in the New Testament. The concept of revelation remains marginal in the New Testament, being reserved almost exclusively for the revelation still to come.[1] Downing then supports his thesis by a rapid examination of Christian usage from Clement of Rome down to recent times (pages 126-61). Lastly he turns to linguistic analysis to support his case. On the basis of certain paradigms from current English he concludes that God may not be said in any genuine sense to have revealed himself. In this context "reveal" cannot be used coherently, unless it is "evacuated of most if not all its meaning (page

284). "Revelation" should drop out of theological talk; its place can be taken by such a word as "salvation," a far more appropriate term to express and summarize the work of God in Christ. It enjoys a better basis in scripture. The effects of salvation stand testing in a way that the claim to know God does not. This saving work of God in Christ enables us to make an obedient commitment to love in the community. The Christian is not one who knows God but one who lives in loving obedience towards God.

Downing's contribution

Before examining the larger questions involved in Downing's central thesis, let me acknowledge briefly what seem to be his main contributions to current discussion of revelation. He reminds us emphatically that "revelation" is not a central scriptural term. The two tables which he appends show that "saving activity" words enjoy an overwhelming priority in the New Testament over such "communication" words as "revealing" and "making known" (pages 291-93). He does not claim to have pioneered this observation, noting that John McIntyre, John Knox, and James Barr have previously remarked that "revelation" is not a characteristically biblical notion (page 16f.). He might have added that Pannenberg has also pointed out that a study of scriptural terminology as such fails to justify modern theologians in talking so readily and frequently of divine revelation.[2] Yet no theologian has so forcefully drawn our attention to this fact as has Downing.

A further valuable feature of Downing's work is that it operates as a strong reminder that revelation may not be considered in isolation from salvation. He observes that "'revelation' is closely bound up with intellectualism even when it is not seen as a 'revealing' of propositions." Theologies of revelation can too easily imply that man's problem is not salvation from sin and death, but "whether and how far God can be known" (page 18). As we have seen, Pannenberg needs such a reminder. For he isolates the question of revelation from that of salvation and remains engrossed in the problem of man's grasping the truth of the divine self-disclosure.

Finally, if Downing rejects revelation as a useful and meaningful category, he does so through a deep concern to speak clearly and sincerely to contemporary man. The word "revelation," he fears, is a "source of great confusion." "Theologies based on 'revelation' are not able to convey to us the full richness of Christian life and faith." He pleads with theologians to take seriously the New Testament, "the facts of the Christian position and the

135

strictly limited possibilities of talking sense about 'God.'" This is "doctrinally and 'existentially' of vital importance" (page 274). Theology for Downing does not constitute an independent, academic industry to be pursued for financial or other rewards. It is both motivated by the experience of Christian love and should in its turn help to enhance that same love.

The Old Testament

What of Downing's central claim that the language of revelation is not properly "biblical" and "meaningful" (page 17)?[3] He first sets out to convince us that "the Old Testament writers do not pretend that the revelation of God and man is close enough or clear enough for God to be said to have revealed himself." He admits that in the Old Testament God may be said to be "dis-closed in the sense that you may see the things he has done," but insists that God remains "hidden in his 'inner self'" (page 46f.). God does not directly reveal himself. Referring to the divine activity described by Isaiah, Downing allows that we have here a description of "the invisible God visibly acting." "Yahweh has rolled up his sleeves for saving action, and the result will be seen (which includes 'felt') by all." "Till now, Yahweh has acted unobtrusively through the despised and ignored servant. But soon it will not be possible to ignore Yahweh's activity." "Reveal" is used of "the open exercise of God's righteousness." "An activity of God . . . is coming out into the open." Yet this fails to constitute revelation; it "does not mean that Jahweh him-self is seen" (page 22 f.; italics mine). At this point one must question whether it is reasonable for Downing to confine revela-tion to a direct revelation of God's "inner self," a disclosure which would be close enough and clear enough for us to call it complete. Such a restricted use of revelation seems arbitrary. Even when men are not seen but remain hidden in their inner selves, they can readily disclose something of themselves in-directly--by their work, their writing, and other activities.

At the outset Downing's approach to the question of revelation appears to imply that the matter can be decided by a lexicographical study.

The mere fact that words meaning "reveal" are not often in the Old Testament, and are not used of God's "revealing his self," or even his will, is suggestive in itself. But it is not enough on its own to settle the question about "revelation"

136

in the Old Testament; and so it has been necessary to examine some possible synonyms, to see if the same thing is being said in a less direct way. And plainly it is not being said at all (page 45; italics mine).

But the fact that the Old Testament writers failed to use a particular set of words to assert that something had happened need not mean that they did not believe--at least implicitly--that this had happened. If they do not say, "There has been a revelation," their words and beliefs, nevertheless, entail this.

By the closing stages of the Old Testament we meet the conviction of the Israelites that Yahweh is their God in an exclusive, incomparable sense: "I am the Lord, and there is no other, besides me there is no God" (Isaiah 45:5). He is the personal creator who governs the world: "I made the earth, and created man upon it; it was my hands that stretched out the heavens, and I commanded all their host" (Isaiah 45:12). Yahweh stands forth as the holy one who calls man to a service of love, the master of history who guides events towards the goal of universal salvation: "The Lord has bared his holy arm before the eyes of all nations; and all the ends of the earth shall see the salvation of our God" (Isaiah 52:10). This is the Lord who chose the Israelites to be his special people, brought them out of Egypt, formed a covenant with them, and gave them the land of Canaan. He punished them for their sins but would one day send them a Messiah. For the Old Testament authors these convictions about God are not mere human inventions, but derived in various ways from God's contact with man. To recognize this is tantamount to acknowledging that the Old Testament writers maintain the existence of divine revelation.

Downing concedes that "the Christian may still just insist on seeing the Old Testament as a whole as 'revealing' God," but hastens to add that it is not legitimate exegesis to read this understanding into the Old Testament itself, which is very chary of saying this sort of thing about God" (page 47). The alternatives supposed here--either the Old Testament says "this sort of thing about God" or we are guilty of reading it into the Old Testament-- are not exhaustive. What the Old Testament affirms could (and does) imply this.

Downing admits that for the Israelites God "allows to be known, with greater or lesser clarity, in more or less detail, the terms of the obedience he requires of men." He agrees that "it might be said that the fact that the hidden God could even be spoken of,

and his commands known, implies 'revelation' in some sense, "
a "'revelation by himself' of enough of Yahweh's own preferences
for a man to be able to 'know' ('obey') him." But, Downing insists, "this 'revelation' by himself" is still "not 'revelation' of
himself" (page 46). Now it is certainly true that revelation by
some person is not inevitably a revelation of that person. An
anonymous writer could conceivably reveal to the curious public
what really happened in some mystifying incident without betray-
ing much or anything of himself in his account. However, if
someone discloses his own preferences and wishes, this inevitably
involves some revelation of the person concerned. Downing has
in fact earlier admitted: "A man cannot reveal his will without
revealing at least something of himself." To this he at once added:
"But the Old Testament writers . . . consistently refuse to make
this deduction" (page 44). Even if these writers fail to make this
deduction, their belief entails it. The conviction that God "allows
to be known . . . the terms of the obedience he requires of men"
involves--at least implicitly--the belief that God betrays something of himself in doing this.

New Testament

Perhaps sensing that he has conceded something damaging to
his thesis, Downing assures us that in any case "the idea that God
did in the Old Testament 'reveal' the terms of the obedience that
he really demands is decisively rejected in the New Testament
by Jesus and Paul" (page 46).[4] When we examine the passages
with which Downing supports this assertion, we fail to find in
Matthew 5 that Jesus is "decisively rejecting" Old Testament
terms of obedience. Scholars as far apart in their opinions and
methods as W. D. Davies and Bultmann agree that Jesus' stance
was not one of "decisive rejection." To quote Davies: "As Jesus
radicalized love, so he radicalized the other demands of the Law."
For "the Law and the Prophets remained valid for Jesus as the
expression of the will of God. At this point, he was one with
Sadducee, Pharisee, and sectarian. Not his estimate of the Law
as the revelation of the will of God set him apart from these but
his interpretation of this revelation."[5] Bultmann rules out the
possibility that Jesus "called into question the validity of the Old
Testament. Its authority stands just as fast for him as for the
scribes, and he feels himself in opposition to them only in the
way he understands and applies the Old Testament."[6] In this
matter we should, of course, try to distinguish Matthew's theology

(and the tradition behind it) from the attitude of Jesus himself. Downing's position fails to find support from Matthew who

> understands the law in a way which does not differ in principle from that of Judaism. . . . The sadness in his contrast to Judaism arises from the discrepancy between doctrine and deeds on the part of his opponents, and at the same time, of course, from the misuse and failure of an interpretation of the law, which does not enquire concerning the original meaning of the divine demand and refuses to perceive the essentials of the law.[7]

For Downing Luke 16:16 also provides backing for his claim that Jesus rejects the notion that in the Old Testament God revealed the terms of obedience he really demands. But this passage bears on something different, Luke's view of the divisions of redemptive history. "The law and the prophets were until John; since then the good news of the kingdom of God is preached, and every one enters it violently."[8] Does perhaps Luke 16:17 ("But it is easier for heaven and earth to pass away, than for one dot of the law to become void") support Downing's view? If we explain the verse with T. W. Manson as "bitter irony" in Jesus' criticism of the "unbending conservatism of the scribes," we reach the meaning: "It is easier for heaven and earth to pass away than for the scribes to give up the smallest bit of that tradition by which they make the Law of no effect."[9] Yet even this interpretation is compatible with the view that Jesus accepted the Old Testament terms of obedience as coming from God. If we attend to the concerns of Luke's own theology, the verse tells somewhat against Downing's view.[10]

The texts which Downing instances from Paul assert that justification comes through faith and not by the works of the law. This affirmation does not contradict the view that in the Old Testament God revealed terms of obedience which he really demanded. Paul attacks the attempt to use the law independently to establish one's own righteousness. But he nowhere rejects the role of the law "as a revelation of God's will and purpose."[11]

It is important to note what Downing is not claiming: (1) that Jesus and Paul taught that only some of the Old Testament terms of obedience were really revealed and demanded by God, or (2) that Jesus and Paul maintained that what God demands is not always a safe index to his nature, or (3) that Jesus and Paul taught that the Old Testament terms of obedience were really but only temporarily demanded by God. Downing's assertion remains unqualified. Jesus and Paul reject "the idea that God did in the Old Testament 'reveal' the terms of the obedience that he really demands." However, the New Testament passages alleged fail to establish this conclusion.

In his chapter on the New Testament Downing presses the argument that the "knowledge" of God claimed by the early Christians fell short of being a claim to a "revelation" of God. Paul "uses eidenai and ginōskein as words to describe man's response to God. But while we translate them 'know,' the nearest word in English is still 'obey.'" "Paul seems to place 'knowing Christ' on the same level as 'knowing' the Father; but it is 'knowledge' of the same sort, in terms of obedience" (page 71f.). Earlier Downing has explained that this "'knowledge of God' is 'personal' in the sense that it means a personal response by the whole man in obedience and worship to the known will of God and his commands" (page 69). Here we must ask how the will of God and his commands can be called "known" unless there is revelation.[12] Without some divine disclosure it is impossible to speak seriously of "obeying" God.

Over and over again Downing brings up New Testament statements which entail revelation. With reference to II Corinthians 4:4-6 he writes of Jesus who is "the image, reproduction of God, the extension of God's own self, through whom he acts; without revealing himself." How can Paul assert that Jesus constitutes such an image of God, unless he believes that God has in some way disclosed himself? It seems difficult to envisage God acting through an image, reproduction and extension of himself without at the same time revealing something of himself. Downing's discussion of this passage continues: "We know what God has done in Christ, and can respond. . . . It is not 'revelation of God in Christ,' but the understanding of God's (reconciling) action in Christ, that is here exciting Paul" (page 70, note 1; italics mine). Such a knowledge and understanding, however, surely imply that God has to some extent revealed what he is doing in Christ. This point emerges even more clearly from Downing's reflection on I Corinthians 1:18ff.): "Paul is saying emphatically that understanding God's action (and, of course, responding to it) can only happen by the act of God" (page 64, note 1). In other words, God makes us understand his action, that is to say, discloses it to us.

It would be tiresome to go through all the passages where we should want to ask Downing what he supposes to be the grounds

140

for Paul's various statements about God. To take a sample of Downing's account of the apostle's thought: the effects of sin "are God's reaction to, dealing with, sin"; "'righteousness' fairly obviously means the activity of God in setting right" (page 78 f.); "the fact that Christ . , . is raised shows that righteousness is no longer by Law, but through this act of God in Christ, through a faith-acceptance of what God has done in Christ. The curse of the Law and the power of the Law are abrogated; and so the Gentiles are accepted by God, as Gentiles" (page 82). But it is simply implausible that Paul could have made such weighty affirmations about God's actions, if he had believed that "God remains quite hidden in his saving activity until the end" (page 17; italics mine). He could not then have spoken of "what God has done in Christ." Downing's only answer here would be: "Wait a few pages and I will explain how such descriptive language--for me, if not for the writers of scripture--is really language of commitment." We return to this issue later.

In commenting on I John Downing writes: "I am not saying--the First Epistle is not saying--that human love is self-sufficient and all that God demands. It is God loving first, and sending his Son, that makes real human love possible; God loving both elicits our love and makes it real" (page 101). One reaction to the passage is to query how I John (and Downing) can talk about what "God demands," about "God loving" and so forth, unless God has manifested his demands, his love and his activity to us. What makes the passage unusual is that we catch Downing apparently willing to subscribe to some scriptural doctrine. For the most part he is content to report (and interpret) what the Old and New Testament writers say. Obviously he thinks that the biblical evidence (and the evidence from Christian tradition) must impress his readers, but generally he avoids suggesting that this evidence carries weight for himself personally. In the early chapters he occasionally talks about "the Christian." But at that stage he does not clearly include himself under this term (page 46 f.). Towards the end of the book he uses the term often and in a way that indicates self-identification with "the Christian." It is the later arguments from Christian disagreement and the right use of language which seem to count most with Downing personally.

Before looking at these arguments I should emphasize that more than a matter of terminology is at stake. Downing's case goes beyond the simple assertion that "revelation" proves an unsatisfactory word when applied to divine-human transactions. When he puts the question "Has Christianity a revelation?" he soon makes it clear that he considers this question "closely related" to another question, "Can Christians at all justly claim to know their God? (page 7). He understands "divine revelation" as making possible knowledge of God. "Revealed" would mean "made available for knowing" (page 221). Hence in questioning revelation Downing is also challenging Christian knowledge of God. He concludes by describing God as "the One who still insists on hiding himself, and leaving us unsure" (page 286).

Christian disagreement

The claim to know God through revelation, Downing argues, could be meaningful only if those who make the claim agreed on all matters which they assert to be important to God. "Differences of opinion about 'God' invalidate the claim to 'know' him" (page 205). Downing fixes his standard so high that the differing viewpoints among the New Testament writers would constitute sufficient disagreement to cast serious doubt on any claims to revelation from their side.[13] Downing demands further that Christian agreement over what was revealed would have to be backed up by uniformly good practice. "Failure to act on 'knowledge' claimed invalidates the claim to 'know.'" Downing requires then (a) agreement over revelation and (b) action on the basis of this revelation. With reference to the issue of divided Christendom, he draws together his two requirements: "The failure of Christians to maintain or restore unity is an even stronger proof that there is no 'knowledge of God,' than their failure to agree on the terms God would will for unity" (page 206).

Downing's criticism is an honest cri de coeur like the question of Shelley ("If God has spoken, why is the universe not convinced?") or the assertion of Thomas Paine ("A revelation, which is received as true, ought to be written on the sun."). Yet one should warn Downing against exaggerating the differences which exist among Christians with regard to the divine revelation they claim to enjoy. He speaks of "kaleidoscopic beliefs," "a mystery of diversity" and "a maze so complex that everyone gets lost in his own way" (page 229). But then take up, for example, S. Paul Schilling's Contemporary Continental Theologians, a dull but studiously fair comparative study of eleven Protestant, Catholic, and Orthodox theologians.[14] Considerable divergences emerge, but the measure of agreement among these influential theologians who represent a very considerable body of Christian believers remains such that any talk of "kaleidoscopic beliefs" and so forth is obviously inaccurate.

142

Secondly, Downing makes his case easier by exaggerating the measure of revelation Christians normally assert. He argues, for example, that if various groups of Christians "agree" that "love between Christians is important to God, but cannot agree on how he wishes church unity to happen, this claim [to know God] is badly shaken" (page 204). This is to require from Christians a far more "detailed" revelation than that which they actually claim for themselves. In this particular case a further point should be made. Christians may not profess to know the concrete way in which God wishes Church unity to happen. But very few of them would deny that God wishes the movement towards unity to be characterized by mutual understanding, trust, prayer, and honesty.

Thirdly, it has been argued that "God's self-disclosure" to men in the Old and New Testament "was often obscured and distorted by their wilful refusal to accept his illumination and understand fully what he was saying to them; or, if they understood, by their sinful failure to respond appropriately."[15] If that held true of the original recipients of revelation, it could also be the case with their heirs. Part of Christian disagreement over God's revelation arises from man's failure rather than any lack of success on God's side in "getting through" to man.

Further, Downing's demand for agreement over what is revealed clearly goes too far when he requires "a sufficiently uniform or intense moral response to 'God' to warrant the claim that he is 'revealed'" (page 248). It is far from obvious that "failure to act on 'knowledge' invalidates the claim to 'know.'" Downing would not wish to assert as a general principle that any claim to knowledge without corresponding virtue is to be rejected. The moment of knowing differs from the lived response; to know is not ipso facto to do. Those who follow Downing's call to commit themselves to a way of life based on a conviction of "salvation" enjoy an unfair advantage. Apparently they are not expected to provide the kind of convincing, practical evidence that they are "saved" which is required in support of their position from those who lay claim to revelation. The latter must live out their claim in the heroic fashion of an "intense moral response." The former face no such stringent demands. "Sincerely to call particular events 'saving,'" Downing explains, "is to commit yourself in some man- ner or other to possibilities" that they still enable us to realize (page 280; italics mine). On the contrary, "Christian disobedience" forms a "living disproof of any claim that the will of the holy God is 'revealed'" (page 231).

Downing requires such an "intense moral response" because he understands "revelation" to imply that the divine will is felt at "full force." Anything short of this does not count as revelation. God can be deemed disclosed, only where he is revealed as "irresistible" (page 236). "The full force of God's revelation demand" has not been felt irresistibly until obedience is offered (page 230). God's revelation would have to be such as not merely to prevent disagreement but also to overwhelm us and compel practice. But I wonder what room remains for speaking of "obedience" when an "irresistible" demand is being felt. It is surely essential to obedience that in some sense what was done should have been freely done. We could have done otherwise. Our performance was not produced by some "irresistible" factor. Downing's requirement seems to exclude personal freedom and decision to the point of being incompatible with talk of human obedience. If only he would admit that revelation with its demands might in some way prove to be qualified and "limited," he could then show grounds for understanding man's actual disobedience and disagreement.

Religious language

The proper use of "revelation" is fundamental to Downing's argument. Nothing else so completely underwrites the logic of his case. If correctly used, "revelation" entails complete understanding and "extreme clarity of perception" (page 208). "'Revelation' used without qualification," he declares, "is normally taken to imply a quite complete making known of whatever it is claimed has been 'revealed'" (page 219). In secular contexts "reveal" may be qualified meaningfully. But such qualification is banished from theistic language. "Any talk of 'revelation of God' must be so heavily qualified that it would be less confusing to use another word" (page 239).[16] Hence modern theologies of revelation could prove acceptable to Downing only under strict conditions. The alleged revelation would have to be a "face-to-face encounter with God" (page 76), an "'I and Thou' relation of mind to Mind" (page 64, note 1), "the sort of relationship that is objectively shaped by physical contact with the Other, and empirically verifiable from moment to moment by the accuracy of conscious and unconscious forecasts of moods and wishes" (page 198). In short, revelation would pass Downing's test only if it were a continuing, direct acquaintance in which God would stand revealed in complete intimacy. No one is willing to say that God has revealed himself in that sense.

Yet if theologians want "reveal" and "revelation" to mean something less than such a clear and distinct disclosure, the words are
decreed to have been "evacuated of meaning" (page 284).

There is good reason for disquiet over this argument. Does
common usage support Downing's case? Revelation can occur
between persons without there being an utterly complete disclosure
of personalities. Take the following statement: "He revealed to
me his wishes in the matter." No full, continuing, personal communion is asserted. But something has been disclosed and that
too in a context which affords some insight into the other's personality. To see something of his personality is not equivalent
to seeing nothing at all. May we not use "reveal" in some such
qualified sense of God, and speak of a genuine experience of God
which communicates something and yet falls short of being full
disclosure?

Finally there is a certain hesitation in Downing's position at
this point. Consider the following statements: (A) God "insists
on hiding himself, and leaving us unsure" (page 286); "God remains quite hidden in his saving activity until the end" (page 17);
"it is very hard to believe that God intended to 'reveal himself'
. . . or at all meant even some lesser insight into his character,
when he gave us his gift-without-authoritative-explanation in Jesus
Christ" (page 287). Contrast these statements with the following
(B): "When the Christian wants to say that 'God has acted most
characteristically in Christ,' has 'expressed himself most fully in
Jesus' life, death and resurrection,' he may meaningfully say this
and no more" (page 288). Statements (A) suggest that we are left
in a state of uncertainty about God. Yet even these statements
contain elements implying some knowledge. God "insists" on something; he "hides himself"; there is a "saving activity" of God; "the
end" will occur; God did give man a "gift" in Jesus Christ. Statement (B) concedes that God has done something which we know
and can talk about in a limited fashion.

Fairness compels us to note the limits of Downing's argument.
He is not maintaining that qualification destroys all religious
assertions and evacuates them of real meaning, but simply that
this is the case with "revelation." He refuses to allow other
theologians to qualify "revelation" on the grounds that it is not
yet given in its fullness. "Salvation," however, as the "complete
but open-ended act of God," may be claimed now in a limited sense.
It is both complete and capable of further development. But can
Downing assert a qualified salvation while rejecting a qualified
revelation? To maintain that God has "saved" man is to claim some

understanding of God's action, at least the recognition of the fact
that God has intervened in the interests of ultimate human welfare.
Further, Downing nowhere shows that he wants to deny that the
whole of man's life forms the sphere of God's saving activity.
Hence man's thinking should be included. If God's action has affected human understanding, the result must be something in the
order of knowledge. We can scarcely speak of the divine action
as it affects man's thinking, and yet insist on outlawing talk of
revelation.

At this stage Downing explains that we can enjoy God's saving
work in Christ while continuing to lack any true revelation. To
illustrate his view he proposes the analogy of a girl finding an
anonymous gift of flowers at her doorstep.

> Supposing a girl answers a ring at the door, and finds a
> large bunch of red roses and white carnations . . . the most
> likely possibility is that the gift without clear information is
> intended as a gift. The flowers are meant to be enjoyed: ar-
> ranged, smelled, gazed at. The donor may wish to remain
> anonymous for the time being, or for good. For the present,
> to understand the flowers as a message is completely to mis-
> understand them. They may even be a preparation for a later
> disclosure; but for the moment they are meant as a gift of
> flowers (page 276).

But there is at least the basic message that someone wishes to
make her a gift. The girl will bring in the flowers and enjoy them.
Yet her chief pleasure will be the knowledge that someone has made
her a gift expressive of some regard and good disposition towards
her.

Similar comment should be made on another analogy which
Downing introduces. Love shown by parents towards their children
may not be understood at the time. But, Downing reflects, this
love can still be there influencing the children to show love in
return, even where this love remains unappreciated and hence "un-
revealed." Likewise, God expresses himself in Christ, so that
in Christ we see "the work of God." "But we are seeing without
comprehending" (page 288 f.). However, the parental love which
Downing invokes can scarcely be effective and enriching for the
lives of children, if it is in no way understood by them. They
must have some genuine apprehension of it, if they are to love
in return. Once again Downing's own analogy can be turned against
his attempt to ban talk of revelation while keeping the category of
salvation.

Commitment

The final elaboration of Downing's thesis shows a reductionist tendency at work. Christian language about God has the function of expressing and eliciting commitment to loving obedience within the community. Religious utterances are resolved into statements of spiritual autobiography, rid of elements referring to the transcendent. It becomes questionable whether Downing's view ultimately allows statements about God to make any genuine truth-claim at all, let alone the claim to be drawn from revelation. God seems to lie beyond experience and knowledge. If theistic language is nondescriptive, [17] no evidence will count for or against it. The values "true" and "false" simply do not apply. "It seems," Downing writes, "that, more or less, Christian talk about 'God' is directly or indirectly the language of commitment" (page 183). "As committal" this language is "neither 'true' nor 'false' but a fact." The name "God" is used by the believer "to express his understanding that a total commitment is demanded of him" (page 187). The Christian intends a "more complex self-committal to 'God,' who, it is believed, must be said really to 'act' now, and really to have 'acted' in Christ" (page 185). This forms "the myth of the prior love of 'real God in Christ'" which Downing maintains as "essential to the Christian commitment." For the myth creates "a possibility of commitment to forms of agape not open to those who do not or cannot accept it" (page 186).

What does "myth" mean for Downing? One thing is explicitly asserted. The myth is indispensable. "Christian statements about 'God' ought not to be in the end reducible to picture statements about man and his world, tales just used for their psychological effect, and exchangeable for quite different stories if they lose their attractiveness and evocative power" (page 177). One misses the reasons for Downing's insistence that he finds it "still necessary to accept the 'myth'" as part of his expressed commitment (page 262, note 1). It looks rather like a gratuitous affirmation to maintain that "traditional Christian assertions . . . seem to be the only vehicle" by which Christian commitment "may be expressed or elicited. There are none other suitable for precisely these lines of action." How can he ground the unique suitability of these assertions? If these assertions are "neither true or false" in themselves and fail to describe God "in any meaningful way . . . that can be shown more or less apt or inapt" (page 191), the connection between Christian myth and commitment appears psychological and hence contingent. At least in principle the Christian myth would be replaceable by some other myth.

But Downing remains reluctant to take this last step. Even though myth is not authenticated in some way through divine disclosure, he clings to it tenaciously. The last pages show him inviting us to join him in his self-commitment through this myth, even though it is not alleged to be more than a human construction. The purpose of the life, death, and resurrection of Christ "can hardly be seen as instructional in any sense. Not even heavily qualified 'revela-lation,' not even the first stage of instruction and enlightenment, can be the purpose of these events" (page 277). Such a Christian myth--so Downing is convinced--should be enough to help others commit themselves to uncertainty and join him in his "leap of faith" (page 289).

From the point of view of Christian living this understanding of the Christian message is patently unsatisfactory. If the Chris-tian can make no truth claims, he ceases to be persuasive. Some measure of belief in truth is needed to sustain commitment. Once we admit that the "myth" of God's love in Christ is not "in any meaningful way" descriptive of the divine reality, it becomes open to serious doubt whether this "myth" will elicit the "complex self-committal" to the forms of agape which Christianity requires. Despite Downing's obvious sincerity in presenting his case, the lack of truth claims robs this interpretation of ethical urgency. Downing rightly emphasizes a life of love as man's supreme obli-gation but then takes away the grounds which should sustain such a commitment.

Conclusion

Some words of summary are now in order. This chapter has proved largely negative in its results. But it serves to raise (again) the issue of knowledge which has been with us since Kant and Freud. The New Testament times differ from our own. In a post-Kantian world we cannot keep the critical question out. How do we solve our bewilderments? How do we "read off" the data of religious experience? Many would refuse to agree that it is better to be committed than to be rational. They search not merely for action but for a theory of action. Precisely the kind of salvation which many people look for today is a solution to their theological bewilderments.

In Downing's account the data of men's experience of belief, along with their pretheological religious language, remain un-explained or are explained as a mistake. Theologies of revelation try at least to make something of people's belief. This is not, of course, to deny all value to Downing's protests against the over-blown rhetoric of some theologians. "Pan-revelationism" will prove no panacea to cure all our theological ills. But neither will a latter-day voluntarism manage to suppress the question of man's knowledge of the self-revealing God.

PART THREE

The Roots of Christian Confession

If we know what historical research is and what Jesus'
resurrection from the dead means, we cannot share the
view that the resurrection can be proved by historical
arguments.

N. A. Dahl

From the very first the main Christian festival has not
been Christmas, nor Good Friday, but Easter. This does
not mean that what took place in the birth and suffering
and death of Jesus Christ is underestimated. It means that
it is given its supreme value.

Karl Barth

Chapter IX

The Resurrection of Jesus

In earlier chapters we sought answers to questions about the nature of theological procedure, revelation, the relation of faith to history, the relation of the two Testaments, and the validity of retaining salvation history as a theological category. These issues remained, for the most part, at a high level of generality. Our task was largely to explore and define basic notions in theology. We now transfer our attention to two specific questions about Christian origins. Christianity remains rooted in history, above all in the events affecting the man from whom it draws its name. Undoubtedly the most important issue in the last section of this book concerns Jesus' resurrection.

There is little difficulty in agreeing that Jesus was victorious over death. The vital question is: In what sense was Jesus victorious over death? In what way did he "come alive" for his disciples? Did his victory consist in the fact that he kept his principles without being deterred even by the fear of execution? Or should we locate his triumph in the rise and spectacular success of the Christian movement? Can he now come alive for us even if we do not believe that he actually rose from the dead in the year A.D. 30? Or was he victorious in being personally "raised from the dead" and made "alive to God" (Romans 6:9f.)? How should we interpret these words of Paul? What kind of life does Jesus now enjoy? May a belief in his resurrection coexist with the admission that his bones lie somewhere in Palestine? It would be folly to pretend that any of these momentous questions can be decided quickly, but decided they must be if this treatment of theological foundations is not to remain patently inadequate.

For Christian faith the resurrection is not only logically, but also chronologically "foundational." Within the history of Christianity the oldest layer of statements about Jesus Christ deals with his rising from the dead. The later Christological affirmations of the Church Councils elaborated the doctrine of the Incarnation. At that stage interest showed itself to be concentrated on the fact that Jesus of Nazareth in his very being was the Son of God and had been such from the first moment of his existence. The earliest confessions of faith, however, arose from the divine action which was discerned in Jesus' resurrection from the dead. Christian reflection gradually explored what lay behind and before this resurrection. This process of discernment that led back through the public ministry of Jesus to the Incarnation came to early fruition in John's gospel which begins with the announcement: "The Word became flesh." But what status in reality does the starting point of this process of reflection enjoy?

Some areas of disagreement

Writers, both theological and nontheological, agree that the resurrection of Christ enjoys paramount importance. In view of the value accorded to it from the beginning of Christianity, they could hardly do otherwise. The far more significant and divisive question is: What does the resurrection mean? This question remains unsatisfactory unless we also ask: What happened in the days following Jesus' death? At one level opposing views converge by agreeing that there exists an historical kernel to the Easter events. When Jesus was arrested, the disciples fled and gave up his cause. But after his death they created the Christian community. As Martin Dibelius wrote: "Something must have happened in between, which in a short time not only produced a complete

reversal of their attitude but also enabled them to engage in renewed activity and to found the primitive Christian community.
This 'something' is the historical kernel of the Easter faith."[1]
Everything hinges on determining what this "something" was.
For many Christians the answer is provided in a straightforward
fashion by the biblical texts. After his death Jesus came alive
again in the tomb, left it to meet his disciples, walked the Emmaus
road with two of them, interpreted scripture for them, ate fish
in their company, showed them the marks of the wounds still
there in his risen body, and after forty days rose up into the sky
in front of them. Lives of Christ commonly provide naturalistic
descriptions of the risen Jesus. He is pictured as once again in
contact with his disciples almost as if he were just another person living on earth. The Johannine account of the meeting for
breakfast on the shore of Lake Tiberias reinforces this willingness to envisage the risen Jesus' contact with his disciples in
ordinary human terms. In dying and rising from the dead he simply
changed horses, as it were, and rode on. Catholic writers in particular have often failed to make any sufficiently firm distinction between the life in space and time which Jesus experienced up to his
death and the risen existence which followed. Effectively, the
resurrection was transmuted into the resuscitation of a corpse.

In sharp contrast with this understanding of the resurrection
are the interpretations of some Christian theologians, to say
nothing of those non-Christian critics who explain the "something"
as a mistake, a fraud, an hallucination, or some other form of
nonobjective experience. Referring to the dead Jesus, Bultmann
asserts: "An historical fact which involves a resurrection from
the dead is utterly inconceivable."[2] This is a clear statement of
principle. Jesus' tomb could not have been empty; his bones must
lie somewhere in Palestine.

The question of the empty tomb highlights easily the divergences
of opinion over the resurrection. Another quick way of illustrating
the scope of these divergences is to refer to the Emmaus story
(Luke 24:13-35). Some scholars accept the story as it stands; in
actual historical fact three persons once walked the road to
Emmaus, as described in Luke's account. For others the two
disciples walked the road alone and they had a vision. Others
again explain the story as substantially or wholly a theological
construction. No one ever walked the Emmaus road.

First Corinthians

Let us now turn to some New Testament texts and examine the main assertions about Jesus' resurrection. One most important document is I Corinthians 15:3-8, a passage which lists the witnesses to whom the risen Lord appeared. This letter was written in the year 54 or 55 (or perhaps 56 or 57)--about ten years before the writing of Mark's gospel and less than thirty years after the events reported in chapter 15. Jesus was executed in A.D. 30 (or perhaps 33); Paul's conversion can be dated in 33 (or perhaps 35). Three years later Paul visited Jerusalem (Galatians 1:18), that is to say, around six years after the events in question. His testimony to the resurrection appearances given in I Corinthians reveals both traditional and autobiographical characteristics. He employs the technical terminology of tradition. Verses 3b-5 which exhibit a pre-Pauline, creedal structure seem to represent a tradition derived from the early Palestinian community.[3] It is difficult to determine how early the tradition of the risen Jesus' appearances reached Paul. But it seems plausible to maintain that this tradition would have been transmitted to him at least by the time of his first visit to Jerusalem where he met Peter and James (Galatians 1:18 f.). Autobiographically, I Corinthians 15:8 ff. (together with 9:1 and Galatians 1:11 ff.) is of the utmost significance. The experience of "seeing" the Lord formed for Paul the basis of his conversion to Christianity and his call to apostleship.

At the outset it is well to note some limitations and peculiarities in Paul's austere formulation. He does not mention the places where Jesus appeared. He provides no details about any of the episodes. He fails to mention either the empty tomb itself or the women who found the tomb empty. On the other hand, Paul reports some resurrection appearances which do not occur elsewhere in the New Testament. The gospel accounts are silent about the appearance to James and to "more than five hundred brethren at one time" (verse 6 f.). For the fact that the risen Christ appeared to Cephas (= Simon Peter) alone (verse 5) we have to rely on an incidental verse in Luke (24:34).

Paul's list of witnesses forms the most valuable single piece of evidence provided by the New Testament for an assessment of the resurrection. In I Corinthians 15 Paul feels no need to name any witnesses for the facts of the crucifixion and burial of Jesus (verse 3 f.). But for the resurrection he lists many witnesses, both individuals and groups. When he remarks that most of the five hundred brethren are still living (verse 6), the implication is that the Corinthians in the mid-50s could check Paul's witness by questioning members of that large group. Paul's assertion remains susceptible of control by his readers. Hans von Campenhausen argues that if we decide to call into question the reliability of Paul's list of witnesses, logic requires that we take all other pieces of New Testament testimony as doubtful.[4] It is instructive that Bultmann, although he finds Paul's appeal to evidence for the resurrection distasteful, chooses to level his criticism against Paul's theology rather than against the reliable nature of his witness. He dismisses Paul's statements in I Corinthians as a blameworthy attempt to compel men to believe in the gospel.

> There is . . . one passage where St. Paul tries to prove the miracle of the resurrection by adducing a list of eye-witnesses (I Corinthians 15:3-8). But this is a dangerous procedure. . . . The resurrection of Jesus cannot be a miraculous proof by which the sceptic might be compelled to believe in Christ.[5]

In Paul's account we meet four times the word ōphthē, which is normally translated as "he appeared" or "he was seen." Earlier in I Corinthians Paul uses another form of the same verb when he asks: "Am I not an apostle? Have I not seen Jesus our Lord?" (9:1). In Galatians, when he refers to his conversion and call to apostleship, he does so in terms of a "revelation" (apokalypsis) of Jesus Christ (1:12, 16), an event which discloses the divine reality. In the Septuagint translation of the Old Testament ōphthē can be used to express a divine confrontation with man. God comes on the scene. Some man becomes aware of God's nearness and special presence, even if he does not literally see God. Hence we should not jump to the conclusion that in I Corinthians Paul is necessarily alleging a literal "seeing" of the risen Christ. He indicates a confrontation which forces itself upon human attention. But there is neither need nor reason for insisting on a specifically visual component to this encounter.[6]

The account of Paul's Damascus road experience provided by Acts chapter 9 is instructive here. Light from heaven suddenly flashes around Paul. Falling to the ground, he hears the voice of one who identifies himself as Jesus (verses 3 ff.). Later in Damascus Ananias introduces himself to Paul with the explanation, "The Lord Jesus who appeared (ophtheis) to you on the road by which you came has sent me" (verse 17). An experience which, strictly speaking, is not the "appearing" of someone is later described as such--at least in the usual English versions. Both here and in I Corinthians it could be preferable to adopt the translation "encounter." This would avoid the unwarranted implication that Paul is necessarily asserting that the resurrection witnesses enjoyed a visual experience of the risen Christ.

In the Easter text from I Corinthians Paul appeals to the tradition he received that Jesus "was raised on the third day in accordance with the scriptures" (15:4). What is the source of this dating? Was it based on historical fact or was it reached by a "deduction" from scripture or some other source? What was the theological significance of "in accordance with the scriptures"? The fact that women found Jesus' tomb empty on the third day (Mark 16:1-8) or that the first encounters with the risen Lord took place on that day did not as such settle the date of the resurrection itself. Jesus' own predictions that he would be killed and "after three days" would rise (Mark 8:31; 9:31; 10:34 and parallels in Matthew and Luke) might have been recalled and accepted as indicating the time of the resurrection. But these predictions are usually understood as vaticinia ex eventu. We are left with the question: What was the element in the "event" which led to the predictions being fitted out with a time sequence? Despite that fact that it is not mentioned by Paul, the discovery of the empty tomb on the third day seems the most likely explanation. Perhaps a part was played by the current belief that after death the soul lingered near the corpse for three days and departed on the fourth day as decay set in. To affirm that Christ rose on the third day would have been a way of asserting that the resurrection took place before his body began to decay. Even if the powers of this world had crucified him, he remained in the hands of the living God and rose before corruption could finally overpower him.

It is notoriously difficult to decide what scriptural texts were believed to have been fulfilled in Christ's resurrection on the third day. Hosea 6:1-2 is usually suggested: "Come, let us return to the Lord; for he has torn, that he may heal us; he has stricken, and he will bind us up. After two days he will revive us; on the third day he will raise us up, that we may live before him."[7] A serious difficulty, however, remains. If this were the basic proof text, it is surprising that it is explicitly mentioned neither by Paul nor by any other New Testament writer.

It is precisely this fact which renders Ernst Fuchs' criticism of Paul's argument in I Corinthians 15 vulnerable and unsatisfying.

If we regard the Easter-fact proved according to the scriptures . . . as a fact which is to be shown or has been shown from the scriptures, does not our faith depend then basically on the same compulsion from which it was supposed to free us--from a faith in our exegetical insight or from that of the so-called apostolic council in Jerusalem, to which the text in I Corinthians 15:3 ff. seems to look back?[8]

How should we appraise Fuchs' argument that an "exegetical insight" lay behind Paul's "according to the scriptures," an insight which was thought of (or could be thought of) as constituting such a stringent proof of the Easter-fact that it compelled belief? This interpretation fails on two counts. Fuchs does not (and cannot) cite scriptural texts which clearly operated this way. Secondly, it is hard to take his view too seriously, given the fact that he elsewhere interprets the phrase "according to the scriptures" in another and quite different sense. He writes in The New Hermeneutic: "Faith in Jesus Christ believes about itself that such faith is not man's work but God's act, so that faith appeals for its truth to God's Holy Spirit and not to man (I Corinthians 2:4 f.). This is the point in the apostolic appeal to the 'scriptures' (I Corinthians 15:3-5)."[9] In this second interpretation the phrase "according to the scriptures" indicates dependence on God rather than an appeal to "our exegetical insight" or "that of the so-called apostolic council in Jerusalem."

Perhaps the reference to "the scriptures" can be explained by the early Church's conviction that the Old Testament promises as a whole were fulfilled in Christ's resurrection. There were no particular proof texts to be cited. God's fidelity in salvation history was acknowledged to reach its climax in Christ's deliverance from death.[10]

The gospel evidence

Even a rapid comparison of the Easter texts in the gospels shows how widely the resurrection stories differ. This stands in striking contrast to the passion narrative which is more or less uniformly related in all four gospels. The appendix to Mark (16:9-22) which was added at the beginning of the second century represents an early attempt at fashioning a concordance of the diverging resurrection reports. To begin with, it is difficult to harmonize the whole set of Galilean appearances with the set of Jerusalem appearances. The Galilean appearances

belong to Matthew (except for the appearance to women [8-9]),
Mark (by implication in 16:7) and John (chapter 21). The Jerusalem
appearances belong to Luke (and Acts), Matthew 28:9, John 20,
and the appendix to Mark (16:9 ff.). We could, of course, try to
harmonize these accounts and have the disciples speeding back
and forth from Galilee to Jerusalem. But this approach would
miss the theological motives which were at work to produce the
geographical disparity. Luke reaches a climax in Jesus' going
up from Galilee to Jerusalem. The city which formed the center
for past revelation has become the scene of fulfillment. Divine
fidelity has secured continuity in salvation history. The city is
the place of the temple, the point at which the third epoch of
salvation history, the period of the Church, begins. It would
spoil Luke's pattern of theological geography to introduce resurrection appearances in Galilee.

On the other hand, in the first gospel which shows itself mani-
festly antagonistic to the Jewish authorities in Jerusalem it is
natural to find the risen Jesus separating himself from the un-
believing city and returning to Galilee. As the leader of the New
Israel (19:28), in a scene which recalls the Sermon on the Mount
and Moses on Mount Sinai, he sends out his apostles from a
mountain into the whole world (28:16-20). Revelation no longer
makes Jerusalem its center, but has moved from there to Galilee
and will move from Galilee out to the rest of mankind.

Apart from the differing location of the resurrection appearances, we meet frequent conflict over details in the accounts
provided by the four gospels. In John the corpse of Jesus is
anointed after his death (19:39f.), whereas in Luke (23:56--24:1)
and Mark (16:1) the women plan to perform that service on the
third day. In Mark three women visit the tomb (16:1), in Matthew
only two (28:1). In Mark (16:4) and John (20:1) the tomb is already
open when the women arrive, whereas in Matthew just as they arrive an angel moves away the stone blocking the entrance (28:2).
Many apologists have been content to take these and other dis-
crepancies and contradictions as a sign of the essential reliability
of the Easter accounts. Inconsistency has been explained as a
sign of truth. The witnesses agree on the substance but differ on
unimportant detail. This apologetical approach, however, ignores
the questions involved in the transmission and development of the
traditions, not to mention the role of the evangelists themselves
in shaping the texts as we have them.

For a proper appraisal of the Easter accounts we must hold
before our attention not only the conflict between the various

gospels but also the apologetical elements that can be detected. To interpret a text as reflecting apologetical interests is, of course, not to foreclose the issue of its historical factuality or falsity. It is a judgment about the motivation for its insertion in the story. In Mark such motivation seems to be involved when Pilate is represented as expressing wonder that Jesus was already dead and seeking confirmation from the officer in charge of the execution (15:44). At this point in the text the fact of Jesus' death is being established and officially confirmed. He was not taken down from the cross when he was only apparently dead. The later disappearance of the corpse is not explained as the revival of an unconscious man. Matthew's account introduces a Roman guard at the tomb to meet the charge that the disciples removed the corpse. The chief priests and Pharisees are portrayed as request- ing a guard from Pilate to prevent precisely such a fraud. They refer to Jesus' prediction that he would rise "after three days," a prediction that is assumed to be common knowledge. The guard will be necessary only "until the third day" (27:62 ff.). After the resurrection some of the soldiers from the guard make a report --not to their superior Pilate (who had sent them to watch the tomb) but to the Jewish chief priests. The soldiers receive bribes to spread the lying story that the body had been stolen during the night. At this point Christians are assumed to know exactly what went on behind the scenes in Jerusalem (28:11-15). We noted above how in the Marcan account women arrive to find Jesus' tomb al- ready open (16:4). There may be apologetical motives at play when Matthew represents the stone as being rolled away from the door just as the women arrive (28:2). The tomb was not only sealed and guarded, but there was not even a chance for robbers (or others) to enter and remove the corpse before witnesses came on the scene.

In their Easter accounts Luke and John are obviously at pains to establish the indubitable corporeal reality of the risen Christ, as well as his identity with the earthly Jesus. Whereas in Matthew the risen Lord merely speaks, in Luke he walks a road, sits at table, invites others to handle him, and eats fish to convince his disciples that he is no ghost (24:15 ff.; 39:41-43). In John he shows his disciples his hands and feet and invites them to touch his risen body in which the marks of his wounds still remain (20:20, 27). In the face of possible (or actual) Docetic and Gnostic denials Luke, John, and the Johannine appendix (chapter 21) ex- press in vivid, natural details the corporeal reality of the risen Christ. This insistence stands in striking contrast with the doc-

trine of I Corinthians 15. In Paul there is no sense of any return
on the part of Jesus to an earthly kind of existence and activities.
The one who has been raised and exalted to heaven comes for the
moment to encounter certain privileged witnesses.

In John and Luke it seems to have been realized that their
emphasis could create the impression that the resurrection was
no more than the resuscitation of a corpse. To check such a mis-
understanding they convey the other-worldliness of the risen body
by portraying Christ as passing through closed doors (John 20:
19, 26) and as suddenly appearing and disappearing (Luke 24:31,
36). A need to do justice to the "otherness" of the risen Christ
is implied also in Luke and John by another recurrent motif.
People who had known the earthly Jesus fail, at least initially,
to identify the risen Lord. In the Emmaus episode the two disciples
recognize Jesus only in the moment of his disappearance (Luke
24:31). Mary Magdalene takes him to be a gardener (John 20:14f.).
Peter and the other disciples out fishing do not at once identify the
stranger who calls to them from the beach (John 21:4ff.).

It should be added that interest in the corporeal reality of the
risen Christ is not totally lacking in the Galilee tradition of Mark
and Matthew. Two women embrace the feet of the Lord (Matthew
28:9). Here a sense of both nearness and transcendence is communicated. They touch the risen Lord only in the moment of their
embracing his feet and worshipping them.

Original traditions

We have been looking in detail at those New Testament texts
which must enter into our understanding of the resurrection, I
Corinthians 15 and the Easter accounts in the four gospels. What
lies behind these texts? What is their historical kernel? Behind
the texts, I suggest, lie two originally independent traditions, a
tradition of Peter and other disciples encountering the risen Christ
(represented in its earliest form by I Corinthians 15:3-8) and a
tradition of women discovering Christ's tomb empty (represented in
its earliest form by Mark 16:1-8). It seems most plausible to hold
that the disciples' encounters with Christ took place in Galilee.
The disciples learned of the empty tomb only after their return to
Jerusalem. They had played no role either in Jesus' death and
burial or in the discovery of the empty tomb. In Mark's gospel
we find an early attempt to connect the two traditions. The women
receive the angel's instruction that the disciples are to go to Galilee
where they will see the risen Lord (16:7), a direction prepared for

by an earlier Marcan addition (14:28). By the time that John's gospel was written the two traditions had been almost completely brought together. The disciples are brought into connection with the crucifixion (19:25-27). Peter and the beloved disciple visit the empty tomb (20:3-10), and the risen Lord appears to Mary Magdalene at the empty tomb (20:11-18). Originally, however, the tradition of encounter with the risen Jesus and the tradition of the discovery of the empty tomb had been independent.

The self-disclosure of the risen Christ to a number of men brought about their Easter-faith and caused them to form the first Christian community. This faith did not arise from the discovery of the empty tomb, but it found in this discovery a confirmation and sign of the reality which had already been revealed. Let us take up in detail the position I am maintaining with respect to the appearances of the risen Lord and the question of the empty tomb.

Encounters with the risen Jesus

A full-scale argument in support of the claim that a number of his disciples to their astonishment really encountered Jesus alive after his death would involve a thorough examination of the different counterexplanations. By various authors the alleged resurrection of Jesus has been explained as the product of fraud, a mistake, an hallucination, a psychological chain-reaction on the part of men vividly expecting Jesus to rise and so forth.[11] Many of these counter-explanations agree in that they interpret the resurrection on the basis of the inner life of the disciples. Whether merely subjective visions, an unbroken conviction that Jesus' cause must triumph, or some other "immanent" factor is advanced as the explanation, such views run at once into serious difficulty. Within the context of late Jewish apocalyptic thought, to claim the resurrection of a single individual before the end of the world was to introduce a quite new element. There existed an expectation that the end of the world would bring a resurrection of all the dead along with a general judgment. Neither the disciples nor anyone else expected the resurrection of one person alone. Without a new, compelling reason they would not have asserted the individual resurrection of Jesus. To explain away their proclamation "Jesus is risen" as the product of faith and vivid expectation is to ignore the expectations of resurrection which actually existed in first-century Jewish religion. What must be accounted for is the shift from the late Jewish confession of "Yahweh who will make the dead alive" to the Christian confession of the God who has raised Jesus from the dead (Romans 8:11; Galatians 1:1; II Corinthians 4:14).

Justice is not done to the New Testament evidence whenever the resurrection and the resurrection appearances are reduced to a transaction between God and the disciples' faith (or love), as their appropriation of the values for which Jesus stood, as the awakening in their minds of the "New Being" which they had experienced in Jesus during his lifetime, as their "infection" with the liberty which characterized Jesus' conduct and so forth. But Peter, Paul, and the other New Testament witnesses did not proclaim the resurrection as some such conclusion, consequence or moral of the events which they had witnessed, but as something which happened to Jesus of Nazareth himself. In the same breath they announced the crucifixion and the resurrection. For them the resurrection was as real an event for Jesus of Nazareth as was his crucifixion. One misrepresents these New Testament witnesses if one maintains that Jesus simply rose in the sense that men came to believe in him and love him. The primary purpose of the witnesses was to announce what God had done to Jesus, not to relate religious changes in other men.

Likewise, the apostolic proclamation is being distorted whenever one represents it as the affirmation of some general principles (for instance, "love conquers"), which the first Christians expressed pictorially ("Jesus rose from the dead"). Nor was their concern simply to announce the saving value of the resurrection (or death) of Jesus. Certainly his saving significance as Second Adam (Romans 5:12-21), the Messiah authorized by God (Acts 2:36) and the Son of God "in power" (Romans 1:4) was vitally important for them. But this significance did not, so to speak, hang in the air; it was based on a real event. The force of Paul's argument in I Corinthians 15 about the role of Jesus as "life-giving spirit" (verse 45) depended on the factual reality of the resurrection.

No one witnessed or claimed to have witnessed the events of the resurrection itself. It was understood as the necessary presupposition to the fact that after his crucifixion Jesus appeared alive to Peter, Paul, and others. If--unexpectedly--he came and met them, he must have risen from the dead. To maintain that these encounters were objective is to affirm that it was a case of the encounters producing the disciples' faith and not of their preexistent faith producing these encounters.

The question has sometimes been raised: What would a chance passerby have seen or heard on the occasion of one of these encounters? In modern terms, what would a tape recorder or a camera have preserved for us? We may well be convinced that we cannot settle any details about the nature of these experiences. In any case the reality of the resurrection encounters is not decided by the fact that men could have photographed them but the fact that the disciples met again him whom they knew to have died.

To some extent our readiness to elaborate on the nature of the encounters with the risen Christ will be governed by the degree of historical reliability which we assign to the triple account given in Acts (9:1 ff.; 22:4 ff.; 26:9 ff.). Here Paul's Damascus-road experience is represented as his meeting a flashing light from heaven and hearing a voice (9:3 ff.; 22:9; 26:13 ff.). Strictly speaking, the episode is not portrayed as a vision of the risen Lord, but as an auditory experience accompanied by light phenomena. Even if we accept the account given in Acts as reliable, there seems to be no effective reason why we should suppose that the other appearances were of precisely the same kind. It is true that in his appeal to the evidence for the resurrection (I Corinthians 15:3-8) Paul lists those who encountered the risen Christ without indicating any differences between their experiences. But it would be dubious procedure to allege on the basis of this summary formulation that Paul implies that the experiences matched each other in their concrete details. It would prove even more dubious to use I Corinthians 15:3-8 to mount an argument that the account in Acts of Paul's conversion should be taken as typifying the experiences of other resurrection witnesses.

For the purpose of his appeal to the Corinthian Christians Paul takes the various encounters with the risen Christ as enjoying similar status and importance. He does not offer any description of these events, either individually or in general. Even in the report provided by Acts the stress lies on Paul's conversion. There is no attempt to satisfy the curious questioner who would wish to know details of the risen Lord's appearance. In both Acts and I Corinthians (as well as in Galatians chapter 1) the encounters with the risen Christ operate to establish the reality of the resurrection and to communicate a missionary charge. I suspect that in Acts Luke could not afford to have introduced an Emmaus-style meeting on the Damascus road. He has already described how the risen Christ is withdrawn from such contact through the Ascension. Hence Paul's Damascus-road encounter occurs without any sense perception of the physical form of a man.

Much unnecessary difficulty and confusion can be occasioned by inadequate accounts of what the New Testament texts affirm the risen existence of Christ to be. Elsewhere I have set out in detail what I take to be the main lines of the New Testament doctrine of the risen body.[12] On the left, inadequate formulations take the form of reducing the resurrection to the survival of Jesus' ideals. On the right, they reduce the resurrection to an inner-historical event, the resuscitation of a corpse. It should be clear both from Jesus himself and from Paul that we may not equate the resurrection with the kind of resuscitation of a corpse which Jesus effects when he raises the daughter of Jairus. The girl resumes life under normal bodily conditions and will die again. She has not entered into her final state of existence. In his resurrection, however, Jesus moves to a state of full and final life with God. In his controversy with the Sadducees (Mark 12:18-27) Jesus does not deny the bodily nature of the resurrection. Yet he clearly implies that the risen body is no simple equivalent to our this-worldly body. A different style of life belongs to that transformed bodily existence which Paul attempts to elucidate (I Corinthians 15:35-53). On the one hand, the risen Lord may not be understood as a pure spirit to be apprehended only through inner visions. On the other hand, his existence transcends a bodily existence in the earthly, historical sense. Through his rising from the dead Christ is transformed to become effectively present to men in history, even if he himself no longer belongs to history in their spatio-temporal sense. In John's gospel Mary Magdalene rushes to the conclusion that the risen Jesus has returned to life in a way which enables her to resume with him the same kind of relationship which she enjoyed before his death (20:16f.). By Jesus' warning to her (20:17) John indicates that the resurrection has inaugurated a new kind of relationship with Christ, a relationship which transcends the ordinary limits imposed by space and time.

The discovery of the empty tomb

The time has come to turn to the tradition of the empty tomb. May Christians believe that Jesus of Nazareth is truly alive with God and at the same time hold that his crucified body decayed in the grave? What part should the empty tomb play in one's Easter faith? Elsewhere I have argued that the discovery of the empty tomb ought not to be interpreted as a nonhistorical legend, a secondary historicization of the original Easter kerygma.[13] The substantial factuality of the discovery tradition has much to be said for it and no convincing argument against it.

Along with the other gospel writers Mark shows a strong interest in what happened to the body of Jesus. He is concerned
to list the names of women who were present at the burial of Jesus
and on the first day of the week found the tomb empty. The empty
tomb was important for the faith and witness of the early Church.
There is no effective reason why it should not remain important
for present Christians also. Paul, of course, refers only to the
burial of Jesus (I Corinthians 15:4). Yet for Paul the proclamation
of the death, burial, and resurrection of Jesus would have been
inconceivable without the presupposition of the empty tomb. The
apostle's account of the risen body (I Corinthians 15:35 ff.) would
have been ruled out if Jesus' corpse had still been in the grave.

Nevertheless, anxious preoccupation with the empty tomb runs
the risk of exaggerating its value. In Mark 16:1-8 the three women
who find the grave open and empty must hear the resurrection message ("He has risen, he is not here") before they come to believe.
Luke reports that the women's message failed to bring others to
faith: "These words seemed to them [the apostles] an idle tale,
and they did not believe them" (24:11). In John, however, the
empty tomb has gained so much importance that it may be enough
to establish faith. Neither the appearances nor the angel's message were required before the beloved disciple, a model of the
true believer, came to faith (20:8). And yet even in John it is
realized that the mere fact of an empty grave remains ambiguous
(20:2, 13-15). This realization surfaces also in Matthew where a
counterexplanation (the theft of the body by Jesus' disciples) is
proposed by the chief priests and elders (28:13-15).

We need to remind ourselves that Jesus' empty grave meant
much more to the first Christians than, so to speak, a return
from the tomb. It stood for a return from the dead and all that
was implied by that. A man's burial meant that he was removed
from the land of the living. He had fallen into the power of death;
the earth or the stone which covered his grave separated him
from the living. To be in the grave was to be in the underworld
(Psalm 49:14 f.; Luke 16:22 f.). Hence Christ's resurrection as
a victory over death (I Corinthians 15:54-57) was understood to
have loosed the bonds of death and deprived death of its power
(Acts 2:24). Christ now possessed the keys of the underworld
(Revelation 1:18), so that he could guarantee that the forces of
death would not prevail against the Church (Matthew 16:18).

Here, as elsewhere in the Easter texts, we meet a blending
of theological reflection and historical assertion. If the proclamation of the resurrection "on the third day" goes back to the

historical fact that on that day women discovered Jesus' tomb to be empty, faith acknowledged here the beginning of a new creation. To associate the resurrection with sunrise on the first day of the week (Mark 16:2) was to announce that with the dominion of night broken the day of the Lord was dawning.

Freedom of faith

In chapter III I drew attention to the freedom which characterizes faith's response to revelation. This element of free decision is essential to man's acceptance of the resurrection, the supreme instance of God's self-revelation. The disciples on the Emmaus road must be willing to adopt a new perspective on the scriptures before they can recognize Christ (Luke 24:13-32). John seems to suggest that something more than a mere physical movement when he portrays Mary Magdalene as "turning around" (20:14) before she can acknowledge the risen Lord. Matthew also implies that an encounter with the resurrected Jesus demands that men be willing to encounter him; they are free not to do so (28:17).

This freedom does not exclude evidence for the resurrection, as if it were an actually transcendent happening which should lead men to disdain grounds for faith. The resurrection transcends history, and yet it is no purely supra-historical or extra-historical event. It touches history in the encounters with Christ as well as in the discovery of the empty tomb. What is not properly datable and localizable leaves evidential traces within history. Despite his anxiety to safeguard faith's freedom, Paul considers it his responsibility to remind the Corinthian Christians of reasons for accepting the resurrection.

For the most part this chapter has rehearsed evidence from the past. Such a procedure risks encouraging the distorted view which assesses the resurrection simply as an episode which is supposed to have happened back there and back then. Christian faith, however, exists only in the link between the subject and the object, between the believing self and the risen Christ to whom allegiance is given. His resurrection took place independently of us. Yet it remains a reality which we know by dwelling in it. We will accept the apostolic testimony to the resurrection only when we discern and acknowledge the risen Lord and hear his words to us now: "I am the resurrection and the life."

Luke and John show a deep interest in such continuous experience of the risen Lord, inserting their theology of the resurrection into a theology of divine service. The risen Christ comes in the liturgy.

Repeatedly the Easter texts of Luke and John imply that he is to be encountered in the Eucharist, in the forgiveness of sin, in the reading and explanation of scripture, and in meal fellowship. The community which the liturgy creates makes known his presence. He manifests himself in the moment of gathering (Luke 24:33; John 20:19).

There exists no point where a theologian's own personal history appears more clearly than when he writes about Christ's resurrection. What he believes the resurrection to be remains inseparably linked to the question why he believes. Ultimately, all interpretations condemn themselves as unsatisfactory when they shift the focus of attention from Jesus Christ himself and attempt, in one way or another, to explain the resurrection as the launching of a new idea. For instance, to interpret the resurrection as an affirmation that "love conquers" demands unpacking. If "love" means here man's love, the principle is patently untrue. Experience unfortunately illustrates too often that human love fails, suffers defeat, or shows itself incapable of meeting effectively the malice or sheer indifference of other men. If the principle asserts that God's love conquers, we must ask: In what sense does (or did) God's love conquer? Finally we recognize that divine love conquers because we know that God intervened in the resurrection. Jesus' particular destiny underpins our confidence that both for him and for us human life transcends the summation of all that we can describe biologically, psychologically, and sociologically.

Since the Church sees its history founded in Jesus' history, it can witness to and explain its religious experience better by writing the history of Jesus as the Messiah than by describing its own religious life.

J. M. Robinson

To seek God apart from Jesus is the work of the devil.

Martin Luther

Chapter X

The Jesus of History

In a certain church in Buckinghamshire one can find the tomb
of a Sarah Fletcher who is declared by her epitaph to have died
"a martyr of excessive sensibility." The high-sounding phrase
conceals the straightforward fact that her husband mistreated
her and she hanged herself. By this stage some readers may
feel that many basic facts about the Christian faith have been too
often hidden behind lofty theological phrases and that they themselves have been made martyrs of academic refinement. This
concluding section on the person of the historical Jesus may offer
some relief. Within a study of theological foundations these reflections offer the opportunity of insisting that the concrete event
of divine self-disclosure takes place through Jesus Christ. Preoccupation with the "cosmic" Christ or with the risen Lord present
in the liturgy fails to do justice to the full scope of that revelation
mediated by the particular life of a first-century Jew. The concrete

nature of God's disclosure must be respected no less than its universal aspects.

The pursuit of knowledge about the historical Jesus has enjoyed an engaging flexibility in modern theology. The issues have proved both theological and historical. Does ordinary historical investigation allow us in fact to know very much about the earthly Jesus? Does it really matter in principle how much or how little such historical investigation establishes? Will faith flourish all the same? This chapter is offered as a criticism of various maximalizers and minimalizers. Positively, it recommends the need to respect the particularity of Christian revelation, a theme already adumbrated in chapter IV.

The classic quest

The modern quest of the historical Jesus began in 1778 with the posthumous publication of extracts from the work of Hermann Reimarus. He portrayed Jesus as a would-be political insurgent who died as a self-confessed failure. The disciples of Jesus, however, stole his body, fabricated the story of the resurrection, and set up the Christian Church. Inevitably the views of Reimarus raised a storm of protest and were widely rejected. Yet he made an assured contribution in recognizing clearly that the real Jesus of history and the Christ preached by the Church were not necessarily the same. The quest of the historical Jesus was on the way.[1]

The classical period for the study of Jesus' life ran from the end of the eighteenth century to the early years of the twentieth century. Scholars like Ernest Renan, D. F. Strauss, and Adolf von Harnack attempted to penetrate beneath the later dogmatic overlay and discover the authentic picture of the real Jesus. "Free from Paul" ("Los von Paulus") was the slogan of such writers as in their various ways they tried to get back behind the Christological dogmas to the simple peasant from Galilee. By precise, unprejudiced use of the earliest sources, in particular Mark's gospel, they expected to uncover Jesus of Nazareth as he really was. Generally this search for the true Jesus was carried on by the unorthodox--by the rationalists (who stripped Jesus' life of miraculous elements), the humanitarians (who concerned themselves with Jesus' ethical code) and the liberal Protestants (for whom formal membership in the Christian Church was often of no great moment). The results of such investigations shocked the orthodox who reacted by penalizing such writers as Strauss and Renan through exclusion from academic appointments.

172

What common picture resulted from all this intensive work on the life of Jesus? Notoriously the enterprise led to no agreed account. Doubts arose, but they were suppressed. Eventually, however, the truth had to be faced. The disparity between the portraits of Jesus by no means derived simply from differences in critical judgments about the New Testament evidence. The writers were affected by their differing attitudes towards God, human life, and the world. In some measure their portrayals of Jesus were the products of highly subjective interpretation. Many showed themselves unbelievably confident about their power to penetrate the mind of Jesus and offer sound reflections on his psychology.

The story of this nineteenth-century search for the real Jesus was told in classic form by Albert Schweitzer in his The Quest of the Historical Jesus, a book first published in 1906 when he was thirty-three years old. Schweitzer summed up his findings.

> Each successive epoch of theology found its own thoughts in Jesus. . . . But it was not only each epoch that found its reflection in Jesus; each individual created Him in accordance with his own character. There is no historical task which so reveals a man's true self as the writing of a Life of Jesus.[2]

Nineteenth-century research had fatally modernized Jesus.

Schweitzer himself, like Johannes Weiss, voiced the conviction that the center of Jesus' preaching lay in eschatology, not in ethics. He developed a one-sided picture of Jesus as an uncompromising apocalyptic preacher who announced the last hour, attempted to bring it about, and fell in the attempt. Schweitzer's permanent contribution was twofold. He successfully challenged the conventional wisdom of nineteenth-century research into the life of Jesus. Henceforth his account of his predecessors would exercise an inhibiting influence, at least in Protestant academic circles. Faced with Schweitzer's perceptive critique of a long line of scholars from Reimarus to William Wrede, others were dissuaded from undertaking the task of writing a biography of Jesus. Secondly, Schweitzer broke decisively with attempts to turn Jesus into a contemporary. Jesus is rightly viewed only within the historical framework of the first century. In particular, the eschatological nature of his message must be respected.

After Schweitzer

As noted, Schweitzer's critique proved inhibiting among Protestant New Testament scholars. Catholic writers, however,
continued to compose what purported to be exact historical lives
of Jesus. The stream of biographies by Ricciotti, Lagrange, Prat,
Daniel-Rops, and others continued. Popular lives of Jesus, not
to mention historical novels about him, remained undisturbed
by academic scruples and disputes.

At this point a few moments reflection on the issues involved
will be worthwhile. Do we really know enough to attempt a life
of Jesus? In large measure answers will be determined by the
materials held to be necessary for writing of any biography.
Four requirements seem indispensable:

(a) That we have access in some degree to the whole of our
subject's life and development;
(b) That some chronological framework can be established;
(c) That we have some access to his motivation and psychology;
(d) That in our portrayal we are able to make use of biographical "types." (By this I mean that, while paying proper attention to our subject's individual traits, we have some way
of generalizing about him as, for instance, a dedicated social
reformer, an antisocial recluse or a violent revolutionary.)

In the case of Jesus the four requirements cannot be met. Our
knowledge of him is restricted to the last two or three years of
his life. Even for these years very little chronology can be
established. The sources we possess make it notoriously difficult
to penetrate his inner life. Momentous questions have not proved
amenable to secure solution. Did Jesus regard himself as Messiah?
If he did, what kind of Messiah did he take himself to be? Did he believe himself to be the Son of Man who would return as universal
judge at the world's end? Finally, Jesus transcends ordinary
biographical types. It remains quite unsatisfactory in our portrayals
of him to make use of such typical figures as the religious re-
vivalist, the wandering miracle worker, or the high priest of a
new cult.

Beyond all this we face a double problem about our primary
sources. Von Harnack once remarked that apart from the gospels
"just about everything we know concerning Jesus' history and
teaching may easily be put on a small sheet of paper." It ob-
scures the real nature of the gospels to describe them as biog-

174

raphies or history books. They constitute relatively brief testi-
monials of faith. For the gospel writers Jesus has become the
central object of religious devotion. They offer an amalgam of
believing witness and historical reminiscence with the aim of
eliciting and developing the reader's own faith. The gospels may
not be dismissed as simply the devotional literature of the early
Church or primitive books of common worship. But neither may they
be interpreted as ordinary historical sources from ancient times.
The classic search for the historical Jesus failed to fit the intention
of the authors of our primary sources.

Furthermore, Bultmann and other form critics have demonstrated that the Synoptic Gospels are collections of materials
linked together in a largely artificial manner.[3] In the preliterary
stage traditions about Jesus were passed on orally as isolated
fragments. The original geographical contexts and chronological
order of these disconnected units became lost, and--what was
much more important--these traditions were preserved, shaped,
and created in line with the needs of the Christian community. By
stressing the role of the early Church in transmitting, forming,
and composing materials, form criticism makes it hard to assess
what historical facts lie behind the traditions. The gospels become
primary sources for the history of the early Church and only
secondary sources for the history of Jesus. Faced with a particular
pericope, our first question should be: What function did this unit
serve in the life of the early Christians? How does it mirror their
situation?

Without question, New Testament scholarship is permanently
indebted to the work of the form-critics in illuminating the development of the gospels. Their findings provided further arguments
in support of Schweitzer's case against the nineteenth-century
quest of the historical Jesus. Yet the value of their contribution
should not lead us to extremes. Specifically, form criticism seeks
to classify materials on purely formal grounds. These classifica-
tions are not always certain. Often difficulties arise in correlating
forms with a setting in the life of the early Church. In fact, it is
impossible to sustain the thesis that no traditions about Jesus survived except insofar as they served some function in the life and
worship of the primitive Church. Further, the mere fact that
certain words or the account of some events can be shown to have
filled some needs of the early Christian community does not necessarily demand the conclusion that these words or events do not
(or cannot) derive from the history of Jesus himself. Community
requirements could have dictated certain selections out of many
(authentic) traditions which were available.

Bultmann's minimalizing

Thus far I have offered a rapid sketch of major trends in the modern pursuit of knowledge about the historical Jesus. The rest of this chapter explores the question through a critical examination of the positions adopted by Rudolf Bultmann and various subsequent writers. Beyond doubt, Bultmann has proved himself to be the arch-minimalizer of the relevance of the historical Jesus for Christian faith.

Historical conclusions and theological convictions need to be carefully sorted out. Otherwise we can easily suppose that Bultmann's theological program is the consequence of his historical research--as Otto Betz's misleading account suggests. "Bultmann maintains that the historical enquirer cannot, even from these detailed sources [the gospels], derive more than the bare 'that' of existence--the fact that a man called Jesus of Nazareth really lived."4 This kind of comment which is frequently offered implies that Bultmann simply makes a virtue (the theological irrelevance of the historical Jesus) out of a necessity (our incapacity to know more than an absolute minimum about the historical Jesus). If this were so, Bultmann would differ from such liberal Protestant scholars as von Harnack merely by the fact that he outbids them in reducing the amount of genuine data about Jesus. He would prove more sceptical than they had been about the historical knowledge we can gather from the kerygmatized accounts of Jesus provided by the Synoptic Gospels.

The truth, however, is different. Bultmann is ready to reconstruct the historical Jesus but takes the position that Jesus remains theologically neutral. These two points call for development. In the opening chapter of his Theology of the New Testament Bultmann summarizes what he regards as the known facts about the historical Jesus. It can be astonishing to note how far this account goes. Jesus' demand for decision, Bultmann argues, indicates how he interpreted his call as God's last word to man. Conscious of his authority, he understood himself as an eschatological sign in relation to which men's destiny was decided. Thus the ministry of Jesus implied a Christology.5 In view of the charge of historical scepticism that has often been levelled against him, it is as well to remind ourselves of Bultmann's confidence that we know a good deal about the historical Jesus.

Why then does Bultmann settle for a theologically neutral Jesus? One common explanation reminds us of Bultmann's uncompromising insistence that Christianity began at Easter.

The earthly Jesus remained within the framework of Judaism as a rabbinical teacher who drastically reinterpreted the law and preached a more radicalized form of Old Testament faith in God. In brief, the history of Jesus forms part of a superseded Judaism.[6] The real vitality of Bultmann's position, however, arises ultimately from his preoccupation with one question: How is God's word of saving revelation made present? Jesus' authoritative claim does not extend beyond his life, but is confined to the past where it can no longer be effective for my salvation. Only the proclamation constitutes that word which encounters me now and can precipitate my faith.

For this kerygma no more than the sheer existence of the historical Jesus must be presupposed: "All that is necessary is to proclaim that he has come."[7] As crown-witnesses for this position Bultmann claims the chief theologians of the New Testament: "Paul and John, each in his own way, indicate that we do not need to go beyond the 'that.'"[8] The content of Jesus' past life and preaching should not be taken to inform faith. Christian faith remains directed to the present kerygma. Here and here alone in the proclaimed word which elicits our decision to believe, "Christ meets us."[9] In short, the Christ of the kerygma and not the person of the historical Jesus constitutes the object of faith.

There is an admirable simplicity about Bultmann's minimalizing view. But a moment's reflection suggests serious flaws in the case he argues. As a matter of fact, the individual personality of the historical Jesus has proved (and remains) highly significant for the faith of very many Christians. To inform them that believers need only to hear it announced that "he has come" would be to cast serious doubt on his genuine human existence. Many have felt uneasy at this Docetic tendency which appears to trivialize the Incarnation out of a preoccupation with the present proclamation. This discomfort has sometimes been expressed by stating that in Bultmann's position the Word does not become flesh, but the flesh becomes word. Even St. John offers his account of the divine Word in the form of a gospel and that means as the history of the Incarnate One.

What does Bultmann finally leave us with? Ultimately we are asked to be content with a kerygma which speaks only of itself, not of Jesus. The proclamation is transmuted into an objectless word-event which may not be taken as a word about someone (or something), but emerges simply as a word, salvific in itself. Let me put this objection in concrete terms. It would seem to satisfy Bultmann's requirements if the Christian preacher today began his sermon by declaring, "Jesus has come," and then spent the rest of

the time uttering nonsense words. A second grave misgiving
arises from the fact that Bultmann offers no convincing justification for the need to retain at least the sheer existence of the historical Jesus. Why does the "that" of Jesus' having come enjoy
such importance, if everything else about him is to be quietly
dropped? Why must man's authentic decision of faith today remain
tied to this historical point in the past?

Post Bultmann locutum

For the moment let me cut short these animadversions about
Bultmann's minimalizing interpretation of the historical Jesus.
In retrospect, it is a little baffling that so many German theologians
could have solemnly accepted this interpretation during the thirties
and forties. The crash came in 1953 with Ernst Käsemann's lecture, "The Problem of the Historical Jesus," in which he insisted
that the form of Jesus' life is relevant for faith.[10] The upshot was
to initiate a return to the problem of the historical Jesus among
theologians who following Bultmann's lead and thus far left the
problem undisturbed. Those who had never accepted Bultmann's
veto naturally expressed satisfaction at the turn of events.
The fifties and sixties witnessed a new wave of "Jesus-books"
along with numerous articles about the historical Jesus from
such scholars as Günther Bornkamm, Hans Conzelmann, Gerhard
Ebeling, Ernst Fuchs, Joachim Jeremias, Ethelbert Stauffer,
and others. Let me offer three comments on this recent phase
of writing, both academic and popular. (1) One can often detect
a recurrence of the phenomenon to which Schweitzer drew attention so well--the creation of Jesus in accordance with the
writer's own thoughts and character. I think here of the many
latter-day accounts of Jesus as the revolutionary leader, Jesus
the truly secular man, Jesus the lawbreaker, and Jesus the divine
propagandist. Such stereotypes may be emotionally satisfying,
but for the most part they are intellectually worthless. This
portrayal of Jesus in line with the writer's own theological presuppositions is quite marked among Bultmann's former students.
Bornkamm announces that he aims to confront the modern reader
with Jesus and his message. In fact he present us with a figure
who exemplifies only too well what Bornkamm learned from
Bultmann. Here is a Jesus who has lost some of his first-century
strangeness and steps forward as the preacher of an existentialist
gospel.[11]

(2) This renewed interest in the historical Jesus differs from the classical, nineteenth-century quest in that the enterprise is now carried on by the orthodox rather than by liberals and rationalists. In particular, the work of Jeremias, Stauffer, Cullmann, and Pannenberg is only too clearly motivated by a desire to defend Christian orthodoxy.

(3) Much recent work reveals some continuity with the classical "histories" of Jesus, albeit that it is nowadays widely acknowledged that we cannot trace Jesus' psychological development and write a genuine biography of him. Stauffer announces his intention of employing scientific historical methods to tell the story of Jesus as it really happened. He expresses his conviction that such new sources as the Qumran materials support this fresh attempt.[12] But what actually characterizes his work is not the use of new evidence but a renewed confidence that he can reach the truth about the historical Jesus, as well as a tendency to pit Jesus against Paul which recalls the nineteenth-century liberal cry of "los von Paulus." Stauffer agrees that it is impossible to write a biography; this would require records of Jesus' psychological development. His aim is to present a genuine history of Jesus, a "clear, strictly objective statement of those facts which can still be actually discerned."[13]

Joachim Jeremias has also shown an extraordinary trust in the power of contemporary exegesis to supply the truth about the historical Jesus. We can expect to hear again the ipsissima vox of Jesus, even if we cannot readily recover Jesus' ipsissima verba. Jeremias argues that historical investigation finds itself today in an "entirely different" and superior position when contrasted with the last century.[14] We now have five "bulwarks" to defend us against the danger of reading subjective fancies into the text and creating Jesus in our own image. These "bulwarks" are: literary criticism, form criticism, our new knowledge of first-century Palestine, our knowledge of Jesus' mother tongue (Aramaic) and the rediscovery of the eschatological character of Jesus' message. The new methods should enable us to reach a secure knowledge of the historical Jesus on which we can safely base our faith.[15]

Käsemann has highlighted the unrealistic nature of Jeremias' assurance. The five "bulwarks" must be admitted to be far from absolutely impregnable. Many serious conflicts in exegetical results continue about such vital issues as Jesus' messianic consciousness and his understanding of his coming death. Every generation may flatter itself that it has reached foolproof methods of exegesis. But no refinement of methods supplies a certain remedy for human caprice. As Käsemann expressed the matter, to rest one's faith on exegesis in the way Jeremias proposes would be more dangerous than to walk blindfolded into a mine-field.[16]

With Jeremias we reach the ultimate limit in the trend to maximalize the significance of the historical Jesus for faith. Where Bultmann minimalizes Jesus' role out of a preoccupation with the primacy of the divine revelation now, Jeremias wishes to base faith totally on what we can establish about the past facts of Jesus' life. Let me take one example which Jeremias names as essential, Jesus' interpretation of his death.

> The very heart of the kerygma, that "Christ died for our sins in accordance with the scriptures" (I Corinthians 15:3), represents an interpretation of a historical event: this death happened for us. But this raises the question whether this interpretation of the crucifixion of Jesus has been arbitrarily impressed upon the events, or whether there was some cir- cumstance in the events which caused this interpretation to be attached to it. In other words we must ask: Did Jesus him- self speak of his impending death, and what significance did he attach to it?[17]

The implication of Jeremias' position must be clearly stated. If we cannot establish historically that Jesus himself attributed a redeeming significance to his impending death, this interpretation of the crucifixion deserves dismissal as "arbitrarily impressed." Nothing short of such proof will satisfy Jeremias. In other words the only reason why he is ready to accept Jesus' death as having happened "for us" and "for our sins" is the actual demonstration that Jesus himself interpreted his coming death in that way.

Jeremias broadens the importance of historical study to the point that he maintains Jesus' "claim to divine authority" to be "the origin of Christianity."[18] Silence is here maintained about God's decisive intervention in the death and resurrection of Jesus. A few pages earlier Jeremias briefly mentions the resurrection but only to insist that the risen Christ was acknowledged to be identical with the earthly Jesus.[19] He interprets the resurrection in the light of the ministry, not the ministry in the light of the resurrection. For Jeremias the unique, astounding fact about Jesus was his claim to authority, not his rising from the dead!

180

It would be news to the apostle Paul that "the origin of Christianity" should be located elsewhere than in the fact that Jesus "died for our sins and rose again for our justification" (Romans 4:25). Paul frequently proclaims Jesus' death "for our sins" without bothering at all to remark, let alone insist, that statements from Jesus himself provide the required backing for this interpretation of the crucifixion. God's action both in raising Jesus from the dead and in the subsequent spread of the gospel supplies the justification for Paul's proclamation. Further, it would be news for the apostle to learn from Jeremias that "we cannot understand the message of Paul unless we know the message of Jesus."[20] If so, Paul has rendered extreme disservice to his readers by rarely quoting or echoing the message of Jesus.

Jeremias' attribution of maximum importance to Jesus' earthly life ends by looking curiously similar to Pannenberg's theology of revelation, albeit that Pannenberg (rightly) recognizes the paramount value of the resurrection. For Jeremias faith rests on our knowledge of certain facts about Jesus. Historical investigation can bring us into assured contact with the vox ipsissima of Jesus and establish that nothing essentially new has been incorporated in the later kerygma. This position resembles Pannenberg's two-stage scheme in which knowledge constitutes man's immediate response to the events of revelation; on this secure basis faith can then arise. Pannenberg interprets revelation as something which happened "back there" and "back then," in Jesus' life, death, and resurrection. Far from being itself revelatory, the later proclamation is merely a report which communicates information about (past) revelation. In similar terms Jeremias affirms the pastness of revelation.

> The preaching of the early church . . . is the divinely inspired witness to the revelation, but the church's preaching is not itself the revelation. To put it bluntly, revelation does not take place from eleven to twelve o'clock on Sunday morning. . . . The doctrine of continuous revelation (revelatio continua) is a gnostic heresy. No, the church's proclamation is, from its earliest beginnings, not itself revelation, but it does guide toward the Revelation.[21]

As I have already argued against Pannenberg, this position fails to respect Paul's repeated reference to the present actuality of revelation. For the apostle revelation occurs through his own preaching and (suffering) existence. God's saving self-manifestation

takes place now for those who acknowledge in faith the crucified
and risen Jesus as their Lord. This recurring revelation does
not constitute a revelatio continua in the sense that it goes beyond
or "adds" something to Christ's unique function as perfect revealer. But God's self-disclosure does not remain "back there"
like some static, independent object which can become the object
of our attention. Christ the revealer, God the revealed, and man
as the one to whom revelation comes in faith belong together
in an inseparable unity. Far from being "a gnostic heresy," the
doctrine of present revelation draws attention to the fact that
revelation cannot exist as a thing by itself. As a living reality
revelation does not hang in the air but is present only in and to
living, believing men.22

Bultmann at bay

As matters stand in this chapter, I have offered some reflections both on those who minimalize and those who maximalize
the role of the historical Jesus for Christian faith. As a useful
way of raising some further points and pulling the debate together, we turn now to a 1960 lecture by Bultmann in which he
responded to Käsemann, Ebeling, Fuchs, Bornkamm, and others
who had taken up the so-called "new quest of the historical
Jesus."23 To simplify matters let us concentrate on Bultmann's
objections to Fuchs and on three questions in particular. What
significance does Jesus' own faith hold for us? May we speak of
Jesus' personality? What change of situation is involved for us
in Jesus' death and resurrection?

(1) Fuchs takes the position that the New Testament sources
have preserved for us those scenes and sayings which convey
the attitude of the historical Jesus. Above all in the parables we
meet an understanding of existence which must be characterized
as faith. We today are called to believe as Jesus himself then
believed. There is sufficient access to his attitude for us to be
enabled to know and relive his existential self-understanding.
We are invited to believe like Jesus whom Fuchs styles "the
representative of faith"24 and his friend Gerhard Ebeling calls
"the witness of faith."25

Over this point Bultmann expresses his misgivings that faith
in Christ is being reduced to the religion of Jesus. He observes
that "the Gospels do not speak of Jesus' faith, nor does the
kerygma make reference to it." A discipleship which would involve "catching" Jesus' faith never arises in the New Testament.
Our call is to believe in Christ, not to believe like Jesus.26

Fuchs acknowledges that "the Synoptic Gospels studiously avoid" talking of Jesus' faith, but (rightly) remains unconvinced that this fact automatically makes it illegitimate to adopt the expression. He argues: "The theme of the sayings of Jesus is the decision which they demand. But this demand is simply an echo of Jesus' decision. We have to understand his conduct as likewise determined by a decision and we can infer what he did from what he demands."[27] But may we so quickly conclude from what Jesus demands to what Jesus did? Without further reasons it is unjustified to infer at once that someone "does" interiorly (that is to say, believes in or decides on) simply from what he calls on others to do. Fuchs' method of argument is questionable, not necessarily his conclusion. Elsewhere he draws attention to Jesus' attitude of obedience and prayer, which justify us in speaking of Jesus' own faith.[28]

(2) A wider issue for debate concerns Jesus' "personality" which--Bultmann insists--do not form for Paul the basis of revelation and faith. The apostle's kerygma requires only the sheer fact of Jesus' life and death, no portrayal of the historical Jesus. Paul fights shy of interpreting the crucifixion from a bio- graphical standpoint as a psychological process in the history of Jesus' personality. By his existentialist reflections, Bultmann argues, Fuchs reverts to the historical-psychological interpreta- tions of Jesus' personality which typified the nineteenth-century quest.[29]

His investigations allow Fuchs to go beyond Jesus' faith to talk also of his joy, love, and that certainty of God which motivated his decision to continue proclaiming his message, come what may. "This man," Fuchs writes, "had decided to suffer and, if needs be, to die for his proclamation. This was his secret."[30] A fairly extensive account of Jesus' personality and motivation emerges. Fuchs agrees that this existential interpretation deals with "psychological considerations," in particular the psychological situation into which the death of John the Baptist plunged Jesus.[31] This is, however, no damning admission which would justify Bultmann's objection. Serious difficulties may often stand in the way of giving confident answers to the questions which Fuchs raises about Jesus' self-understanding. But it is arbitrary to invoke Paul and John as a theological veto against raising these questions. They arise naturally from an historical examination of the Synoptic Gospels. The very fact that the kerygma names Jesus as the one through whom God's saving revelation reaches man obliges us to investigate his life for the purpose of inter- preting the kerygma.

To follow Fuchs' lead is not to revert to the nineteenth-century attempts to write a life of Jesus. Disagreement with that classical enterprise should not lead us to abandon as irrelevant for faith all enquiry into what historical methods now disclose about Jesus' ministry. As Ebeling argues, "the fact that we cannot, as the eighteenth and nineteenth centuries imagined, reconstruct from the sources a biography of Jesus surely must not be confused with the idea that the historical Jesus is completely hidden from us behind the New Testament witness and totally unknown to us."[32] Bultmann may assure us that "all that is necessary is to proclaim that Jesus has come." But this is clearly not enough. Listeners will spontaneously and rightly ask who this "Jesus" was, what he did, what he said, what he thought, and so forth. They will pose the kind of questions which Fuchs considers apropos for faith.

(3) The third quarrel Bultmann has with Fuchs concerns "the shift of aeons." In the kerygma Christ is proclaimed as the one who died for our sins and was raised for our salvation. There exists a fundamental difference between the period of Jesus' life and preaching and the period of Paul's preaching. The shift of aeons has taken place. Far from repeating Jesus' preaching, Paul announces that in the historical phenomenon of the cross the eschatological event has occurred. Fuchs' position, however, presents us with a post-resurrection retreat to the preaching situation of the historical Jesus.[33]

Let me elaborate Bultmann's objection, since it seems basically sound. Fuchs resembles Jeremias in maximalizing the function of Jesus' history for faith and essentially rendering his death and resurrection unnecessary. It would make little apparent difference for Fuchs' explanation, if at the end of his ministry Jesus had suddenly disappeared and had never been seen again. Provided that his words along with some indication of his conduct had been preserved and were now proclaimed to us, we could discern his self-understanding before God and relive it through our own faith. In Fuchs' scheme of things the preaching of Jesus would be suf-ficient for us to know and respond to God's revelation. The cross and resurrection have no integral part to play. Fuchs is consistent when he interprets Paul's achievement as a restoration of that language about God "which had already been reached with the historical Jesus." Paul resembles Jesus by raising "ordinary life to 'the stuff' of the revelatory event."[34] In short, Paul reestablishes the preresurrection situation.

Conclusion

What moral may be drained off from this debate between those (like Bultmann) who minimalize the function of the historical Jesus for Christian faith and those (like Jeremias and Fuchs) who maximalize this function? Ultimately there is a proper tension to be preserved. Jesus' death and resurrection form the high point of divine revelation but not in a way which renders the earthly story of Jesus a matter of indifference, a mere prolegomenon to be relegated to the history of Judaism. The particularity of Jesus' human life demands respect, yet not to the point that his death and resurrection are reduced to a dispensable appendix. We are asked both to believe like the earthly Jesus and to believe in the risen Christ. Both the Synoptic account of the preacher from Nazareth and Paul's reflections on his Lord's death and resurrection belong to the canon. The history of Jesus is neither theologically neutral nor theologically paramount.

In brief, the true tension between the concreteness of a given human life and the universality of Christ's lordship must not be relaxed by devaluing either past origins nor present proclamation. We meet God in the cosmic Christ who encounters us now, as well as in the particularity and strangeness of a first-century Galilean.

ABBREVIATIONS

ADT	Anfänge der dialektischen Theologie, ed. by Jürgen Moltmann
BDT	The Beginnings of Dialectic Theology, ed. by J. M. Robinson
Bultmann	Rudolf Bultmann in Catholic Thought, ed. by T. F. O'Meara and D. M. Weisser
CBQ	Catholic Biblical Quarterly
CD	Karl Barth, Church Dogmatics
Commentary	Commentary on the Documents of Vatican II, ed. by H. Vorgrimler
DD	The Documents of Vatican II, ed. by W. M. Abbott
Dz	Enchiridion Symbolorum, Definitionum et Declarationum, 34 ed., ed. by A. Schönmetzer
Essays	Rudolf Bultmann, Essays Philosophical and Theological
EvTh	Evangelische Theologie
GA	Ernst Fuchs, Gesammelte Aufsätze
GST	Wolfhart Pannenberg, Grundfragen systematischer Theologie
GuV	Rudolf Bultmann, Glauben und Verstehen
HJKC	The Historical Jesus and the Kerygmatic Christ, ed. by C. E. Braaten and R. A. Harrisville
JGM	Wolfhart Pannenberg, Jesus God and Man
John	Rudolf Bultmann, Das Evangelium des Johannes
KuD	Kerygma und Dogma
NTS	New Testament Studies
PL	Patrologia Latina, ed. by J. B. Migne
RaH	Wolfhart Pannenberg, Revelation as History
RGG	Religion in Geschichte und Gegenwart, 3 ed., ed. by K. Galling
Studies	Ernst Fuchs, Studies of the Historical Jesus
TDNT	Theological Dictionary of the New Testament, tr. by G. W. Bromiley
TH	Jürgen Moltmann, Theology of Hope
ThLZ	Theologische Literaturzeitung
TNT	Rudolf Bultmann, Theology of the New Testament
ZThK	Zeitschrift für Theologie und Kirche

Notes to Chapter I

1 The Theologian at Work (New York, 1969), p. xiii.
2 The Grammar of Assent, edited by C. F. Harrold (New York, 1947), pp. 63 ff.
3 K. Rahner and H. Vorgrimler, Theological Dictionary (New York, 1965), p. 456.
4 New Frontiers in Theology, III, Theology as History, ed. J. M. Robinson and J. B. Cobb (New York, 1967), p. 229.
5 See his God and Word (Philadelphia, 1967).
6 K. Rahner, Theologians at Work, ed. P. Granfield (New York, 1967), p. 44 f.
7 Ibid., p. 229.
8 ADT, p. xvii.
9 Word and Faith (London, 1963), p. 202, note 1.
10 IV/1, p. 741.
11 Theology of Hope (New York, 1967), p. 33; hereafter TH.
12 In a sweeping statement Ebeling declares: "To speak of God is meaningful solely with an eye to the conscience." Word and Faith, p. 412.
13 "Jews and Gentiles: The Social Character of Justification in Paul," Journal of Ecumenical Studies 5 (1968), pp. 241-67; "The Kerygma of Galatians," Interpretation 21 (1967), pp. 131-46.
14 Denken und Sein (Zollikon, 1959), p. 192.
15 Secular Christianity (London, 1966), pp. 18, 20.
16 Cf. E. Fuchs, GA, II, p. 168 f.
17 Memory and Hope (New York, 1967), pp. 102-40.
18 G. Ebeling, Theology and Proclamation (Philadelphia, 1966), p. 21.
19 Ibid., p. 20 f.
20 Ibid., p. 22.
21 The Relevance of the New Testament (New York, 1968), p. 72.
22 Ebeling, Theology and Proclamation, p. 28.
23 See H. Ott, "What Is Systematic Theology?" New Frontiers in Theology, I, The Later Heidegger and Theology, ed. J. M. Robinson & J. B. Cobb (New York, 1963), pp. 77-111. See also Roger Lapointe, Les trois dimensions de l'herméneutique (Paris, 1967).
24 Guide to the Debate about God (London, 1966), p. 51.
25 Ebeling, Theology and Proclamation, p. 18.
26 Ibid., p. 22 f.

187

27 Wahrheit und Methode (Tübingen, 1960), pp. 152 ff., 367 ff., etc.

28 TNT, II, p. 251.

29 The Word of God and Tradition (Philadelphia, 1968), p. 166.

30 The Church and the Reality of Christ (New York, 1962), pp. 146, 10 f.

31 In the End God (rev. ed.; New York, 1968), p. 37 f.

32 Kerygma and Myth, ed. R. H. Fuller (London, 1962), II, p. 92.

33 Theological Dictionary, p. 456.

34 Theological Explorations (New York, 1968).

35 Karl Barth, Romans (London, 1933), p. 143 f.

36 Letters and Papers from Prison (3 ed.; New York, 1967), p. 157; cf. pp. 153, 181 f.

37 GA, III, p. 268; see my "Reality as Language: Ernst Fuchs' Theology of Revelation," TS 28 (1967), pp. 91 ff.

38 "Declaration on Religious Freedom," note 11, in DD, p. 692.

39 An additional question regarding Romans 13, 1 ff. is its authenticity. J. Kallas has argued that this passage is interpolated; see his "Romans xiii, 1-7: An Interpolation," NTS II (1965), pp. 365-74.

40 "The Apostle Paul and the Introspective Conscience of the West," Harvard Theological Review 56 (1963), pp. 199-215.

41 "Jews and Gentiles: The Social Character of Justification in Paul," Journal of Ecumenical Studies 5 (1968), 241-67.

42 The Testament of Jesus (Philadelphia, 1968), p. 75.

43 The Relevance of the New Testament, p. 19.

44 For a survey of the problem of "early Catholicism" with extensive bibliographical information, see J. H. Elliott, "A Catholic Gospel: Reflections on 'Early Catholicism' in the New Testament," CBQ 31 (1969), pp. 213-23.

45 Structures of the Church (Notre Dame, 1968), p. 144.

46 The Church (New York, 1967), p. 19.

47 "Quod ubique, quod semper, quod ab omnibus creditum est, hoc est . . . vere proprieque catholicum." PL 50, 639. No one, of course, has ever established that some belief was held literally "everywhere, always and by all." It is hard to imagine how this could ever be established.

48 First Part, Question 1, Article 2.

49 Faith and Theology (New York, 1968), p. 15.

50 Dictionary of Theology (New York, 1965), p. 441.

51 Dogmatics in Outline (Harper Torchbook, 1959), p. 5.

52 Theology of Renewal, ed. L. K. Shook (New York, 1968),
I, p. 47.

53 Theological Dictionary, p. 456.

54 Theology and Proclamation, p. 108.

55 Theology and Revelation (New York, 1966), p. 19.

56 In the End God, p. 41.

57 Ibid., p. 38. What Dr. Robinson maintains about the scientific nature of theology makes the continuing existence of disputes
between theologians somewhat puzzling. If there is a "scientific
necessity" (page 41, note 6) about the conclusions to be drawn
from the data of Christian existence, theologians should be able
to demonstrate fairly readily to some mistaken colleague that
such a conclusion is required for a scientific explanation of the
data. So long as Dr. Robinson insists on the "scientific necessity"
inherent in the process of drawing conclusions, he would have to
account for persistent theological disputes by alleging that theologians are failing to agree on what constitutes the data of Christian existence. That would mean that this group of competent
professionals engaged in a "scientific" enterprise would be unable
to agree on what is to count as valid data for their purposes.

58 For Aquinas a scientia proceeds with certainty from principles which it does not prove but which it takes as so much information provided to form the major premises of a deductive process.
He understands theology to be such a system because it moves from
its axioms (the articles of faith) to demonstrate conclusions by the
syllogistic method. However we might disagree with this view of
theological procedure, one point is clear: scientia for Aquinas is
not the same as modern science. On the concept of scientia in
medieval theology, see V. Preller, Divine Science and the Science
of God (Princeton, N.J., 1967), pp. 233 ff.

59 Chenu, op. cit., p. 15.

60 Dogmatics in Outline, p. 5.

61 Theological Dictionary, p. 456.

62 See Van A. Harvey, The Historian and the Believer (New
York, 1966), pp. 43 ff., 71-77, 80-89.

63 Karl Rahner, Theological Investigations (Baltimore, 1966),
V, p. 25.

64 Theology and Proclamation, pp. 22, 23 f.

65 The Word of God and Tradition, p. 160.

66 Kerygma und Mythos, ed. H. W. Bartsch (Hamburg, 1948),
II, pp. 85-101.

67 The Reality of God (New York, 1966), p. 229 f.

1 See Gerald Downing, Has Christianity a Revelation? (London, 1964), pp. 18, 249 ff., 263 ff.

2 RGG, IV, col. 1609.

3 From Die christliche Wahrheit: quoted by W. Bulst, Revelation (New York, 1965), p. 22.

4 Dz 3004.

5 Vatican I, Dz 3008.

6 Dz 3000-3045.

7 Dz 3005.

8 "Haec porro supernaturalis revelatio, secundum universalis Ecclesiae fidem a sancta Tridentina Synodo declaratam continetur 'in libris scriptis et sine scripto traditionibus, quae ipsius Christi ore ab Apostolis acceptae, aut (ab) ipsis Apostolis Spiritu Sancto dictante quasi per manus traditae, ad nos usque pervenerunt'" (Dz 3006).

9 The Idea of Revelation in Recent Thought (New York, 1956), pp. 27 ff.

10 The Divinity of Jesus Christ (Fontana Library, 1964), p. 114 f.; cited by Baillie, op. cit., p. 15.

11 DD, pp. 112 ff.

12 Revelation (New York, 1969).

13 The Theology of Revelation (New York, 1966).

14 Theology of Revelation (New York, 1966).

15 Revelation and the Quest for Unity (Washington, 1968).

16 Theology of Revelation, p. 181; Catechesis of Revelation (New York, 1966), pp. 57, 60, 70, 77 f., etc.; Vision and Tactics (New York, 1968), pp. 44 ff.

17 Theology of Revelation, p. 119.

18 Hugo Meynell observes: "Does not a relationship of love and trust with another person involve one in a disposition to assert some propositions, and to deny others, concerning him?" (The New Theology and Modern Theologian [London, 1967], p. 26; cf. p. 27).

19 "Faith is concerned not only with the God of my individual and unique life. . . . Faith is also and in every instance an act of man that is enacted within community" (Georg Muschalek, Readings in Theology, ed. C. Gavin, et al., V, Christian Faith [New York, 1968], p. 195).

20 Cf. Romans 10:8 ff.

21 Notre Dame, Indiana, 1968, pp. 8 ff., 48 ff., 74 ff.

22 Summa Theologica, II, II, 1, 2.

23 Ibid., II, II, 11, 2.

24 Theology of Revelation, pp. 212 ff.

25 Pannenberg draws attention to the way Hegel and Marheineke formed part of the background for Barth's thought on revelation (RaH, pp. 4 ff.; JGM, p. 127, note 29). See Barth's own remarks in Theology and Church (New York, 1962), pp. 208 ff.

26 See Ebner's Das Wort und Die Geistigen Realitäten (Vienna, 1952). On Ebner's work see Theodor Schleiermacher, Das Heil des Menschen und Sein Traum vom Geist (Berlin, 1962) and "Ich und Du. Grundzüge der Anthropologie Ferdinand Ebners," KuD 3 (1957), pp. 208-29.

27 Theology of Revelation, pp. 213-15.

28 The "dialectic" theologians included Emil Brunner, Bultmann, Friedrich Gogarten, and Eduard Thurneysen. Their journal, Zwischen den Zeiten, appeared from 1922 to 1933. The name given to their movement expressed the dialectical structure of Barth's method of talking about God. The divine truth was to be expressed through statement and counterstatement, every positive assertion being corrected by a negation. See further, J. M. Robinson, The Beginnings of Dialectic Theology, I (Richmond, Va., 1968), pp. 24 ff.; hereafter this work is cited as BDT.

29 A little help is provided by Gloege's general survey of the Christian theology of revelation in RGG, IV, col. 1609-13. H. D. McDonald's Theories of Revelation (London, 1963), which together with his earlier Ideas of Revelation (London, 1959) offers an historical study covering the years 1700 to 1960, are disappointing and dispiritingly uncritical. Not only is much space devoted to questions of biblical inspiration, authority, and inerrancy, but comparatively little is said about continental, and in particular German, thought on revelation. So far as I know, we still lack a detailed study on the interpretation of revelation in dialectic theology. Various works on dialectic theology as a whole are listed by Pannenberg (RGG, II, col. 168-174). See also James Smart, The Divided Mind of Modern Theology (Philadelphia, 1967); the two volumes edited by Moltmann as Anfänge der dialektischen Theologie (Munich, 1962-1963); Avery Dulles, Revelation Theology (New York, 1969), pp. 94 ff.; Heinrich Fries, Bultmann-Barth and Catholic Theology (Pittsburgh, 1967).

30 Heinz Zahrnt, The Question of God (New York, 1969), p. 20.

31 Zwischen den Zeiten 8 (1924), p. 62.

32 The Word of God and the Word of Man (Harper Torchbooks, 1957), pp. 226 ff., 231 ff., 236.

191

33 The Epistle to the Romans (London, 1933), p. 10; hereafter
Romans.

34 Theology and Church, p. 300.

35 Romans, p. 91.

36 ADT, II, p. 335.

37 Ibid., I, p. 319.

38 Philosophie und Offenbarung (Tübingen, 1925), p. 15. Later
in Revelation and Reason (Philadelphia, 1947) Brunner wrote in
similar strain: "The divine revelation alone is both the ground
and the norm, as well as the content" of the Church's message.
"Her first and most urgent task is obvious: that is, to reflect
upon revelation" (page 3).

39 BDT, I, p. 118. Nearly forty years later Bultmann recalled: "From this book it became decisively clear to me that the
essence of Christian faith does not consist in an attitude of the
soul, but in its relation to its object, God's revelation" ("Mile-
stones in Books," Expository Times 70 [1958-1959], p. 125).

40 BDT, I, p. 234.

41 Das Evangelium des Johannes, Meyer commentary (14 ed.;
Göttingen, 1956), p. 31; hereafter John.

42 To cite Bultmann: "According to John revelation does not
consist in a complex of statements or thoughts" (John, p. 119).
The word of revelation is no "completed teaching," no "complex
of propositions" (ibid., p. 432).

43 Pannenberg, JGM, p. 127, note 28.

44 ADT, I, p. 317.

45 The Word of God and the Word of Man, p. 289.

46 Frühe Hauptwerke (Stuttgart, 1959), p. 353; from "Religion-
sphilosophie," originally published 1925.

47 P. 432; cf. pp. 104, 118, 206; Existence and Faith (Cleve-
land, 1960), pp. 75 ff.

48 ADT, I, p. 313.

49 Theology and Church, p. 258; Die christliche Dogmatik
(Munich, 1927), pp. 44 f., 127, 148 f., etc.: CD I/1, pp. 129 ff.

50 The Word of God and the Word of Man, p. 43.

51 Against the Stream (London, 1954), p. 225.

52 Natural Theology (a single volume including Nature and
Grace by Brunner and Barth's reply No!) (London, 1946), p. 116.

53 ADT, I, p. 317. A few pages earlier Brunner insisted:
"All the means of verification, of 'proof' are taken out of our
hands. Revelation is grasped only by faith, and what faith believes,
because it is the opposite of all movements of thought which start
from us, seems folly to our thinking" (page 295). Later he wrote:

Revelation "is indeed, by its very nature, something that lies beyond all rational arguments" (Revelation and Reason, p. 205 f.). Anything a human being can verify or deduce for himself by any process of argument, investigation, or proof, cannot possibly be revelation, and, vice versa, that which is revelation cannot be verified by any such process" (ibid., p. 207).

54 Against the Stream, p. 208 f.; cf. p. 215 f.; Die christliche Dogmatik, pp. 81, 147; CD, I/1, pp. 282 f.; 350 f.; IV/3, pp. 72 ff.

55 Faith and Understanding, pp. 300-01; cf. p. 138.

56 Der Verkehr des Christen mit Gott (7 ed.; Tübingen, 1921), p. 20.

57 Die christliche Dogmatik, p. 237.

58 Faith and Understanding, p. 30.

59 BDT, I, p. 254.

60 John, p. 275.

61 Theology and Church, p. 254; Barth is quoting Herrmann.

62 Die christliche Dogmatik, p. 243.

63 CD, I/1, p. 373.

64 Jesus Christ and Mythology (New York, 1958), p. 59. It is precisely because "he is the revealer who speaks God's word that Jesus' coming and exaltation have their saving significance" (John, p. 116).

65 GuV, III, p. 162.

66 Barth, Die christliche Dogmatik, pp. 284 ff.; CD, I/2, pp. 203 ff.; I/1, p. 518.

67 Brunner, ADT, I, p. 294.

68 Bultmann, John, p. 28. "Redemption is an event which takes place in man's existence through the encounter with the revealer" (ibid., p. 467).

69 Bultmann, TNT, II, p. 18.

70 Existence and Faith, p. 85. He continues: "There is no other light shining in Jesus than has always already shined in the creation. Man learns to understand himself in the light of the revelation of redemption not a bit differently than he always already should understand himself in the face of the revelation in creation and the law--namely, as God's creature" (ibid., p. 86).

71 The Word of God and the Word of Man, p. 290.

72 ADT, p. 220.

73 Erlebnis, Erkenntnis und Glaube (Tübingen, 1921), p. 82.

74 Faith and Understanding, p. 283 (translation corrected).

75 Pp. 286-89, 262, note 3.

76 See ADT, I, p. 311 f.

77 BDT, I, p. 140.

78 Frühe Hauptwerke, p. 382.

79 Pp. 29, 97; cf. p. 96.

80 CD, IV/3, p. 86; cf. pp. 38 ff. Barth's shift towards an unqualified Christocentric view was reflected in his opposition to natural theology; cf. A. Szekeres, "Karl Barth und die natürliche Theologie," EvTh 24 (1964), pp. 229-42 and Henri Bouillard, Karl Barth (Paris, 1957), III, pp. 129 ff. Barth defined "natural theology" as "the doctrine of a union of man with God existing outside God's revelation in Jesus Christ" (CD II/1, p. 168).

81 How I Changed My Mind (Richmond, Va., 1966), p. 43.

82 Against the Stream, p. 211.

83 Romans, p. 160.

84 The Word of God and the Word of Man, p. 77.

85 Romans, p. 30. The "transition . . . from the old aeon that ends with the cross of Christ to the new one which begins with his resurrection--this transition is revelation" (CD I/2, page 56).

86 Revelation and Reason, p. 305.

87 Die christliche Dogmatik, pp. 126 ff., 140 and 154 ff.; CD, I/1, pp. 339, 351 ff., 367 f., 381 f. The other two "forms" of the word of God were given as the word of scripture and the word of preaching: cf. Die christliche Dogmatik, pp. 43-46; CD I/1, pp. 98 ff.

88 See Natural Theology; CD II/1, pp. 107 ff.; Brunner's Revelation and Reason, pp. 77 ff.

89 TNT, I, p. 227.

90 Faith and Understanding, p. 46 f.

91 Existence and Faith, p. 80.

92 TNT, I, p. 232.

93 Faith and Understanding, p. 169.

94 Kerygma and Myth, I, p. 27.

95 John, p. 115.

96 Faith and Understanding, p. 315.

97 John, p. 39.

98 Kerygma und Mythos, II, p. 203 f.; Existence and Faith, p. 71 f.; Essays Philosophical and Theological (London, 1955), p. 53 f.

99 TNT, II, p. 26.

100 GuV, III, p. 149; cf. Essays, pp. 136, 257; Kerygma and Myth, I, p. 192.

101 Jesus Christ and Mythology, p. 53.

102 John, p. 479f.

103 TNT, I, p. 190.

104 Original, 1927; English translation, 1962.

105 Expository Times 70 (1958-1959), p. 125. Bultmann's understanding of the historical character of human existence will be discussed in a later chapter.

106 Kerygma and Myth, I, p. 24.

107 Ibid., p. 27. For detailed treatments of the connection between Heidegger and Bultmann see: G. W. Ittel, "Der Einfluss der Philosophie M. Heideggers auf die Theologie Rudolf Bultmanns," KuD 2 (1956), pp. 90-108; U. Luck, "Heideggers Ausarbeitung der Frage nach dem Sein und die existential-analytische Begrifflichkeit in der evangelischen Theologie," ZThK 53 (1956), pp. 230-51; J. Macquarrie, An Existentialist Theology (New York, 1955); The Theology of Rudolf Bultmann, ed. C. Kegley (New York, 1966), pp. 127-43; Helmut Peukert, "Bultmann and Heidegger," Bultmann, pp. 196-221.

108 Kerygma und Mythos, III, p. 57; John, pp. 115, 241, 261, 288, etc.; TNT, II, p. 26.

109 TNT, I, p. 209.

110 John, p. 481; cf. Existence and Faith, p. 59: "Revelation means that opening up of what is hidden which is absolutely necessary and decisive for man if he is to achieve 'salvation' or authenticity."

111 Kerygma and Myth, I, pp. 24 ff.

112 John, p. 479f.; cf. p. 288 and Existence and Faith, pp. 86, 141.

113 TNT, II, p. 76.

114 John, p. 32.

115 Essays, p. 11; John, p. 206; GuV, III, p. 17.

116 TNT, I, p. 317.

117 Faith, Bible Key Words (London, 1961), p. 86.

118 John, p. 200.

119 Kerygma und Mythos, II, p. 207.

120 Ibid., p. 73.

121 Existence and Faith, pp. 78, 221.

122 Kerygma und Mythos, II, p. 224.

123 "The proclaimed word of Christ . . . is revelation"; "the preaching is itself revelation and does not merely speak about it" (Existence and Faith, pp. 90, 78).

124 Ibid., p. 87.

125 The Old Testament and Christian Faith, ed. B. W. Anderson (New York, 1963), pp. 11, 33.

126 H. Schulte, The Theology of Rudolf Bultmann, ed. Kegley, p. 224.

127 Essays, pp. 205 ff.

128 Faith, pp. 75, 83.

129 Der Glaubensvollzug (Essen, 1963), p. 144, n. 20; see his "New Insights into Faith," Bultmann, pp. 125-50.

130 John, p. 288.

131 Essays, pp. 94, 98, 114 f., 118, 135-40; Existence and Faith, p. 62.

132 The Theology of Rudolf Bultmann, ed. Kegley, p. 143.

133 Ibid., p. 275.

134 The Theology of Revelation, pp. 315, 22.

135 "Spes Quaerens Intellectum," Interpretation 22 (1968), p. 44 f.

136 The Humanity of God (Richmond, Va., 1960), pp. 39 ff.

137 Secular Christianity, p. 121.

138 Ibid., p. 123.

139 Pp. 62 ff.

140 Secular Christianity, p. 57.

141 CD, II/1, p. 168; cf. pp. 190, 199, 242. See H. Bouillard, The Knowledge of God (New York, 1968).

142 Bultmann, Essays, p. 134.

143 History and Hermeneutics (Philadelphia, 1966), p. 15.

144 See my Theology and Revelation, pp. 54-57.

145 Twentieth Century Religious Thought (London, 1963), p. 335 f.

146 See my Theology and Revelation, pp. 68 ff.

Notes to Chapter III

1 See Joseph Ratzinger's detailed analysis in Commentary on the Documents of Vatican II, ed. H. Vorgrimler, III (New York, 1969), pp. 155-272; extensive bibliographical information is provided here. This work will be cited hereafter as Commentary. See also B.-D. Dupuy, ed., La Révélation divine, 2 vols. (Paris, 1968).

2 DD, pp. 112, 116, 113; cf. p. 127.

3 Dz 3004.

4 Loc. cit.

5 DD, pp. 112-14.

6 Dz 3004; DD, p. 112.

7 "The holy, catholic, apostolic Roman Church believes and confesses that there is one true and living God, Creator and Lord of heaven and earth, almighty, eternal, immense, incomprehensible, infinite in intellect, in will and in all perfection; who, as being one, sole, absolutely simple and immutable spiritual substance, is to be declared as really and essentially distinct from the world, of supreme beatitude in and from himself, and ineffably exalted above all things which exist, or are conceivable outside of himself" (Dz 3001).

8 Dz 3008.

9 DD, p. 113.

10 Dz 3009.

11 Dz 3013. Curiously Dei Filius fails to mention Christ's death and resurrection as the great sign of God's revelation.

12 DD, p. 121f.; cf. p. 112f.

13 DD, p. 117.

14 See Dz 3004.

15 Commentary, III, p. 176.

16 Dz 3007.

17 DD, p. 111.

18 Ad Limina Apostolorum (Richmond, Va., 1968), p. 45.

19 Dz 3000.

20 DD, p. 111.

21 DD, p. 118.

22 DD, p. 112; see Commentary, III, p. 174. Vatican I has slightly more to say about the sinful condition of man to whom revelation comes; see Dz 3014.

23 DD, p. 201.

24 See also other documents, especially the "Declaration on the Relationship of the Church to Non-Christian Religions" and the "Declaration on Religious Freedom."

25 DD, p. 116.

26 Commentary, III, pp. 184ff.

27 Ibid., p. 185f.

28 See Carl E. Braaten, History and Hermeneutics, pp. 11ff.

29 London, 1964. Downing's rejection of revelation is discussed in a later chapter.

30 Catechesis of Revelation, p. 151.

31 Moran and Maria Harris, Experience in Community (New York, 1968), p. 72f.

32 See above, pp. 31ff.

33 See my "Reality as Language: Ernst Fuchs' Theology of Revelation," Theological Studies 28 (1967), pp. 76-93; Man and

197

His New Hopes (New York, 1969), pp. 31 ff.; "Spes Quaerens Intellectum," Interpretation 22 (1968), pp. 36-52; Theology and Revelation, pp. 77-87.

34 This is not to suggest that Fuchs ignores the epistles. But it is significant that he understands Paul's achievement to consist in a return to the historical Jesus' transformation of ordinary life into "the 'stuff' of the revelatory event" (GA, III, p. 259f.).

35 Apart from two references to Saint Mark (p. 194f.) the gospels do not appear in Theology of Hope.

36 See above, pp. 37 ff.

37 Existence and Faith, p. 59.

38 Essays, p. 301.

39 The Theology of Revelation, p. 374.

40 Existence and Faith, p. 85f.

41 See Ratzinger, Commentary, III, p. 178f.

42 Existence and Faith, p. 141.

43 TNT, II, p. 318f.

44 BDT, I, p. 214. Moltmann draws attention to Bultmann's style of theologizing in alternatives (TH, pp. 67, 188), but curiously sometimes lapses himself into the same style; see TH, pp. 18, 21, 75, 84.

45 Romans 16:25 speaks, it is true, of "the revelation of the mystery which was kept secret for long ages." But the passage does not belong certainly to the original text.

46 See Vatican II's "Declaration on Religious Freedom," no. 10 (DD, p. 689f.).

47 See Romans 1:19f.; Matthew 11:20-24; John 15:22-24, 16:9.

48 See I Corinthians 2:14f.; H. Schlier, Epheserbrief (5th ed.; Düsseldorf, 1965), pp. 79, 211.

49 See Bultmann, TNT, I, pp. 213, 318.

50 Ibid., I, p. 300; II, pp. 74, 128.

51 Essays, p. 113.

52 The Theology of Revelation, p. 370.

53 Essays on New Testament Themes (Naperville, 1964), p. 174.

54 I Clement 42; Ignatius, Romans 4:3; Didache 4:13; Barnabas 19:11.

55 GA, III, p. 185f.; I, p. 88.

56 "Pastoral Constitution on the Church in the Modern World," no. 11 (DD, p. 209).

57 In the foreword to Heinrich Fries, Revelation (New York, 1969), p. 9.

1 Philosophical Fragments (Princeton, N.J., 1962), p. 130.

2 HJKC, pp. 17, 41.

3 The Interpretation of the New Testament 1861-1961 (London, 1964), p. 129.

4 See my "The Christology of Wolfhart Pannenberg," Religious Studies 3 (1967), pp. 369-76, especially 370.

5 HJKC, p. 20.

6 The Church and the Reality of Christ, especially pp. 13-36.

7 "In its kerygma the Church represents the historical Jesus" (HJKC, p. 42).

8 Essays, p. 83.

9 Lessing's Theological Writings, ed. H. Chadwick (Stanford, 1967), pp. 53, 55.

10 R. Rendtorff: "History as a whole is God's revelation. Since it is not yet at an end, it becomes recognizable as revelation only from the end" (ThLZ 85 [1960], col. 836).

11 An Existentialist Theology (New York, 1955), p. 170.

12 ZThK 2 (1892), p. 253.

13 The Mediator (New York, 1934), p. 156.

14 G. N. Clark, The New Cambridge Modern History, I, (Cambridge, 1957), xxv.

15 Essays, p. 19.

16 The New Theology and Modern Theologians, p. 132.

17 GST, p. 63.

18 Essays, p. 259f.; History and Eschatology, p. 143.

19 Essays, p. 241, n. 2.

20 History and Eschatology, p. 143; cf. pp. 119, 155.

21 Essays, p. 241; cf. Claude Geffré, "Bultmann on Kerygma and History," Bultmann, pp. 167-95.

22 Bultmann himself, Essays, p. 64f.; History and Eschatology, pp. 40ff.; Existence and Faith, pp. 226-40, especially p. 237; cf. R. Gregor Smith, Secular Christianity, p. 116.

23 "History and Eschatology in the New Testament," NTS 1 (1954-1955), p. 15.

24 GA, I, p. 148; GA, II, pp. 91, 95; GA, III, p. 236f. (Studies of the Historical Jesus [Naperville, 1964], p. 218; hereafter Studies).

25 Cf. my Man and His New Hopes, pp. 112ff.

Notes to Chapter V

1 On the subject of salvation history see: F. Christ, ed., Oikonomia (Hamburg, 1967); O. Cullmann, Christ and Time (rev. ed.; London, 1962), and Salvation in History (New York, 1967); A. Darlap, "Fundamentale Theologie der Heilsgeschichte," Mysterium Salutis, ed. J. Feiner and M. Löhrer I (Einsiedeln, 1965), pp. 3-156; J. Feiner, "Kirche und Heilsgeschichte," Gott in Welt, ed. H. Vorgrimler, et al. (Freiburg, 1964), pp. 317-45; K. Löwith, Meaning in History (Chicago, 1949), pp. 182-90; J. Moltmann, TH, pp. 69-76; H. Ott, Geschichte und Heilsgeschichte in der Theologie R. Bultmanns (Tübingen, 1955); G. von Rad, Old Testament Theology, 2 vols. (New York, 1962-1965); J. A. Soggin, "Geschichte, Historie und Heilsgeschichte im Alten Testament," ThLZ 89 (1964), col. 721-36.

2 For some critical estimates of Cullmann's theology of salvation history see: H. Anderson, Jesus and Christian Origins, pp. 134-48; R. Bultmann, Existence and Faith, pp. 226-40; W. Kreck, Die Zukunft des Gekommenen (2 ed.; Munich, 1966), pp. 25-28, 33-37, 209-13; W. Pannenberg, Theology as History, p. 247, n. 46. On Cullmann's interpretation of biblical concepts for time, see J. Barr, Biblical Words for Time (Naperville, 1962).

3 See J. Ratzinger, "Heilsgeschichte und Eschatologie," in Theologie im Wandel, ed. Ratzinger and J. Neumann (Munich, 1967), pp. 68-69.

4 DD, pp. 112, 452; see F. Dexinger, "Die Darstellung des Themas 'Heilsgeschichte' in der Konstitution über göttliche Offenbarung," Bibel und Liturgie 41 (1968), pp. 208-32.

5 DD, p. 450.

6 Ibid., p. 208; cf. pp. 236, 247.

7 Ibid., p. 209.

8 With regard to twentieth-century theologies of salvation history we need a study comparable to G. Weth's Die Heilsgeschichte, ihr universeller und ihr individueller Sinn in der offenbarungsgeschichtlichen Theologie des 19. Jahrhunderts (Munich, 1931).

9 Not a few positions defended by Cullmann in Salvation in History are open to serious questioning or need heavy qualification. On the second-century struggle with Gnosticism he concludes: "Christianity emerged victorious from that decisive crisis because it preserved the only thing that kept it from ruin, namely the idea of salvation in history" (italics mine, p. 26f.). He writes of the "great chronological precision" of the resurrection

tradition in I Corinthians 15:3 ff. (p. 157). The early Church is asserted to have "believed in Christ's Messiahship only because it was convinced that Jesus himself believed it, and that it belonged to the essential content of his message" (italics mine, p. 112; cf. Cullmann's The Christology of the New Testament [rev. ed.; Philadelphia, 1963], p. 8: "The early Church believed in Christ's Messiahship only because it believed that Jesus believed himself to be the Messiah."). Other issues for debate with Cullmann are his hermeneutics, his understanding of myth, and his failure to explain clearly the relationship between salvation history and ordinary history.

10 The Theology of St. Luke (London, 1960). See H. Flender, St. Luke Theologian of Redemptive History (London, 1967), p. 124 f. for a somewhat different analysis of Luke's scheme of periods in salvation history.

11 W. Marxsen, Theologische Existenz Heute, new series 59, Exegese und Verkündigung (1957), p. 47.

12 Flender, op. cit., p. 3.

13 Bultmann, Jesus and the Word (New York, 1958), p. 55 f.

14 See above, p. 12 f.

15 TNT, II, p. 8.

16 Studies in Luke-Acts, ed. L. E. Keck and J. L. Martyn (Nashville, 1966), pp. 45 ff.

17 Jesus and the Word, pp. 131, 55 f. For documentation on Bultmann's interpretation of eschatology, see my Man and His New Hopes, pp. 55 f., 58 ff.

18 Kerygma and Myth, ed. H. W. Bartsch (Harper Torchbooks, 1961), p. 41.

19 John, p. 271.

20 Cullmann's reaction to Bultmann's use of the fourth gospel is to argue that in this gospel "salvation history is not only present, but stressed" (Salvation in History, p. 270; cf. pp. 268-91).

21 "On the Topic of Primitive Christian Apocalyptic," Journal for Theology and Church 6 (1969), pp. 99-133. The whole issue is devoted to the contemporary debate about apocalypticism.

22 "God's Righteousness in Paul," Journal for Theology and the Church 1 (1965), pp. 100-10. See also P. Stuhlmacher, Gerechtigkeit Gottes bei Paulus (Göttingen, 1965), pp. 203 ff.

23 Stuhlmacher, op. cit., p. 232.

24 Moltmann, TH, p. 158.

25 Cullmann, Salvation in History, p. 251.

26 Jesus and Christian Origins, p. 140.

27 Theological Investigations, V (Baltimore, 1966), p. 106 f.

28 CBQ 30 (1968), p. 608.

29 The Interpretation of the New Testament 1861-1961, p. 267 f.

30 Secular Christianity, p. 112.

31 Theological Investigations, V, p. 107.

32 Secular Christianity, p. 114 f.

33 Ibid., p. 110.

34 Ibid., p. 127 f.

35 GST, p. 67; cf. p. 89, n. 19 and p. 76; "The Question of God," Interpretation 21 (1967), pp. 292 ff.

36 DD, pp. 112, 114.

37 Secular Christianity, p. 128.

38 Ibid., p. 95.

39 TH, p. 73 f.

40 Salvation in History, pp. 12, 20 f., 121, etc.

41 See my Man and His New Hopes, pp. 59 ff.

42 Secular Christianity, p. 113; cf. Moltmann, TH, pp. 69 ff.

43 Salvation in History, p. 124 f.

44 See Pannenberg, RaH, p. 142 f. and GST, pp. 218, 68 f.

45 Kerygma und Mythos, ed. H. W. Bartsch (Hamburg, 1948-1963), VI, 1, p. 22.

46 See H. van den Bussche, "The Church in the Fourth Gospel," The Birth of the Church, ed. by J. Giblet (New York, 1968), pp. 83-109.

47 See also the cult-hymns in Exodus 15:1-17; Psalms 78, 105, 106, 135, 136.

48 Jesus and Christian Origins, p. 140.

49 The Church and the Reality of Christ, pp. 27, 88 ff.

50 Ibid., p. 88 f.

51 GST, p. 89, n. 19. G. D. Kaufman's position bears a resemblance to Pannenberg's: see his "On the Meaning of 'Act of God,'" Harvard Theological Review 61 (1968), pp. 175-201. For further views see Schubert Ogden, The Reality of God, pp. 164-87; Ronald Gregor Smith, Secular Christianity, pp. 117-24.

52 Richard R. Niebuhr, Resurrection and Historical Reason (New York, 1957), p. 81.

53 See S. C. Neill, The Interpretation of the New Testament 1861-1961, pp. 283 ff.; Alan Richardson, History Sacred and Profane, pp. 184 ff.

54 Secular Christianity, p. 43; cf. p. 126.

55 Salvation in History, p. 153 f.

56 Ibid., p. 78.

57 Ibid., p. 155 f.

58 Christ and Time, p. 23; cf. p. 94.

59 Salvation in History, p. 152.
60 Secular Christianity, p. 128.

Notes to Chapter VI

1 DD, p. 121 f.
2 C. Westermann, Essays on Old Testament Hermeneutics (Richmond, Virginia, 1963), p. 72.
3 Bernard W. Anderson, ed., The Old Testament and Christian Faith (New York, 1963), p. 31.
4 Ibid., p. 13.
5 Ibid., p. 14 f.
6 Ibid., p. 31 f.
7 GA, II, pp. 386 ff. (= Studies, pp. 175 ff.)
8 See above, pp. 85 ff.
9 Salvation in History, pp. 107 ff.; Christology of the New Testament, pp. 60-69, 152-64.
10 TH, pp. 95 ff.
11 PL 34, p. 623.
12 See H. de Lubac, Catholicism (London, 1950), pp. 91 ff.; Exégèse Médiévale (Paris, 1959), I, pp. 341 ff.
13 See above, pp. 85 ff.
14 Hebrews 1:1 f.
15 W. D. Davies, Paul and Rabbinic Judaism (London, 1948), p. 324.

Notes to Chapter VII

1 Theology as History, ed. J. M. Robinson and J. B. Cobb, p. 226 f.
2 GST, p. 22.
3 History Sacred and Profane, p. 13.
4 RaH, p. 19.
5 Op. cit., pp. 134, 136, 138.
6 GST, pp. 67, 76, and 89, n. 19.
7 Ibid., p. 22.
8 See my "Reality as Language: Ernst Fuchs' Theology of Revelation," Theological Studies, 28 (1967), pp. 76-93.
9 GST, p. 22.
10 History Sacred and Profane, p. 134. For Pannenberg and Richardson Heilsgeschichte has, of course, a quite unexceptionable meaning if it is understood as history which--at least in

203

principle--is open to examination by historians and does not lie "beyond" or "above" ordinary history.

11 Ibid., pp. 125-53.

12 GST, p. 22.

13 Ibid., pp. 22, 38, 4f.

14 RaH, pp. 3-8.

15 Ibid., pp. 8, 14.

16 Ibid., p. 125.

17 Ibid., p. 15f.

18 Ibid., pp. 9-13.

19 Ibid., pp. 125-31.

20 Ibid., pp. 132-35.

21 GST, p. 218.

22 RaH, pp. 135-37; cf. GST, pp. 170f., 232.

23 RaH, pp. 137-39; cf. GST, p. 63.

24 RaH, pp. 16ff., 139-48; cf. GST, pp. 27, 171ff., 232, and 89, n. 19.

25 RaH, pp. 149-52.

26 Ibid., pp. 152-55.

27 GST, p. 63; RaH, p. 138.

28 GST, pp. 223, 231.

29 JGM, p. 109f.; "The Question of God," Interpretation 21 (1967), p. 293f.

30 Downing, Has Christianity a Revelation? pp. 238f., 205.

31 RaH, p. 156, n. 14.

32 GST, p. 47.

33 JGM, pp. 301, 322f.

34 GST, p. 63.

35 "Revelation through History in the Old Testament and in Modern Theology," Interpretation 17 (1963), p. 197.

36 Theology as History, p. 232.

37 JGM, p. 83.

38 Ibid., p. 66; cf. RaH, p. 146f.

39 See my "The Christology of Wolfhart Pannenberg," Religious Studies 3 (1967), p. 375f., and several articles in Journal for Theology and the Church 6 (1969), an issue devoted to the theme of apocalypticism.

40 See above, p. 90f.

41 GST, p. 86.

42 The Existence of God as Confessed by Faith (Philadelphia, 1965), p. 146.

43 RaH, p. 140.

44 GST, p. 111, n. 32.
45 Revelation as History, pp. 256, 258.
46 Ibid., p. 247, n. 46.
47 Studien der alttestamentlichen Überlieferungen, ed. R.
Rendtorff and K. Koch (Neukircken, 1961), p. 83.
48 Theology and Revelation, pp. 50 ff.
49 Ibid., p. 27 f.
50 Theology as History, pp. 227 ff.

Notes to Chapter VIII

1 Has Christianity a Revelation? pp. 20-125. Hereafter this
work will be cited by page numbers given within brackets in the
text.
2 RaH, p. 8 f.
3 If Downing later concedes that "'reveal' may be qualified,
and meaningfully," he continues to insist that "the theologian who
is at all aware of the actualities of the Christian situation will
admit that any talk of 'revelation of God' must be so heavily
qualified that it would be less confusing to use another word"
(p. 239).
4 Downing refers to Matthew 5:21 ff., 27 ff., 33 ff., 38 ff.;
Luke 16:16 f.; Galatians 2:16, 21; Romans 3:28; Philippians 3:6, 9.
5 The Setting of the Sermon on the Mount (London, 1964),
pp. 431 and 428 f.
6 TNT, I, p. 16.
7 G. Bornkamm, G. Barth, and H. J. Held, Tradition and
Interpretation in Matthew (London, 1963), p. 31.
8 "It is the message of the kingdom of God that constitutes
the new element in the present epoch of salvation, in contrast to
the old epoch whose last representative was John the Baptist"
(H. Conzelmann, The Theology of St. Luke [London, 1960], p.
161).
9 The Sayings of Jesus (London, 1949), p. 135.
10 Conzelmann writes: "The Law prepares the way for the
Gospel just as Israel does for the Church and her mission. . . .
Luke xvi, 17 then goes on to express the 'permanence' of the Law,
the fact that its position is one of principle. In other words, the
epochs are separate, but there is no break between them, for the
elements in the former one persist into the next" (Theology of St.
Luke, p. 160 f.).

11 C. F. D. Moule, "Obligation in the Ethic of Paul," Christian History and Interpretation, ed. W. R. Farmer, et al. (New York, 1967), p. 403.

12 Downing in fact earlier admitted: "It might be said that the fact that the hidden God could even be spoken of, and his commands known, implies 'revelation' in some sense" (p. 46).

13 "It would be difficult enough to make good a claim that the New Testament writers themselves had a common 'knowledge of God'" (p. 204).

14 London, 1966.

15 D. E. Nineham, ed., The Church's Use of the Bible (London, 1963), p. 150.

16 This is a remarkably mild statement of Downing's view. As we will see, his desire to phase out the language of revelation goes far beyond concern about possible confusion.

17 That is to say, nondescriptive of God. It is incidentally descriptive of the human commitment intended (p. 185, n. 2; p. 191).

Notes to Chapter IX

1 Jesus (London, 1949), p. 131.

2 Kerygma and Myth, I, p. 39.

3 See B. Klappert, "Zur Frage des semitischen oder grieschischen Urtextes von 1. Kor. 15:3-5," NTS 13 (1967), pp. 168-73; H. Conzelmann, "Zur Analyse der Bekenntnisformel I Kor. 15: 3-5," EvTh 25 (1965), pp. 1-11.

4 "The Events of Easter and the Empty Tomb," Tradition and Life in the Church (Philadelphia, 1968), p. 45.

5 Kerygma and Myth, I, p. 39; cf. TNT, I, pp. 295, 305.

6 See W. Michaelis, TDNT, V. pp. 355 ff., esp. p. 358.

7 See also Jonah 1:17; 2:1; 2 Kings 20:5; Psalms 16:10.

8 GA III, p. 448.

9 New Frontiers in Theology, II, ed. J. M. Robinson and J. B. Cobb (New York, 1964), p. 114. Elsewhere Fuchs offers a third explanation of the phrase: "The meaning of the scripture proof in I Corinthians 15:3 f." is that "now the time for faith is definitely come" (GA III, p. 278).

10 See further K. Lehmann, Auferweckt am dritten Tage nach der Schrift, Quaestiones Disputatae 38 (Freiburg, 1968).

11 For a convenient summary of counterexplanations see H. Anderson, Jesus and Christian Origins, pp. 199 ff.

12 Man and His New Hopes, pp. 68 ff.
13 Ibid., pp. 71 ff.

Notes to Chapter X

1 The literature on the quest of the historical Jesus is enormous. Useful (initial) bibliographies are found in J. Jeremias, The Problem of the Historical Jesus (Facet Books, 1967), pp. 25-27 and p. 1, n. 1.
2 The Quest of the Historical Jesus (New York, 1961), p. 4.
3 Bultmann's History of the Synoptic Tradition (Oxford, 1963) first appeared in 1921, two years after the publication of two other basic works in New Testament form criticism by M. Dibelius and K. L. Schmidt.
4 What Do We Know about Jesus? (London, 1968), p. 12.
5 TNT, I, pp. 3-32.
6 Ibid., pp. 3 ff., 12, 16 f., 22 ff.
7 Kerygma and Myth, I, p. 117.
8 HJKC, p. 20.
9 Kerygma and Myth, I, p. 41.
10 Essays on New Testament Themes, pp. 15-47.
11 Jesus of Nazareth (New York, 1960), pp. 10, 68, 70, 75, 79, 93, etc.
12 Jesus and His Story (New York, 1959), pp. 8 ff.
13 Ibid., p. 12.
14 The Problem of the Historical Jesus, p. 15.
15 Ibid., pp. 16-19.
16 New Testament Questions of Today (London, 1969), pp. 24 ff.
17 The Problem of the Historical Jesus, p. 13; italics mine.
18 Ibid., p. 21.
19 Ibid., p. 14.
20 Ibid., p. 14.
21 Ibid., p. 23 f.
22 See my Theology and Revelation, pp. 50 ff.
23 HJKC, pp. 15-42.
24 GA II, p. 164 (= Studies, p. 28).
25 The Nature of Faith (Fontana Library, 1966), pp. 44-57.
26 HJKC, pp. 33 f., 41.
27 GA II, p. 252 (= Studies, p. 60) and p. 157 (= Studies, p. 23).

28 GA II, pp. 254 ff., 397 f. (= Studies, pp. 62 ff., 184).

29 HJKC, pp. 31 ff.

30 GA III, p. 451.

31 Ibid., pp. 8, 12.

32 Word and Faith, p. 205.

33 HJKC, pp. 16, 41 f.

34 GA III, pp. 23, 259 f.